# Christian Ethics at the Boundary

# Christian Ethics at the Boundary

## Feminism and Theologies of Public Life

Karen V. Guth

Fortress Press
*Minneapolis*

CHRISTIAN ETHICS AT THE BOUNDARY
Feminism and Theologies of Public Life

Cover image: Light entering through door © iStock/Thinkstock
Cover design: Ivy Palmer Skrade

Library of Congress Cataloging-in-Publication Data
Print ISBN: 978-1-4514-6570-9
eBook ISBN: 978-1-4514-6975-2

The paper used in this publication meets the minimum requirements of American
National Standard for Information Sciences — Permanence of Paper for Printed
Library Materials, ANSI Z329.48-1984.

Manufactured in the U.S.A.

This book was produced using PressBooks.com, and PDF rendering was done by
PrinceXML.

# Contents

# Acknowledgments

This book shows how the field of Christian ethics would benefit if its participants conceived of their task as engagement in what theologian Kathryn Tanner has called a *"genuine community of argument."* For Tanner, participation in such a community is constitutive of Christian identity. It is "marked by mutual hearing and criticism among those who disagree" and "a common commitment to mutual correction and uplift, in keeping with the shared hope of good discipleship, proper faithfulness, and purity of witness." Indeed, this work is informed by my own experience of having participated in such genuine communities of argument that have shaped me as a scholar and strengthened my argument here.

The book began as a dissertation under Charles Mathewes at the University of Virginia. Nothing I say here could adequately convey my gratitude to Chuck for the countless ways he has guided, challenged, and encouraged me as a scholar. I feel very fortunate to have studied with him and with the other exceptional members of my dissertation committee—James F. Childress, Margaret Mohrmann, Paul Dafydd Jones, and Lawrie Balfour—whose indispensable feedback on that project has seen its way into this manuscript. I am also deeply indebted to the intellectual community of graduate students that I enjoyed while at Virginia. Emily Filler, Laura

Hawthorne, Peter Kang, Betsy Mesard, Jenny Phillips, Shelli Poe, Reuben Shank, Mark Storslee, and Daniel Weiss all helpfully engaged early versions of the material.

The book also owes much to members of other communities of argument in which I was privileged to participate both before and after my career at Virginia. Shelly Matthews first introduced me to feminist studies in religion when I was an undergraduate at Furman University. My studies with her and with Helen Lee Turner gave me a strong foundation in feminist scholarship. Although I did not follow Shelly into New Testament studies, she did send me to her alma mater, Harvard Divinity School, where I was able to bring my interest in feminist studies to bear on other areas of theological inquiry. My advisor there, Ronald F. Thiemann, introduced me to public theology and provided a compelling model for the kind of constructive work that I wanted to pursue. Preston Williams' course on Martin Luther King Jr. also proved invaluable; my engagement with his course material gave rise to the questions at the heart of chapter four. From 2011-2012, a postdoctoral fellowship in Religious Practices and Practical Theology at Emory University's Candler School of Theology provided yet another community with which to reflect on the book's material.

I am grateful to teach at an institution that values and supports faculty scholarship. A course release funded by the Collaborative Undergraduate Research Program at St. Catherine University provided additional research time during the fall of 2014. I thank my colleagues Lynda Szymanski, who founded the program, and Cynthia Norton, who served as interim director during my grant period, for their work on behalf of faculty scholarship at St. Kate's. Special thanks to my student and research partner, Catherine Madison, for our lively theological conversations and her insightful comments on chapter two. I would also like to thank my dean in the School of Humanities, Arts and Sciences, Alan Silva, for valuable support and funding for conference travel in excess of regular faculty travel grants.

A number of friends and colleagues read portions of the manuscript. Their comments not only improved the argument, but also provided needed encouragement. Many thanks to Janel Kragt Bakker, Jennifer M. McBride, Thomas H. West, and Nathaniel Van Yperen. I also thank Chuck Mathewes for providing substantive feedback on portions of the manuscript and organizing a book workshop with his recent and current graduate students at the University of Virginia. Joe Lenow, Philip Lorish, Kristopher Norris, and Matthew Puffer all offered comments and questions that helped me clarify the introductory material.

Several chapters benefited from the excellent discussion of colleagues at professional meetings. I presented revised versions of material from chapter three at the 2015 annual meeting of the Society of Christian Ethics, as well as earlier versions of chapter four at both the 2010 annual meeting of the American Academy of Religion and the 2011 annual meeting of the Society of Christian Ethics. An early version of chapter four also benefited from the engagement of members of the Love and Justice Reading Group at the Institute for Advanced Studies in Culture at the University of Virginia, including Jamie Ferreira, Jennifer Geddes, Charles Mathewes, and Regina Schwartz. I received helpful feedback on an earlier version of chapter two from my fellow contributors to *Gendering Christian Ethics*, particularly from Jenny Daggers and Rachel Muers. I also presented early versions of the introductory material at the 2009 Ecclesiological Investigations group session of the annual meeting of the American Academy of Religion and the 2009 annual meeting of the Southeastern Commission for the Study of Religion.

I gratefully acknowledge Georgetown University Press, the *Journal of Scriptural Reasoning* and Cambridge Scholars Press for permission to reprint portions of the following previously published material, respectively: "Reconstructing Nonviolence: The Political Theology of Martin Luther King Jr. after Feminism and Womanism." *Journal of the Society of Christian Ethics* 32, no. 1 (Spring/Summer 2012): 75-92; "The Feminist-Christian Schism Revisited." *The Journal of Scriptural Reasoning* 13, no. 2 (November 2014); "Churches as 'Self-Critical Cultures': Reinhold Niebuhr, Kathryn Tanner, and the Church's Politics," in *Gendering Christian Ethics*, edited by Jenny Daggers (Newcastle: Cambridge Scholars Press, 2012), 23-50. Thanks also to everyone at Fortress Press.

This work—and all of my work—would not be possible without the loving support of my family, including my brothers Brad, Eric, and Gary; my sisters-in-law Leigh, Meghan, and Sarah; and my nieces and nephews Alice and Lydia, Emily and Austin, and Jackson and Benjamin. My parents, James L. Guth and Cydelle A. Dukleth Guth, introduced me to the life of the mind and have encouraged and nurtured my love of learning for as long as I can remember. Although Mom can be grateful that the days of the science fair have long since passed, Dad bears the burden of being a professional scholar and still receives proofreading requests from his daughter.

For this particular book, however, I owe the largest debt of gratitude to my partner, Craig Danielson. I wrote the bulk of the manuscript during our first year of marriage, and although our vows said nothing of scholarly or editorial duties, Craig took them on as though they had. I cannot thank him enough for his loving engagement with me and with my work. Because of his dedication, both the book and I are better versions of ourselves.

# Publication Credits

The following publishers are acknowledged for the permission to reproduce material in this book:

Karen V. Guth, "Churches as 'Self-Critical Cultures': Reinhold Niebuhr, Kathryn Tanner, and the Church's Politics." In *Gendering Christian Ethics*, edited by Jenny Daggers, 23–50. Newcastle: Cambridge Scholars, 2012. Published with the permission of Cambridge Scholars Publishing.

*The Journal of Scriptural Reasoning* and Dr. Jacob L. Goodson for: Guth, Karen V., "The Feminist-Christian Schism Revisited." In *The Journal of Scriptural Reasoning* 13, no. 2 (November 2014). http://jsr.shanti.virginia.edu /volume- 13- number -2- november-2014- navigating- john- howardyoders- the- jewish- christian-schism- revisited/the-feminist-christianschism-revisited.

The Society of Christian Ethics for: Guth, Karen V., "Reconstructing Nonviolence: The Political Theology of Martin Luther King Jr. after Feminism and Womanism." In *Journal of the Society of Christian Ethics* 32, no. 1 (Spring/Summer 2012), 75-92.

# Introduction

In "Paul's Letter to American Christians," Martin Luther King Jr. issues what is probably one of his lesser-known critiques of the church. Most students of King's work are familiar with his condemnation of the church's racial segregation. Many will also recall King's searing prediction that if the church continues to conform to society's injustices rather than to Christ, it will become "an irrelevant social club."[1] But in this text, King imagines that the apostle Paul would attack American denominationalism:

> Let me say something about the church. Americans, I must remind you, as I have told so many others, that the church is the Body of Christ. When the church is true to its nature, it knows neither division nor disunity. I am told that within American Protestantism there are more than two hundred and fifty denominations. The tragedy is not merely that you have such a multiplicity of denominations, but that many groups claim to possess absolute truth. Such narrow sectarianism destroys the unity of the Body of Christ. God is neither Baptist, Methodist, Presbyterian, nor Episcopalian. God transcends our denominations. If you are to be true witnesses for Christ, you must come to know this, America.[2]

---

1. Martin Luther King Jr., *Why We Can't Wait* (New York: Signet, 2000), 80.
2. Martin Luther King Jr., *Strength to Love* (Philadelphia: Fortress Press, 1981), 140. For another well-known critique of American denominationalism, see H. Richard Niebuhr, *The Social Sources of Denominationalism* (New York: Meridian, 1957).

King identifies several problems related to denominationalism, but he focuses on how it can lead to divisiveness. King makes clear that the stakes of this problem are high: the discord that often results comes at the expense of church unity, threatening the very integrity of its witness. Like so many of King's perceptive analyses, this one remains as trenchant now as when he first spoke it. It poses a bold challenge for Christians to approach difference constructively.

But is King's critique of the church relevant for theologians and Christian ethicists? Although denominational divisions often inform work in academic theology, other divides are perhaps more salient. Most ethicists, for example, identify with one of the major approaches in twentieth- and twenty-first-century Christian ethics: synergy, realism, integrity, or liberation.[3] These divisions run across denominational affiliations. They are perhaps less solidified than the various Christian denominations, but they do mark important differences.

As such, they are indispensable. Just as the various Christian denominations in America possess gifts and resources specific to their strand of the tradition, theologians of the various stances espouse diverse perspectives that can foster mutually critical and mutually enriching dialogue. But far too often, they do not. In just the manner King describes with the church, academic theologians often allow these differences to create discord. And just as King identified disunity as a threat to the integrity of the church's mission, so, too,

---

3. I take these ways of naming the "variations on the Christian stance" from Robin W. Lovin, *An Introduction to Christian Ethics: Goals, Duties, and Virtues* (Nashville: Abingdon, 2011), 45–66. The *synergy* stance characterizes theological work in the natural law tradition, broadly construed, that emphasizes and fosters collaboration between Christian and non-Christian conceptions of the good; the *integrity* or "witness" stance emphasizes the distinctiveness of Christian communities—especially their espousal of pacifism—amid the larger culture; the *realist* stance emphasizes the role of sin in human affairs and the moral ambiguity of all human action; and the *liberation* stance places front and center the preferential option for the poor and marginalized, emphasizing Christianity's role in liberating the oppressed. Lovin borrows the term *stance* from Catholic moral theologian Charles Curran.

divisiveness within Christian ethics often compromises our projects and sacrifices the resources our field possesses for addressing the challenges of our "communal moral life."[4]

Indeed, one of the most common responses I hear (from groups ranging from the first-year college students who take my Christian ethics courses to meet their theology requirement to my non-Christian friends and colleagues) is that theology is irrelevant. It neither holds significance for their lives nor contributes to the common good. Although this attitude often results from prejudice and ignorance, it provides an opportunity for self-reflection. Do responses like these have anything to do with how we go about the theological task—and specifically, how we navigate differences marked by the intra-disciplinary boundaries of our field? A number of my own academic experiences lead me to suspect so. Allow me to share two.

Several years ago, I presented a paper at the feminist theologies section of an academic conference. The first thing that struck me about the session participants and the audience members was that we were predominantly white women. A white male feminist in attendance later commented to me that he felt as though he had been the unwelcome visitor at a club meeting. Apart from the identity politics operating in the room, I was also intrigued by the audience reaction to my paper. I had given a paper on the subfield of Christian ethics known as "public theology,"[5] raising the question of why there

4. I borrow this phrase from Traci C. West. See "Constructing Ethics: Reinhold Niebuhr and Harlem Women Activists," *Journal of the Society of Christian Ethics* 24, no. 1 (2004): 46.

5. I use "public theology" in a general sense to refer to theologians like Niebuhr, Yoder, and King who either played significant roles in American public life or whose theologies address the relationship between Christianity and politics, but it is also a term of art that refers to a particular conversation within twentieth-century American Christian ethics and theology. Prominent figures include David Hollenbach, Robin W. Lovin, Martin E. Marty, William Placher, Max Stackhouse, Kathryn Tanner, Ronald F. Thiemann, and David Tracy. In my judgment, feminist theology qualifies in a general sense as public or political theology, but very few self-identified feminist theologians explicitly engage conversations in so-called public

were not more feminist participants in this conversation, given that feminist theologies also address the relationship between Christianity and public life. A well-known feminist confessed that she had not engaged these conversations because she found public theology "boring."

On another occasion, the context was somewhat reversed. I was speaking with a prominent nonfeminist theologian whose work addresses issues related to religion and public life. Again assuming a common set of interests between public theologies and feminist theologies, I asked him what he regarded as the most important contribution of feminist theologies to the wider field. His response—"nothing"—was as dismissive as the feminist's.[6]

I have learned a great deal from both of these theologians. And, although I remain alarmed by how swiftly and confidently they dismissed each other's fields, I suspect their motivations were good. Both are firmly committed to theology, deeply invested in its integrity, and keenly aware that theology profoundly affects people's lives. Both would likely argue that the future of theology and the flourishing of human persons and all of creation are at stake, and I agree. But there was also something disturbing about how both of these theologians—despite shared interests—dismissed the other's approach rather than engaging it to identify areas for mutual critique or even collaboration.

I share these examples not because these theologians stand out as exceptions; they are representative of how we are trained to do

theology. Exceptions include Linell E. Cady, Rosemary P. Carbine, Rebecca S. Chopp, Mary Doak, and Mary E. Hines. Public theology has also received renewed attention in the broader English-speaking world, including from feminist perspectives. See, for example, vol. 4 of the *International Journal of Public Theology* (2010); Elaine Graham, *Between a Rock and a Hard Place: Public Theology in a Post-Secular Age* (London: SCM, 2013); and *Public Theology and the Challenge of Feminism*, ed. Anita Monro and Stephen Burns (New York: Routledge, 2015).

6. This theologian later clarified that he meant "nothing" insofar as he regarded feminist theologies to be versions of theological liberalism.

theology. I share them because they raised for me in an especially clear way the motivating questions of this book: What would Christian ethics look like if we mobilized our differences for engagement rather than disengagement? How would Christian ethics benefit when done at the boundaries of our diverse perspectives rather than exclusively from within any one dedicated stance? Would doing so make any difference for the integrity of theology and its power to address complex moral problems?

Just as King saw church unity as essential to the vitality of the church's witness, it may be that how theologians approach projects of different perspectives bears directly on the impact of those projects in the world. My questions are thus versions of King's. They affirm the need for the methods of Christian theology to be in keeping with its end. As King asks in the letter, "I wonder whether your moral and spiritual progress has been commensurate with your scientific progress. . . . How much of your modern life can be summarized in the words of your poet Thoreau: 'Improved means to an unimproved end.'"[7] As Christian ethicists, do we seek improved means to an unimproved end? Have we allowed the disciplinary structures of the academy to produce division at odds with our common search for truth? Or, as King might put it, have we allowed our theological progress to outstrip our moral progress? For King, only the practice of love is consistent with the end of love. Only "by uniting yourselves with Christ and your brothers through love will you be able to matriculate in the university of eternal life."[8] In order for our guild to avoid becoming its own irrelevant social club, we must commit to engaging difference without succumbing to a divisiveness that betrays the integrity and power of our work.

7. King, *Strength to Love*, 138.
8. Ibid., 144.

This book is thus an attempt to explore an alternative approach to the "denominations" of academic theology. I draw on Kathryn Tanner's concept of Christian identity as participation in a *"genuine community of argument"*[9] and her claim that "the distinctiveness of a Christian way of life is not so much formed *by* the boundary [of cultural forms] as *at* it"[10] to argue that, rather than using our diverse approaches to dismiss each other, Christian ethicists should use them to identify sites for constructive work. Far from compromising the integrity of each stance, approaching academic boundaries this way actually strengthens them.

I do this by exploring the debate between "realist" and "witness" theologians in American[11] Protestant public theology about how Christianity best engages the world. As my opening anecdotes reveal, those in public theology often show little interest in dialoguing with feminist theologies. Nor do many feminist theologians seem eager to respond to contemporary witness and realist approaches within public theology or the work of three of America's most influential public theologians whose work is foundational to these approaches—Reinhold Niebuhr, John Howard Yoder, and Martin Luther King Jr. (though there are notable exceptions to these generalizations).[12] This is not a problem specific to witness, realist, or feminist theologians, but I will use the debate, or lack thereof, between witness, realist, and feminist theologians on this particular topic as an example of a much larger problem within the field of

---

9. Kathryn Tanner, *Theories of Culture: A New Agenda for Theology* (Minneapolis: Fortress Press, 1997), 123. I explain my use of this concept in the "Method" section of this introduction.
10. Ibid., 115.
11. I use the term *American* narrowly to refer to the United States.
12. These exceptions include, but are not limited to, work in public theology by feminist theologians Linell E. Cady and Rosemary P. Carbine; engagement with postliberal/witness approaches by feminists Gloria Albrecht, Linell E. Cady, Debra Dean Murphy, and Amy Plantinga Pauw; as well as the appropriation of Niebuhr's Christian realism by feminist Rebekah L. Miles.

Christian ethics. What is the cost of these missed opportunities for collaboration?

I demonstrate that such disengagement negatively affects both the legacies of three of America's most important Protestant public theologians and our ability to identify new lines of valuable inquiry. But also—and more importantly—I demonstrate the constructive possibilities that emerge when this segregation is ended. I focus on how the witness-realist dominance and the absence of feminist theologies in public theology affect the legacies of Niebuhr, Yoder, and King. I argue that the criticisms witness, realist, and feminist theologians level against each other helpfully identify sites for construction in the thought of these three figures. When developed, the resources at these sites give rise to possibilities that both contribute to Niebuhr's, Yoder's, and King's legacies *and* enhance the internal projects of witness, realist, and feminist theologians. Locating these spaces at the boundaries of their work reveals new trajectories for needed work in Christian ethics.

In short, this book is an attempt to demonstrate how the field of Christian ethics might benefit if it is conceived of as a "genuine community of argument" conducted "at the boundaries" of its diverse approaches. I advance this claim through a series of arguments that show the constructive potential of Niebuhr's, Yoder's, and King's legacies when approached at the boundaries of witness, realist, and feminist approaches. I focus on these figures not only because of their significance in American Protestant Christian ethics in the last century, but also because their legacies manifest the destructive impact of the witness-realist divide of the last half century in a particularly acute way.

The first strand of this argument is that feminist theologies are indispensable to Niebuhr's, Yoder's, and King's legacies. Reading these figures alongside various feminists and womanists enables me to illuminate aspects of their thought that are obscured when approached only at the witness-realist boundary, namely: Niebuhr's thought on the church, Yoder's identification of feminism and "tactical alliances"[13] with liberalism as constitutive of the church's identity and mission, and King's increasingly "feminist" and "womanist" account of love.

This reading, in turn, enables the second strand of my argument: doing Christian ethics at the boundaries identifies new agendas for Christian ethics. In this particular case, approaching the thought of Niebuhr, Yoder, and King at the boundaries of witness, realist, and feminist perspectives enables me to identify ecclesiology as a new agenda for realists, feminism as a new agenda for witness theologians, and creative maladjustment as a productive stance for all Christian ethicists.

The third strand of my argument is that doing Christian ethics at the boundary holds promise for the entire field. It is of course important to note the "boundaries" of my own study. This book engages most centrally with three approaches within Christian ethics that have been particularly influential in American Protestant theology of the last half century: witness, realist, and feminist theologies. There are many other important subfields and specific debates beyond the scope of this book. But far from limiting the significance of this study, demarcating the boundaries of its subject matter only serves to identify possible sites for additional engagement. Scholars in Catholic moral theology, for example, or scholars across theological ethics engaged in debates within natural law, virtue ethics, or any of the many topics outside of public theology, can also generate stronger projects by doing Christian ethics at the boundary.

13. John Howard Yoder, *The Priestly Kingdom: Social Ethics as Gospel* (Notre Dame, IN: University of Notre Dame Press, 1984), 61.

The fourth strand of my argument is that the very integrity of theology and its power to address complex moral problems is at stake. While Tanner posits the "genuine community of argument" as a constitutive model for Christian community, it also provides a powerful model for academic theology—whose current structures more often reward the mobilization of academic boundaries for uncharitable criticism and disengagement from those with whom one disagrees. Rather, we should approach the boundaries in a spirit of humility and contrition, eager to learn and willing to offer constructive criticism and encouragement. Doing Christian ethics at the boundaries thereby provides a more constructive approach to difference—one that acknowledges its importance and uses it to enable more robust theologies across each stance. I begin by turning to the specific case of this study: debates within American Protestant public theology, particularly those relevant to the legacies of Niebuhr, Yoder, and King.

### Christianity in Public Life: The Witness-Realist Debate

In recent decades, theologians of two stances have dominated discussions within Christian ethics over the role of the church in public life. On one side of these discussions are scholars working in the tradition of twentieth-century Swiss Protestant theologian Karl Barth. These theologians often identify themselves as "witness," "postliberal," or "integrity" theologians. Concerned about the accommodation of the church and its particularistic language and practices to non-Christian cultural forms, these scholars tend to emphasize the distinctive resources of the tradition. They stress the primacy of revelation, the role of the biblical narrative and church practices for the moral formation of Christian disciples, and the nature of the church as a distinctive polis that witnesses to the world.

As such, they ground their thinking about Christian politics in ecclesiology.[14]

On the other side are theologians working in the tradition of twentieth-century American theologian Reinhold Niebuhr. These theologians claim the label "realist."[15] Sharing the witness concern to distinguish Christian views from those of the wider culture, these scholars emphasize the critical relevance of Christian beliefs and practices to the political order and highlight the tradition's invaluable, indeed superior, resources for identifying and addressing social, political, and economic problems. Rather than maintaining that Christian practices constitute their own particular politics, these scholars see a need for Christians to bring their distinctive views to bear on politics beyond the church. In contrast to the witness focus on ecclesiology, realists favor the doctrines of sin and anthropology, using them to underscore both the limits and the possibilities of Christian ethical action.[16]

Scholars of both schools provide compelling—and in some respects, compatible—accounts of Christian life in the world. But their differences have been more pronounced, and several irreconcilable differences do indeed exist at the heart of their proposals. They espouse different theories of truth (narrative theory[17] versus moral realism), different stances toward the use of violence (pacifism versus

14. Representative works in this category include the work of John Howard Yoder; Stanley Hauerwas, *The Peaceable Kingdom: A Primer in Christian Ethics* (Notre Dame, IN: University of Notre Dame Press, 1983) and *With the Grain of the Universe: The Church's Witness and Natural Theology* (Grand Rapids: Baker Academic, 2001); and William T. Cavanaugh, *Torture and Eucharist: Theology, Politics, and the Body of Christ* (Malden, MA: Wiley-Blackwell, 1998).

15. I use the term *realist* exclusively to refer to theologians who identify as political realists.

16. Representative works in this category include the work of Reinhold Niebuhr; Robin W. Lovin, *Christian Realism and the New Realities* (Cambridge: Cambridge University Press, 2008); Douglas F. Ottati, *Hopeful Realism: Recovering the Poetry of Theology* (Eugene, OR: Wipf & Stock, 2009); and William Schweiker, *Theological Ethics and Global Dynamics: In the Time of Many Worlds* (Malden, MA: Wiley-Blackwell, 2004).

17. I recognize that witness theologians may contest this description.

limited justification of force), and different political emphases (ecclesial versus extra-ecclesial). More often than not, these differences function less to orient conversation than to prevent it altogether.

So entrenched is the divide between these approaches that it structures the field of Christian ethics itself. The very act of locating one's work within "theological ethics" or "social ethics" signals one's loyalties. In other cases, subfields such as "public theology" have been polarized between the two perspectives. And, although less clear because of its proliferation of meanings, categories like "political theology" that originated in other contexts now seem to separate witness and realist territory from that of others, such as feminists and other liberationists.

Several recent works have turned to Augustine in an attempt to strike a middle ground between realist and witness approaches. All provide Christian proposals for political activity and better acknowledge feminist insights. As such, these accounts advance the discussion on numerous fronts. Three prominent accounts deserve special attention. Charles Mathewes's *A Theology of Public Life*[18] charts a middle course between witness and realist approaches by arguing that political participation is itself a form of Christian discipleship, showing how public engagement enriches Christian faith. Eric Gregory's *Politics and the Order of Love*[19] also seeks a balance, recognizing the importance of the liberal order for restraining sin but also emphasizing the centrality of love to political action. Finally, Luke Bretherton's *Christianity and Contemporary Politics*[20] combines a concern for the church's own politics with its

18. Charles Mathewes, *A Theology of Public Life* (Cambridge: Cambridge University Press, 2007).
19. Eric Gregory, *Politics and the Order of Love: An Augustinian Ethic of Democratic Citizenship* (Chicago: University of Chicago Press, 2008).
20. Luke Bretherton, *Christianity and Contemporary Politics: The Conditions and Possibilities of Faithful Witness* (Malden, MA: Wiley-Blackwell, 2010).

participation in politics beyond the church. All three manage to mediate between the witness-realist extremes and incorporate feminist contributions more thoroughly than previous witness and realist approaches.

Nevertheless, each of these accounts still leans too heavily to one side or the other of the witness-realist balance, and they fail to follow through on the feminist engagement their work invites. For all its merits, Mathewes's account remains overly individualistic at the expense of ecclesiology and relies heavily on an under-nuanced account of suffering that fails to satisfy feminist and womanist concerns. Gregory's account offers a valuable reclamation of love for politics but does not provide an accompanying ecclesiology that accounts for how this virtue is cultivated; nor does his proposal, for all its attention to feminist ethics of care, adequately treat the work of Christian feminists who offer valuable reconstructions of agape. Bretherton's account of Christian politics deftly handles the complexity of the church's relationship with local, national, and global realities but ultimately relies on an account of the church and worship that is overidealized, neglecting the potentially malformative impact of the church on its members' moral formation. While these significant accounts make progress, there is still critical work that needs to be done. But why does this work matter?

## Theologians of American Public Life: Niebuhr, Yoder, and King

It matters because the legacies of three of America's most important Protestant public theologians—Niebuhr, Yoder, and King—are at stake. Witness theologians continually dismiss Niebuhr as a liberal whose apology for Christianity, far from displaying the relevance of the tradition to political realities, fundamentally compromises its distinctive witness. Realists respond by emphasizing the theological nature of Niebuhr's thought, but often fail to highlight his ecclesiological credentials. Realists dismiss Yoder as politically irrelevant, and witness theologians only exacerbate the stereotype by casting Yoder in their antiliberal image. Despite his significance and influence, King is routinely overlooked by both realist and witness theologians. For their part, feminists do not show much interest in any of the three; nor do prominent witness or realist theologians fully appreciate the distinctive contributions of feminist theologies. Is there any hope for the legacies of these three figures so central to American Christian ethics?

One hopes so—their legacies are also critical to the entire field of Christian ethics. All wielded significant influence within American Christianity during their lives and produced bodies of work that continue to feature prominently in public, ecclesial, and academic debate. Their enduring influence suggests not only the importance of their work but also its potential to set the terms of conversation for decades to come.

Each also represents a major position, broadly construed, in twentieth-century and contemporary (especially Protestant) Christian ethics. Niebuhr is arguably the most important figure in Christian realism, a theological movement originating in the early twentieth century. Among its other important contributions, Christian realism emphasizes the role of sin in human affairs, challenging the social gospel's optimistic belief in the inevitability of human progress. Yoder represents Christian witness, the branch of Christian ethics that emphasizes—especially in its espousal of pacifism—the distinctiveness of Christian communities amid the larger culture. And King, in his embrace of social gospel convictions about the relevance of Christian faith to social matters and in his anticipation of liberationist themes, offers a composite position between the social gospel of the early twentieth century and contemporary liberationists. Focusing on these figures provides a broadly representative portrait of future paths in contemporary Protestant Christian ethics.

Moreover, the work of each of these theologians exists in profoundly ambivalent but potentially productive relationship with that of feminists, whose diverse perspectives are so vital and important yet are often marginalized. Elements of Niebuhr's, Yoder's, and King's thought seem at once resonant and discordant with some of the central concerns of feminist thought. Yet, with the exception of Niebuhr, there is a dearth of feminist dialogue with these figures. How does this lack of engagement affect not only the legacies of Niebuhr, Yoder, and King, but also the entire field?

One of the most common criticisms witness theologians make of Niebuhr is that he lacks an ecclesiology. Niebuhr's own contemporaries frequently articulated this criticism,[21] but it is also made by theologians like Yoder, whose work spanned the later part of Niebuhr's career and continued after Niebuhr's death. Yoder claims not only that Niebuhr's theology is, in the first instance, anthropology, but also that he lacks attention to central theological doctrines like the resurrection, the Holy Spirit, and ecclesiology.[22] Contemporary postliberals repeat the refrain. Subtitles in two recent articles put it clearly but, as I will argue, perhaps too cleverly: "Why Christian Realism May Not Be Quite as Theologically Serious as It May Appear,"[23] and "Reinhold Niebuhr's Ecclesiology, or Lack Thereof."[24] The claim has become so commonplace that it seems

---

21. For a discussion of criticisms from Niebuhr's contemporaries, see Gary Dorrien, *Social Ethics in the Making: Interpreting an American Tradition* (Malden, MA: Wiley-Blackwell, 2009), 238.

22. John Howard Yoder, "Reinhold Niebuhr and Christian Pacifism," *Mennonite Quarterly Review* 29 (April 1955): 116.

23. Samuel Wells, "The Nature and Destiny of Serious Theology," in *Reinhold Niebuhr and Contemporary Politics: God and Power*, ed. Richard Harries and Stephen Platten (Oxford: Oxford University Press, 2010), 83.

24. William T. Cavanaugh, "A Nation with the Church's Soul: Richard John Neuhaus and Reinhold Niebuhr on Church and Politics," *Political Theology* 14, no. 3 (2013): 391.

to operate more as shorthand (enabling postliberals to identify their ideological perspective) and less as any substantive argument about Niebuhr's work. Equally troubling, because of their own focus on politics, realists themselves do not effectively highlight Niebuhr's ecclesiological insights. Several studies seek to reclaim Niebuhr's theological contributions but few attend to Niebuhr's thought on the churches. By and large, realists fail to respond adequately to witness caricatures, leaving Niebuhr's ecclesial contributions underemphasized.

Of course, witness theologians are in some sense correct. It is true that Niebuhr focuses on the politics of the state and does not devote himself to developing a full-blown ecclesiology. Nevertheless, he does discuss the church. The quick dismissals that appear with nearly every mention of Niebuhr's name in witness circles may usefully signal the writer's theological loyalties, but they prevent the appreciation of Niebuhr's potential contribution to ecclesiology. This is a substantial theological loss, as Niebuhr's reflection on the church can be developed to enhance not only his own legacy but also contemporary witness and realist theologians' own projects. In fact, Niebuhr's insights on the church are desperately needed in current ecclesiological reflection. His emphasis on the role of Christianity in fostering self-criticism and in the practices of the church in cultivating humility and hope both contribute to realism in the form of ecclesiology and offer welcome antidotes to the overconfident and idealized expressions of the church's political mission promulgated by witness theologians.

Yoder also loses when it comes to the witness-realist debate. Although many witness theologians take Yoder's work as their point of departure, their antipathy to liberalism and to feminism[25] depart from key elements of Yoder's account of Christian politics as well as its relationship to extra-ecclesial politics. Equally unfortunate, realists tend to underappreciate the extra-ecclesial politics for which Yoder's account calls. Their emphasis on the politics of the state leads to mistaken claims that Yoder renounces politics altogether when, in fact, he eschews only one political option: the use of force. As with Niebuhr, the polarization between witness and realist theologians obscures the issues. Witness theologians have posited a Yoder who is not only postliberal but also antiliberal. Realists have not appreciated the extra-ecclesial resistance to systemic violence for which Yoder's account calls. Neither group fully appreciates Yoder's challenge to its perspective. My reading of Yoder challenges witness theologians to take up the issue of feminism as part and parcel of the pacifist politics of the church and to honor the confluences that sometimes obtain between Christianity and liberalism. It also bids realists to recognize the distinctive contributions of the church to "secular" politics.

The fierce debate also impoverishes an appreciation of King's continuing contributions. Although there are increasing numbers of studies on King's theology, the majority of scholarly studies on King provide historical treatments of his work as an activist in the civil rights movement, focusing on King as a political leader who led a national movement for social change. Despite his self-identification as a Baptist preacher—one who led the Southern Christian Leadership Conference and mobilized black churches during the civil rights movement—King is regularly referred to as a politician.[26] When it comes to witness and realist theologians, King is either praised in passing as a "heroic figure" or simply neglected. It is odd that King does not garner more attention from both groups of theologians. King is, after all, the quintessential Christian witness in the very sense that witness theologians emphasize. But King's embrace of

25. For example, Stanley Hauerwas, perhaps the best-known theologian to claim Yoder's legacy, both positions his own project over against liberalism and dismisses feminist theologies as versions of liberalism.

26. See, for example, the back cover of *Reinhold Niebuhr and Contemporary Politics.*

extra-ecclesial politics distances him from these scholars. King's involvement in extra-ecclesial politics and pursuit of justice would also seem to earn him favor among realists, and yet his dedication to nonviolence distinguishes his exercise of extra-ecclesial politics from that of realists who make concessions for occasional justified use of force.

Yet, as with Niebuhr and Yoder, King's theological reflection and practice provide especially important insights for witness and realist theologians alike. King's own attention to the triple evils of racism, materialism, and militarism are deeply needed as correctives to current witness political ecclesiologies, most of which continue to overlook these problems. Although witness theologians have taken up important issues related to capitalism and consumerism, racism and nonmilitary forms of violence such as the systemic violence of sexism remain among the challenges their ecclesiologies continue to ignore. Similarly, King serves as a reminder to realists of the importance of the church and its formative practices in sustaining extra-ecclesial politics, especially with regard to enabling the "possibility" part of what Niebuhr referred to as the "impossible possibility" of love in politics. As with Niebuhr and Yoder, the polarization between witness and realist theologians detracts from King's important contributions.

## Feminist Contributions

Given their focus on Christian politics, witness and realist theologians' neglect of feminist theologies and feminist theologians' tendency to avoid weighing in on discussion in public theology strike one as particularly odd. Of all theologians, feminists provide some of the most careful, nuanced work reflecting on the relationship between the theological and the political. If any group of theologians demonstrates the redundancy of the monikers "public theology" and "political theology," it is feminist theologians. Throughout the rich variety and diversity of feminist work lies a well-demonstrated and shared theme: all theology is political. Contemporary feminist work builds on the indispensable work of pioneering feminist and womanist theologians[27] whose work highlights the importance of theological language and its role in shaping cultural and social norms; the negative import of theological concepts on women's identity and agency; the complicated inter-workings of theology and social and political organization; and the relationship between theology and socio-economic and political categories. In essence, feminist and womanist theologians expand the conception of what constitutes theology. Their work demonstrates the power of theology to influence political realities that shape people's daily lives. Without their significant contributions, understanding of the myriad ways in which theology is always already "political theology" would be severely impoverished.

And yet, prominent witness and realist accounts of Christian politics rarely engage this work, and feminists rarely engage conversations in public theology. Eager to distinguish their postliberal theologies from theological liberalism, witness theologians often reduce the diversity of feminist theologies to versions of theological liberalism. Feminist theologies, so the claim goes, are really just liberal theologies in another key:[28] they import Enlightenment reasoning into Christian theological reflection; they smuggle non-Christian vocabulary, concepts, and norms into their supposedly theological work; they do social, political, and economic analysis and pass it off as theology. Another version of this criticism

---

27. See, for example, the work of Katie G. Cannon, Mary Daly, Beverly W. Harrison, Elizabeth A. Johnson, Rosemary Radford Ruether, Letty M. Russell, Elisabeth Schüssler Fiorenza, and Delores S. Williams.
28. See, for example, Stanley Hauerwas, "Failure of Communication *or* A Case of Uncomprehending Feminism," *Scottish Journal of Theology* 50, no. 2 (1997): 234.

charges that feminist theologians have yet to do actual constructive work, that feminist theology is simply critique.[29] In short, feminist theologies are just not theological enough.

If witness theologians dismiss feminists altogether, realists tend to be more receptive. But they often subsume feminist work under their own conceptual rubrics. Rather than focusing on distinctive feminist characteristics, realists sometimes regard various feminisms as different forms of realism.[30] This move highlights important synergies between these approaches, but it underemphasizes the particularly feminist aspects of feminist work. The lack of engagement with the important work of a variety of feminists and womanists is unfortunate. Not only does it detract from these theologians' contributions and stymie new lines of work, it overlooks the significant resources of a diversity of feminist theologies to mediate the witness-realist divide.

Rather than focusing on issues related to the public accessibility of Christian truth claims, questions about the moral permissibility of force, and whether Christians should focus on ecclesial or extra-ecclesial politics, feminist accounts tend to examine the ethical impact of Christian truth claims and feature broader conceptions of violence and politics than realist and witness theologians. This concern for how Christian truth claims affect the most vulnerable of persons, attention to the systemic violence of sexism, racism, and classism, and broad conceptions of what counts as political enables feminists to sidestep the intractable debates that consume witness and realist

---

29. For an excellent discussion of such claims, see Rachel Muers, "Doing Traditions Justice," in *Gendering Christian Ethics*, ed. Jenny Daggers (Newcastle: Cambridge Scholars, 2012), 7–22.
30. Robin W. Lovin, for example, identifies feminists Jean Bethke Elshtain and Catherine Keller as proponents of various realisms in *Christian Realism and the New Realities*, 28-37. I do not disagree with this characterization; I merely note that it underemphasizes Elshtain's and Keller's distinctively feminist commitments.

theologians, revealing the value of their approaches to public theology.

But feminists rarely engage discussions in public theology or those involving the work of Niebuhr, Yoder, and King. This is especially unfortunate, since reading the theologies of Niebuhr, Yoder, and King alongside those of various feminists and womanists not only illuminates new possibilities for the legacies of Niebuhr, Yoder, and King within Christian ethics but also contributes to the projects of feminist, realist, and witness theologians alike.

Granted, there are good reasons for this lack of engagement. Although there will be a need for feminist critique of tradition as long as the sin of sexism persists,[31] feminists have their own agendas. They do not need to be limited to exposing sexism in the work of "seminal" figures in the tradition. Despite my own focus on Niebuhr, Yoder, and King, I find compelling the arguments of many feminists that Christian ethics must move beyond studies of the lone male figure.[32] In one sense, my study participates in this highly contested move. But in another sense, my focus on these figures is not just about three male theologians, but the whole field of Christian ethics. As theologian Kathryn Tanner has argued, feminist theologies wield the most significant influence on the larger field and increase their own legitimacy when they reconfigure oppressive uses of the tradition to liberating ends.[33] My work takes just such an approach by identifying "feminist" trajectories in the legacies of Niebuhr, Yoder, and King,

---

31. Muers, "Doing Traditions Justice," 7–8.
32. See, for example, West, "Constructing Ethics," 37; and "Gendered Legacies of Martin Luther King Jr.'s Leadership," *Theology Today* 65 (2008): 44; Rachel Muers, "Bonhoeffer, King, and Feminism: Problems and Possibilities," in *Bonhoeffer and King: Their Legacies and Import for Christian Social Thought*, ed. Willis Jenkins and Jennifer M. McBride (Minneapolis: Fortress Press, 2010), 33–42.
33. Kathryn Tanner, "Social Theory Concerning the 'New Social Movements' and the Practice of Feminist Theology," in *Horizons in Feminist Theology: Identity, Tradition, and Norms*, ed. Rebecca S. Chopp and Sheila Greeve Davaney (Minneapolis: Fortress Press, 1997), 189–90.

and by demonstrating the indispensability of feminist theologies in doing so.

But focus on the lone male authority is far from the only problem feminists might identify with these particular figures. Given the reform-oriented nature of feminist scholarship, feminists may find it difficult to engage figures whose personal lives seem at odds with their own best insights. Perhaps Niebuhr is a partial exception. Unlike Yoder and King, Niebuhr did not personally behave in denigrating ways toward women, and there is, after all, a good deal of feminist response to his work. But there is also increasing evidence that Niebuhr's wife Ursula may have been the unacknowledged coauthor of much of his work,[34] as well as criticism that Niebuhr's privilege prevented him from registering the important work being done by black female contemporaries in Harlem.[35] Although Yoder identifies Jesus as a feminist and argues for the centrality of gender egalitarianism to Jesus' ministry, his focus on pacifism as a refusal of state violence prevents him from fully developing these aspects of his pacifist position. Moreover, Yoder's pervasive sexual violence against women calls into question his commitment to feminism as part and parcel of Christian mission.[36] King's legacy presents problems of both

---

34. See Rebekah Miles, "Uncredited: Was Ursula Niebuhr Reinhold's Coauthor?" *Christian Century* 129, no. 2 (January 25, 2012): 30–33.
35. West, "Constructing Ethics."
36. Yoder's pervasive sexual violence is documented in the January 2015 issue of the *Mennonite Quarterly Review*. For a historical narrative of Yoder's case, see Rachel Waltner Goossen, "'Defanging the Beast': Mennonite Responses to John Howard Yoder's Sexual Abuse," *Mennonite Quarterly Review* 89, no. 1 (January 2015): 7–80. According to Goossen, mental health professionals who worked with Yoder estimate that he violated more than 100 women (10–11). I take up the difficulties Yoder's complex legacy raises in my forthcoming article, "Doing Justice to the Complex Legacy of John Howard Yoder: Restorative Justice Resources in Witness and Feminist Ethics," *Journal of the Society of Christian Ethics* 35, no. 2 (Fall/Winter 2015). For additional discussion of Yoder's abusive behavior and his theological legacy, see Ruth Elizabeth Krall, *The Elephants in God's Living Room, Volume Three: The Mennonite Church and John Howard Yoder, Collected Essays,* http://ruthkrall.com/downloadable-books/volume-three-the-mennonite-church-and-john-howard-yoder-collected-essays/; David Cramer, Jenny Howell, Jonathan Tran, and Paul Martens, "Scandalizing John Howard Yoder," *The Other*

theoretical content and concrete practice. Despite championing civil rights, King not only failed to address the evil of sexism, he himself failed to treat women as equals in both his professional and personal life.

For these reasons, and perhaps others, it is understandable if feminists choose to avoid these figures. But in my view, these discrepancies make engagement between these figures and feminists more, not less, valuable. And, as I hope to show, reading these figures alongside various feminists and womanists charts new territory beyond the witness-realist divide.

### Method: Doing Christian Ethics "at the Boundary" through a "Genuine Community of Argument"

Following King's insight that one cannot reach improved ends without improved means, I argue that the method of theology is just as important as the content. As such, I will use theologian Kathryn Tanner's work in *Theories of Culture* to guide my methodological

*Journal,* July 7, 2014, http://theotherjournal.com/2014/07/07/scandalizing-john-howard-yoder/ and "Theology and Misconduct: The Case of John Howard Yoder," *Christian Century* 131, no. 17 (August 20, 2014): 20–23; Gerald W. Schlabach, "Only Those We Need Can Betray Us: My Relationship with John Howard Yoder and His Legacy," GeraldSchlabach.net, July 14, 2014, http:// www.geraldschlabach.net /2014 /07 /10 /only-those-we-need-can-betray-us-my-relationship-with-john-howard-yoder-and-his-legacy; Mark Oppenheimer, "A Theologian's Influence, and Stained Past, Live On," *New York Times* (October 11, 2013): A14; Mark Thiessen Nation, with Marva Dawn, "On Contextualizing Two Failures of John Howard Yoder," Anabaptist Nation Blog, September 23, 2013, http://emu.edu/now/anabaptist-nation/2013/09/23/on-contextualizing-two-failures-of-john-howard-yoder/; and Kate Tracy, "Christian Publisher: All of Top Theologian's Books Will Now Have Abuse Disclaimer," *Christianity Today,* December 18, 2013, http://www.christianitytoday.com/gleanings/2013/december/publisher-john-howard-yoder-books-abuse-women-mennonite.html?paging=off; and "Yoder Suspended," *Christian Century* 109, no. 24 (August 12, 1992): 737–38. For the original reporting of the offenses, see Tom Price's five-part series in *The Elkhart Truth*: "Theologian Cited in Sex Inquiry" (June 29, 1992): B1; "Theologian's Future Faces a 'Litmus Test': Yoder's Response to Allegations Could Determine Standing in the Field" (July 12, 1992): B1; "Theologian Accused: Women Report Instances of Inappropriate Conduct" (July 13, 1992): B1; "A Known Secret: Church Slow to Explore Rumors Against a Leader" (July, 14 1992): B1; "Yoder Actions Framed in Writings" (July 15, 1992): B1; and "Teachings Tested: Forgiveness, Reconciliation in Discipline" (July, 16 1992): B1.

approach. I do so for two reasons: 1) Tanner's concept of Christian identity as constituted by participation in a *"genuine community of argument"*[37] highlights the importance of debate among those who disagree but also the need for this debate to be conducted in a manner consistent with Christian aims; and 2) her identification of Christian distinctiveness as being formed "not so much . . . *by* the boundary as *at* it"[38] helpfully identifies my own methodology.

The "genuine community of argument" is Tanner's answer to the question of Christian identity. Relying specifically on postmodern cultural theory, Tanner argues that Christian identity is not constituted by shared beliefs or practices, appeals to tradition, or rules, but rather by participation in a "genuine community of argument" about the meaning of Christian identity. Contrary to modern views of tradition as either stores of material that are interpreted differently in different contexts or deposits that change gradually over time, Tanner argues that the task of interpreting those materials, not tradition, provides the common denominator among those who claim Christian identity. In her words, "It is not the sharing of a particular account of their interpretation or organization that makes one a Christian. . . . What makes for Christian identity is the fact that such *investigation* is viewed as crucial, not *agreement* on its outcomes."[39] It is important to note that this "argument" is not limited to verbal expressions but includes Christian practices, such as the sacraments.

Although some may view this account as leaning too heavily on procedural criteria for defining Christian identity at the expense of common substantive content, it offers a particularly fruitful and theologically robust approach to handling the different stances that

---

37. Tanner, *Theories of Culture*, 123.
38. Ibid., 115.
39. Ibid., 125.

mark the field of Christian ethics. Tanner's emphasis on investigation over agreement is perhaps most important for my purposes because it highlights not agreement on final outcomes but the character of engagement required. Because it does not aim for uniformity of belief, Tanner's account honors the diversity of belief that obtains, for example, between the witness, realist, and feminist theologians considered here, and emphasizes the virtues needed to prevent that diversity from becoming divisive. She posits the need for the genuine community of argument to be "marked by mutual hearing and criticism among those who disagree, by a common commitment to mutual correction and uplift, in keeping with the shared hope of good discipleship, proper faithfulness, and purity of witness."[40]

Tanner's concept also proves to be a fitting mediator between witness and realist theologians because her work locates the distinctiveness of Christian belief in neither the ecclesially embodied countercultural witness of witness theologians nor the "relevance" of Christian insights to secular politics of realist theologians. Rather, for Tanner, "the distinctiveness of a Christian way of life is not so much formed *by* the boundary as *at* it," as Christians negotiate their identity in relation to "cultural materials shared with others."[41] This means that Christian identity is "no longer a matter of unmixed purity, but a hybrid affair established through unusual uses of materials found elsewhere."[42] In highlighting both the distinctiveness of Christian identity and its use of common cultural materials, Tanner's account strikes a balance between postliberal and liberal understandings of how Christianity relates to the wider culture. Her theology reflects the postliberal bent of the so-called Yale School, but also features valuable liberal insights without buying into the deficiencies of liberal

40. Ibid., 123–24.
41. Ibid., 115.
42. Ibid., 152.

accounts of Christianity's relationship to culture. It assumes, with postliberals, a conception of Christianity as a distinctive culture, but refuses, with liberals, the postliberal conception of this cultural boundary as so firm that it produces a distinctively pure Christian culture that shares little with the wider culture. It assumes, with liberals, that Christianity will share much of the same cultural materials with others, but refuses, with postliberals, to understand these common sources as undermining the distinctiveness of Christian identity. Despite their different accounts of how Christian identity interacts with the surrounding culture, Tanner argues that both postliberals and liberals make the mistake of positing an internally formed Christian identity that is then either in countercultural or in correlative identity with the cultures with which it interacts.

Because of these strengths, I use her concept as a model to host a conversation between witness and realist theologians that honors both the witness emphasis on the church and its practices as its own political option and the realist emphasis on extra-ecclesial politics. Using witness, realist, and feminist critiques to identify potential sites for construction "not so much . . . *by* the boundary as *at* it," my study locates spaces for needed work in Christian ethics. It thereby refigures the theological contributions of Niebuhr, Yoder, and King for new purposes while strengthening witness, realist, and feminist theologians' own agendas.

In my judgment, it is just this kind of engagement that we academic theologians too often fail to manifest in our work. Our stances are meant to promote movement but often they become immobilizing. They prepare us to respond to the "play" at hand but not the play that comes from a direction we cannot already anticipate. This is not to say that the boundaries that mark the playing field of Christian ethics are not useful. Indeed, I want to be clear: I am not arguing that we should seek to transcend these boundaries. My proposal depends on the existence of boundaries and celebrates the differences they mark. We necessarily employ a variety of intradisciplinary labels to categorize and understand the diverse range of theological approaches that comprise our fields. These labels help identify methodological perspectives and name motivating questions; they delineate common features of certain theological frameworks or schools and clarify their relationship to those of other schools. They enable me, for example, to refer meaningfully to Niebuhr as a Christian realist, or to identify a dearth of dialogue between feminists and Yoder, or to describe the hybrid nature of King's theological thought. In short, these categories orient and enable our work.

These categories prove valuable not only for naming the variety of positions and schools within theology and ethics but for *creating* them. They serve the important function of securing the space for scholars of traditionally marginalized perspectives to do their work. We have "feminist theology," "womanist ethics," "*mujerista* theology," "Asian theologies" and so on in part because we can name these fields as such. It is no surprise that theologians and ethicists from these perspectives often champion the "power of naming"; without this power, one does not exist. Just as the God of Genesis 1 creates by separating and by naming, theologians name themselves and their areas of expertise into existence. We need these boundaries. The differences they name enable us to appreciate other points of view and to understand our own more clearly. It is not the boundaries, then, that are the problem, but rather approaches to the boundaries that succumb to divisiveness.

Indeed, these same categories can function in less than helpful ways. They can be used to misidentify or mischaracterize theological positions, obscuring rather than illuminating a thinker's approach and perspectives. When I describe King as belonging to the social gospel tradition, for example, I neglect his indebtedness to and innovations on Christian realism; and perhaps more important, I obscure his primary grounding in African-American church traditions and his critique of racism. Moreover, in describing him as a liberationist, I overshadow feminist, womanist, Latina, and Asian theologians who more fully embody or explicitly identify with this tradition. The very category of liberation, like that of "feminist theologies," conceals significant differences among its adherents.

Other unproductive uses of these categories appear across our theological and ethical endeavors in the academy. While these categories are often mobilized quite purposefully to signal a theological or ideological commitment—to make a theological point—they can simultaneously function as conversation stoppers. Presumably, "theological ethicists" describe themselves as such to distinguish their starting points from the theologically inadequate ones of "social ethicists." But theologians also often mobilize these categories intentionally to relieve themselves of the burden of engaging with those with whom they disagree. In my experience, the distinctions between "liberal theology" and "postliberal theology," and "public theology" and "feminist theology," often function this way. But even if one does not intend such use, it is difficult to avoid less-than-productive consequences.

### Overview of the Chapters

In chapter 1, I detail the witness-realist debate that has dominated Christian ethics in recent decades. I assess both the indispensable contributions made to Christian ethics by these scholars and the problems in their accounts that might be addressed by constructive conversation between feminist theologies and Niebuhr, Yoder, and King. Witness accounts contribute a valuable emphasis on the importance of the church and its practices for ecclesial politics. But their overidealized ecclesiologies fail to grapple with the complex interrelationships between "church" and "world," thereby neglecting extra-ecclesial politics and the church's response to and complicity in racism and sexism. The main contributions of realist accounts reside in their thoughtful reflection on the need for extra-ecclesial political participation, the relevance of Christianity to politics, and the need to pay explicit attention to possibilities and limits. But these accounts often undervalue the importance of the church as its own particular arena for moral formation and political witness. The chapter then explores the significant contributions of recent "new Augustinian" interventions, valuing the advances of these accounts beyond the witness-realist impasse and their incorporation of feminist insights—while also noting missed opportunities for further conversation with feminist theologies. Finally, it inquires into the ability of feminist and womanist theologies to illuminate new paths in Christian ethics.

Chapter 2 offers a witness- and feminist-inspired appropriation of Reinhold Niebuhr's thought on the church. The chapter begins by highlighting significant points of connection between witness and feminist theologians. It argues that despite their apparent differences, witness and feminist theologians make many of the same formal critiques of Niebuhr's work, including a shared substantive critique that Niebuhr rejects the moral potential of religious communities. Treating their criticisms as invitations to explore the potential of Niebuhr's thought to contribute to the work of theologians across the stances of Christian ethics, I attempt to provide a charitable exegesis of Niebuhr's theology that renders it more amenable to witness and feminist agendas. Might Niebuhr's thought possess resources that could be developed into an account of the church and its moral capacities that would honor the insights of both witness and feminist theologians? What would the character of such a community be?

What virtues would its members embody? How would they act? Highlighting thematic similarities between Niebuhr's discussion of churches and theologian Kathryn Tanner's thesis that Christianity, and particularly belief in divine transcendence, possesses the capacity to create "self-critical cultures," I develop Niebuhr's reflection on the nature and role of the church into a Niebuhrian account of churches as self-critical cultures who engage in formative practices of contrition that cultivate the virtues of humility and hope, giving rise to creative ethical action. This account contributes to realism by detailing a potential realist ecclesiology. It also contributes to witness and feminist theologies by correcting the overidealism prevalent in witness ecclesiologies and the tendency of feminist interpreters to appropriate Niebuhr's thought outside of explicitly ecclesial frameworks.

Chapter 3 uses realist and feminist criticism and witness appropriations of Yoder to argue that feminism is a vital form of Christian political witness. I argue against common realist contentions that Yoder neglects extra-ecclesial politics, showing that he rejects only one political option: the use of violence. I then argue against feminist and womanist critiques that understand Yoder's interpretation of "revolutionary subordination" as an endorsement of women's oppression, and prominent witness tendencies to espouse hostilities toward both feminism and liberalism. I show that Yoder's theology posits feminism as integral to Christian identity and encourages tactical alliances between Christianity and liberalism. Indeed, Yoder's account features striking points of connection with certain feminist theologies, including shared conceptions of Christianity as a culture, shared conceptions of their respective theologies as Christian projects of retrieval, and shared conceptions of the church's vocation as entailing countercultural witnesses of peace. I then argue that despite prominent witness claims to Yoder's legacy, it is feminists and womanists whose work—while certainly not doing so intentionally—best develops Yoder's pacifist vision. Feminist analysis of nonmilitary forms of violence by Gloria Albrecht and Linda Woodhead, recent feminist work on trauma by Cynthia Hess, Serene Jones, and others, and recent womanist attention to "the cultural production of evil" and gender injustice in black churches by Emilie M. Townes, Marcia Y. Riggs, and Kelly Brown Douglas can all be seen as expanding and developing Yoder's account of Christian pacifism.

In chapter 4, I address the neglect of King by witness, realist, and feminist theologians alike. I first demonstrate convergences between a variety of feminist and womanist reconstructions of agape (including those of Beverly W. Harrison, Carter Heyward, Linell E. Cady, and Patricia Hunter) and a transformation of King's own conception of love from the standard Protestant accounts that emphasize disinterestedness, nonreciprocity, and self-sacrifice to one akin to feminist reconstructions of love as passionate, mutual, and community-forming. Moreover, the "creative" nature of this love as King describes it resonates with an emphasis on the creative power of love in work by Monica A. Coleman, Karen Baker-Fletcher, and other womanists. This account not only yields new agendas for those committed to King's legacy, it also contributes meaningfully to witness, realist, and feminist theologies. Witness theologians might find that King challenges them to address questions of race as well as conceptions of extra-ecclesial politics consistent with their own emphasis on witness. Realists might find themselves challenged to attend to the importance of the church as a sphere of moral formation that funds extra-ecclesial politics. And finally, while not exonerating King from his failure to address sexism, the chapter challenges feminists and womanists to recognize King as a theopolitical ally whose work features "feminist" arcs.

## Contributions

Each chapter uses witness, realist, and feminist criticism to identify sites of construction in the thought of Niebuhr, Yoder, and King that, in turn, strengthen each stance's own internal agenda. Moving beyond the polarization between Christian ethicists over the role of Christianity in public life in recent decades, this study affirms the importance of both ecclesial and extra-ecclesial politics to the Christian vocation. It embraces the importance of ecclesiology and particular church practices while challenging overidealistic accounts of church that neglect both extra-ecclesial political action and pervasive forms of nonmilitary violence such as racism, sexism, classism.

The collaboration I initiate by placing witness, realist, and feminist theologians in a "genuine community of argument," and by identifying new agendas for Christian ethics "at the boundary" of their approaches, also offers new readings of Niebuhr's, Yoder's, and King's relevance to public theology. In each chapter I address the dismissal, misinterpretation, or neglect of these figures among contemporary postliberals, realists, and feminists. But perhaps most importantly, I do so while enhancing the internal vitality of each stance, thus demonstrating the substantive benefits of a methodological approach that privileges constructive engagement with difference. Such an approach ensures that Christian ethicists are not only modeling productive ways to engage difference but also enhancing the potential of their work to meet current moral challenges.

# 1

---

# Old Divides and New Trajectories in Christian Ethics

The current divide between witness and realist theologians has its origins in much older debates. Before "public theology" existed as a subfield, and before feminist theologies even arrived on the theological scene, Karl Barth and Reinhold Niebuhr found themselves on opposite sides of the theological crises provoked by the twentieth-century world wars. In order to understand what is at stake for contemporary witness and realist theologians, this chapter briefly reviews that debate before examining two of the most important contemporary witness and realist accounts as well as significant feminist contributions.

The main burden of the chapter is twofold: first, I argue that although contemporary witness and realist theologians often move beyond the Barth-Niebuhr argument in innovative directions, they also remain beholden to it in unproductive ways. I aim to show not only how contemporary witness and realist theologians' projects continue unnecessarily to neglect elements important to the other but also how attending to such would strengthen their proposals without sacrificing their integrity. Second, I aim to show through a discussion of significant feminist insights how an increased feminist presence in public theology would enhance the constructive reach of Niebuhr, Yoder, and King—all of whose legacies have been damaged by the witness-realist division—*while* benefiting witness, realist, and feminist proposals. My argument both demonstrates the indispensability of feminist theologies in reconfiguring "malestream" thought toward liberating ends and prevents "feminist theology from being classified as a marginal, fringe movement."[1] In short, I aim both to identify how the witness-realist divide and the feminist absence in public theology continue to be unproductive for the field and to explore the promising trajectories that emerge when opportunities for dialogue between witness, realist, and feminist theologies are taken seriously. But before we consider how Niebuhr's, Yoder's, and King's legacies might be reinvigorated, a look back is in order.

## Barth and Niebuhr

The world wars of the twentieth century precipitated a theological crisis. The optimism about human capacities for progress at the center of many of the liberal theologies then in vogue proved ill equipped to deal with the horrors of the day, raising anew the perennial question of how Christian faith should relate to political realities. Swiss theologian Karl Barth and his American colleague Reinhold Niebuhr developed two of the most significant theological responses.

The basic narrative of these two theologians' influence is a familiar one. In the wake of World War I, Barth published his commentary

---

1. Kathryn Tanner, "Social Theory Concerning the 'New Social Movements' and the Practice of Feminist Theology," in *Horizons in Feminist Theology: Identity, Tradition, and Norms*, ed. Rebecca S. Chopp and Sheila Greeve Davaney (Minneapolis: Fortress Press, 1997), 189.

on the book of Romans, which emphasized the radical disjuncture between God and human beings. Barth's thesis flew in the face of two theological trends: emphasis on human experience as a theological source for knowledge of God, and efforts to align certain social, political, and economic positions with the divine will. With this challenge to the Protestant liberal theologies prominent at the time, Barth, in the words of Karl Adam, "dropped a bomb on to the playground of the theologians."[2] He insisted that the word of God is free. It cannot be discerned easily either in nature or in preestablished ethical guidelines. Rather, it speaks a unique word of judgment to each situation. Barth did develop a conception of *analogia fidei* that identified "prominent lines"[3] for Christian moral action, but he continued to insist on the radical difference between the word of God and the world of humans. His focus on preserving God's freedom resisted not only clear manifestations of human evil, such as Nazism, but any straightforward identification of Christian truth with political opinion. Rather than attempting to discern the "right" Christian response to the political and social contingencies of the day, Barth encouraged Christians to focus on their communities of faith. And even here, Barth contended that Christian action is likely to be at odds with any particular political option. When the church acts, it moves "not with the stream but against it."[4]

Reinhold Niebuhr took a different tack. While he appreciated Barth's refusal to acquiesce to the "easy optimisms"[5] of liberal theology, Niebuhr condemned Barth's failure to provide concrete

2. As quoted in Stanley Hauerwas, *With the Grain of the Universe: The Church's Witness and Natural Theology* (Grand Rapids: Baker Academic, 2001), 152.
3. Robin W. Lovin, *Christian Faith and Public Choices: The Social Ethics of Barth, Brunner, and Bonhoeffer* (Philadelphia: Fortress Press, 1984), 118.
4. Karl Barth, "The Christian Community in the Midst of Political Change," in *Against the Stream: Shorter Post-War Writings, 1946–52* (London: SCM, 1954), 116.
5. Reinhold Niebuhr, "Barth—Apostle of the Absolute," in *Essays in Applied Christianity: The Church and the New World*, ed. D. B. Robertson (New York: Meridian, 1959), 143.

guidance for moral action. Dubbing Barth the "apostle of the absolute,"[6] Niebuhr responded with a Christian realism that, like Barth's theology, emphasized divine judgment and criticized liberal confidence in human progress. Niebuhr, however, departed from Barth in his assessment of the significance of God's judgment for human action. He put more emphasis on the role of mercy and forgiveness in freeing human beings for what he describes as responsible political action. Insisting that "we are men and not God,"[7] Niebuhr argued that our starting place is not the revelation of God per se but our limited understanding of it. Responding to the word of God "begins in our common experience of human reality."[8] For Niebuhr, Barth's emphasis on revelation and the church enabled what he considered an irresponsible withdrawal from responsible action. He insisted that despite human limits, concrete choices must be risked in specific situations. To do otherwise, according to Niebuhr, would be to sacrifice the good that might be possible in spite of evil.

The differences between Barth's and Niebuhr's responses to the theological challenges of their lifetimes continue to shape Christian theology. Although history ensures changes in context, the contours of the debate remain largely the same.[9] Witness theologians challenge realists' reliance on human experience; realists criticize witness theologians for too absolute a conception of revelation. Witness theologians criticize realists for accommodating Christian truth to social and political realities; realists accuse witness theologians of abdicating moral responsibility by refusing to make discriminate judgments between good and evil. Witness theologians accuse realists

---

6. Ibid., 141.
7. Reinhold Niebuhr, "We are Men and Not God," in *Essays in Applied Christianity*, 168.
8. Lovin, *Christian Faith*, 14.
9. This is not to minimize the significant differences that obtain between the various contemporary witness and realist theologians' accounts or their differences from Barth's and Niebuhr's positions.

of betraying the church's distinctive political witness; realists chastise witness theologians for what they characterize as an irresponsible withdrawal into the church. At stake for both is faithful Christian engagement in the world, and each finds the other wanting in radical ways.

Given the tenor of the discussion, it is tempting to posit a diametrical opposition between witness and realist approaches. And to be sure, there are a number of fundamental disagreements. Witness and realist theologians subscribe to different theories of truth.[10] Consequently, witness theologians emphasize the particularity and therefore publicly inaccessible nature of Christian truth claims, whereas realists are confident that Christian truth is relevant and accessible to a wider public. Witness theologians identify the church itself as the primary political identity for Christians, whereas realists see the primary tasks of Christian ethics as necessitating involvement in secular politics. Witness theologians espouse nonviolence, whereas realists allow for the use of force.

These are irreconcilable differences, and I make no effort to reconcile them. But more often than not, what appear to be fundamental differences can ultimately be seen as different sides of the same coin. What look like differences in starting points—revelation versus experience—end up being different ways to construe the relationship between revelation and experience. What look like different attitudes toward engaging society—witness versus apology—end up being different approaches to avoiding cultural accommodation. What look like differences in political strategies—a focus on the pacifist identity and mission of the church versus participation in secular politics—end up being different ways to

---

10. Christian realists are often moral and theological realists, whereas witness theologians subscribe to a narrative theory of truth. For an excellent discussion of these differences, see Robin W. Lovin, *Reinhold Niebuhr and Christian Realism* (Cambridge: Cambridge University Press, 1995). I recognize that these descriptions are contestable.

construe political responsibility. These similarities are just as important as the differences, as they often suggest opportunities for fruitful partnership and collaboration between witness and realist theologians. Unfortunately, theologians of both approaches rarely take advantage of such opportunities.

## Contemporary Witness and Realist Theologies

Although both Stanley Hauerwas and Robin W. Lovin—the best-known contemporary representatives of these schools—effectively expand the view from their respective vantage points, both also continue to be less than fully responsive to the other stance's critiques. Hauerwas's explorations of Christian "peaceableness" chart territory beyond the violence of the state, including reflection on topics as wide-ranging as abortion and mental disabilities. But despite his constant claim that the "first social ethical task of the church is to be the church,"[11] he does not identify the subsequent tasks[12] that prove integral to Christian ethics for realists. As such, he continues to neglect not only important questions raised by realists about Christians' moral responsibilities beyond the church but also constitutive components of the church's witness of peace: resistance to the violence of sexism and racism.

For his part, Lovin develops a Christian realism focused not, as Niebuhr's was, on the nation, but on the "new realities." Despite his affirmation of "unapologetic politics," however, his realism continues to under-analyze how the church sustains its politics—a topic of concern for witness theologians. Thus, despite his advance beyond Niebuhr's focus on the nation to articulate a Christian realism for

11. Stanley Hauerwas, *The Peaceable Kingdom: A Primer in Christian Ethics* (Notre Dame, IN: University of Notre Dame Press, 1983), 99.
12. As Eric Gregory puts it, "He does not give an account of what a second, or third, social ethical task might be." See *Politics and Order of Love: An Augustinian Ethic of Democratic Citizenship* (Chicago: University of Chicago Press, 2008), 132.

the new realities of globalization and the power of new religious movements, his proposal continues to leave largely unanswered witness questions about how the church and other contexts cultivate the necessary moral resources to meet current challenges. What is perhaps most curious about both of these oversights is that, despite certain nonnegotiable differences between their accounts, providing more adequate answers to each other's questions is entirely possible without sacrificing integrity. In fact, far from compromising their accounts, responding more readily to the other's criticism would actually strengthen them.

## Christian Witness

Witness theologians have devoted a great deal of attention to the church and how its narrative and practices form Christian communities in moral virtue, preparing them for a distinctive witness. If Barth's own hesitancy to associate Christian ethics with the questions of politics was motivated by the aim to resist the accommodation of Christianity to National Socialism, Hauerwas identifies political liberalism as the Constantinian temptation for American Christians. It is impossible to do justice to Hauerwas's contributions to the field of Christian ethics. His prolific writings make it difficult to even cover the body of his work in any detail. But among his significant contributions are a renewed focus on the church and its practices as constituting its own politics, the importance of virtue and character for Christian ethics, and attention to the ways Christians must resist cultural accommodation. In addition to addressing war-related issues, Hauerwas develops his understanding of Christian "peaceableness" in relation to important moral questions such as abortion and issues related to the family and mental disability.

Hauerwas is perhaps most famous for his insistence that the church is its own political and social reality. He is frequently quoted as saying that "the church does not have a social ethic; the church is a social ethic."[13] Highly critical of the social gospel ideal of Christianizing the social order—with which he identifies Reinhold Niebuhr as complicit, despite Niebuhr's disavowal of the social gospel—Hauerwas argues that it is not the primary responsibility of Christians to attempt to improve the social situation in which they live. "The first task of Christian social ethics . . . is not to make the 'world' better or more just, but to help Christian people form their community consistent with their conviction that the story of Christ is a truthful account of our existence."[14] One of the strengths of Hauerwas's approach is its focus on the church as a site of moral formation with its emphasis on the church's distinctive moral resources and the role of Christian Scripture and practices in shaping Christians in virtue. Also significant is Hauerwas's emphasis on the inherently political nature of the church's internal activity, especially in his insistence that church communities should provide alternative solutions to moral problems. Hauerwas finds himself in good company here with feminists, who also emphasize the inherently political nature of the church's institutional life and the task of theology itself. Feminists also understand the church's role as a countercultural witness against dominant (sexist, in the feminist case) cultural trends.

This emphasis on the church as its own polis enables witness theologians to distinguish Christian truth from American political liberalism. Because the "social ethical task of the church. . . is to be the kind of community that tells and tells rightly the story of

13. Hauerwas, *Peaceable Kingdom*, 99.
14. Stanley Hauerwas, *A Community of Character: Toward a Constructive Christian Social Ethic* (Notre Dame, IN: University of Notre Dame Press, 1981), 10.

Jesus,"[15] the church will often find itself at odds with the values and priorities of the larger culture. Upholding Barth's thesis that the church often runs against the stream, Hauerwas criticizes Christians who equate being a good Christian with being a good American. His proposal highlights the distinctiveness of the Christian community over against the values of the nation. Despite frequent critical claims to the contrary, this antagonism does not constitute a sectarian withdrawal from society. In Hauerwas's words, "This does not involve a rejection of the world, or a withdrawal from the world; rather it is a reminder that the church must serve the world on her own terms."[16] In this sense, emphasizing the church's particular moral identity and resources is less a withdrawal from worldly affairs and more a statement about the priority of Christian truth claims over those of other communities to which Christians may belong. Given the complexity of our identities and social roles—or as Hauerwas puts it, the fact that "we inherit too many histories and participate in too many communities"[17]—Hauerwas's insistence on the priority of the church serves as a reminder that despite their other communal identities, Christians' ecclesial identity is primary.

Despite the strengths of his proposal (and his prolific body of work), Hauerwas's proposals tend to leave important questions—especially those of concern to realists—under-addressed. Hauerwas continues to evade questions about how the church's witness of peace relates to extra-ecclesial politics. As Robert Jenson notes in his analysis of "the Hauerwas project," no matter how compelling his account, Hauerwas will never escape claims that he is sectarian if he does not more effectively address the question of how the church should navigate its relationship to the world.[18] Hauerwas's

---

15. Ibid., 52.
16. Ibid., 85.
17. Ibid., 126.
18. Robert W. Jenson, "The Hauerwas Project," *Modern Theology* 8, no. 3 (July 1992).

account rightly challenges Christians when they might be tempted to conflate American ideals and the truths of their faith. But his account is less effective at acknowledging what his own witness colleague, John Howard Yoder, once referred to as the "confluence of optimisms"[19] that sometimes obtains between American liberalism and Christianity. Nor does it fully address how the church might participate in larger political structures without compromising its particular identity and mission. Nor has it adequately acknowledged the ways liberalism itself operates as a moral tradition.[20] Hauerwas's interest in emphasizing the distinctiveness of the Christian tradition has meant that he has been too hesitant to identify the formative influence of the Christian tradition in political liberalism, the intricate relationship between church and world, and the variety of ways they already, and might yet, engage each other in mutually beneficial ways.[21]

But perhaps even more importantly, it is not just that Hauerwas avoids consideration of how the primary task of Christian ethics relates to its secondary tasks; he also stops short of adequately developing his account of the first task. There is, of course, more to being a peaceable community than rejecting the military violence of the state. But despite his important reflection on topics such as abortion, disability, and medical ethics, his elaboration of "peaceableness" has not done enough to engage questions raised by

19. John H. Yoder, *For the Nations: Essays Evangelical and Public* (Eugene, OR: Wipf & Stock, 2002), 126.

20. For such an account, see Jeffrey Stout, *Democracy and Tradition* (Princeton, NJ: Princeton University Press, 2004).

21. For a powerful critique of Hauerwas's project, see Nathan R. Kerr, *Christ, History and Apocalyptic: The Politics of Christian Mission* (Eugene, OR: Cascade, 2009). Kerr argues that Hauerwas's doctrinal focus on ecclesiology is both overdetermined by his antiliberalism and "reductive of Jesus' historicity," preventing Hauerwas from conceiving of the church's identity as constituted by its missionary encounter with the world (20, 93). Kerr's account of Christian politics, which calls for a shift from "church-as-*polis*" to "mission makes the church" (169), resonates at points with the account of "feminism as Christian politics" that I develop in chapter 3.

feminists and other liberation theologians about sexism and racism.[22] Hauerwas's account gives little indication of how the church should respond to either the internal violence of trauma or the pervasive forms of systemic violence within the church and in society at large. In this sense, it is not simply the case that Hauerwas ignores the "second" and "third" task of the church in favor of elaborating the first; his account also requires a fuller development of the first.

Hauerwas's neglect of racism and sexism are especially odd given that the theologian whom he credits for his conversion to pacifism, John Howard Yoder, saw both the rejection of ethnic provincialism and commitment to feminism as inherent to—indeed, constitutive of—the church's identity and mission. I am far from the first to raise this issue, and Hauerwas has responded to some of these criticisms. But while acknowledging the importance of these issues, Hauerwas generally defends his decision not to engage racism and sexism. For example, although Hauerwas identifies the black church as the best example of what his theology promotes, he also says that he has not written about Martin Luther King Jr. because King's story "is not *my* story."[23] But given Hauerwas's emphasis on the church as Christians' primary identity, it is hard to understand how King's story is not Hauerwas's story. Honestly acknowledging the difficulty of addressing racism as a white person has its own integrity and should be respected as such. But in another sense, it remains complicit in the white privilege that allows white persons to imagine that the issue of racism is not about them. It too easily excuses oneself from dealing with issues of critical importance.[24] Certainly, one cannot expect one scholar to write everything there is to write about the church's first

---

22. Hauerwas himself acknowledges that he can be "rightly criticized for not writing about the challenges raised by feminism." See Stanley Hauerwas, "Remembering How and What I Think: A Response to the *JRE* Articles on Hauerwas," *Journal of Religious Ethics* 40, no. 2 (2012): 302.
23. Stanley Hauerwas, "Remembering Martin Luther King Jr. Remembering: A Response to Christopher Beem," *Journal of Religious Ethics* 23, no. 1 (Spring 1995): 136.

task, but these issues represent missed opportunities for Hauerwas to develop his account in directions realists and feminists might appreciate while simultaneously strengthening his own agenda.

Despite substantial feminist response to his project, Hauerwas has also tended to avoid feminist concerns. This is not, he notes, because he has a problem with feminism, but because most feminist theologies are often versions of the theological liberalism he rejects.[25] While it is true that many feminist theologies—especially the earliest ones—reveal the influence of theological liberalism, the proliferation and significance of diverse feminist theological perspectives challenges Hauerwas's reasons for not engaging feminist theologies. I argue in chapter 3 that Hauerwas would do well to take a page out of Yoder's playbook on this count because Yoder identifies feminism as intrinsic to Christian identity and ecclesial politics. Doing so would enable a promising trajectory for work on which witness and feminist theologians might collaborate. What does a Christian witness of peace that takes sexism seriously as a form of systemic violence look like? The account of feminism as Christian politics that I develop in chapter 3 both enhances the relevance of Yoder's legacy and makes needed contributions to witness accounts like Hauerwas's by better addressing questions raised by realists about extra-ecclesial politics and by feminists about the church's response to racism and sexism.

## Christian Realism

Robin W. Lovin is arguably the most important realist in contemporary Christian ethics. His work has been instrumental in

---

24. Aaron D. Conley makes a similar argument in "Loosening the Grip of Certainty: A Case-Study Critique of Tertullian, Stanley Hauerwas, and Christian Identity," *Journal of the Society of Christian Ethics* 33, no. 1 (Spring/Summer 2013): 38.

25. Stanley Hauerwas, "Failure of Communication *or* A Case of Uncomprehending Feminism," *Scottish Journal of Theology* 50, no. 2 (1997): 234. See also Hauerwas, "Remembering How and What I Think," 302.

developing Christian realism, particularly in its attention to the significance of Reinhold Niebuhr's theology. As was the case with Hauerwas's work, it would be difficult to do justice to Lovin's significant contributions to the field in a brief overview. But some of his important contributions include studies that locate the roots of contemporary social ethics in the thought of Karl Barth, Emil Brunner, and Dietrich Bonhoeffer,[26] as well as a major study on Reinhold Niebuhr that carefully delineates the three realisms—political, theological, and moral—that comprise Niebuhr's realist stance.[27] Lovin continues the work of expounding Christian realism in *Christian Realism and the New Realities*, where he provides a short history of Christian realism and a typology of four prominent realisms present in contemporary Christian ethics.[28] But the bulk of this work consists of Lovin's own account of a realism responsive to the "new realities" that takes Niebuhr's Christian realism beyond Niebuhr's own formulation of it.[29]

Niebuhr's context dictated that Christian realists address the reality of the nation-state, but Lovin's account focuses on current realities. The nation-state remains important, but power is increasingly wielded by religious movements and transnational corporations. Consequently, the realists' caution about idolatrous attempts to defy human limits and reminders about the need to embrace God-given freedom require articulation in the context of these new realities. If Niebuhr talked about politics primarily in terms of national governments, realists today must operate with a much broader conception of politics. This politics includes the nation-state but also extends beyond it to include the variety of diverse settings wherein

---

26. Lovin, *Christian Faith*.
27. Lovin, *Reinhold Niebuhr and Christian Realism*.
28. Robin W. Lovin, *Christian Realism and the New Realities* (New York: Cambridge University Press, 2008).
29. Ibid., vii.

we pursue a multiplicity of goods in our everyday lives, including business, religion, family, and school.[30] Each constitutes a "context" that demands responsibility.[31] Nor can politics be limited to some public realm separated from so-called private life. Proposing an alternative to the either-or of choosing between the demands of "public reason" that refuses to admit religious claims in political deliberations and an "unapologetic theology" unconcerned with the public accessibility of religious claims, Lovin argues that each context possesses both internal and external "forums" that are best governed by an "Unapologetic Principle."[32] This principle protects the integrity of each context when it interacts with the others. It ensures each context's right to define itself. But, as Lovin notes, each context will likely choose to justify its existence to the others. When it does, it engages in a public forum where its claims are best made in terms the other contexts will understand.[33] In this complex, highly differentiated configuration of social reality, politics is no longer restricted to the sphere of law and government. It is, in short, "the deliberations by which we order our lives with others to make human goods and good lives possible."[34] Rather than separate the public from the private or the religious from the political, Lovin's account offers a broad conception of politics that brings into view the previously obscured political activity of our everyday lives.

Lovin's account is compelling. Not only does it acknowledge the various and diverse contexts in which we pursue human goods, it does justice to our complex identities and the multiplicity of roles and responsibilities to which these contexts give rise. It also attends to the moral conflict and ambiguity that result from the competing

30. Ibid., 13.
31. Ibid., 100.
32. Ibid., 129.
33. Ibid., 139.
34. Ibid., 144.

demands of each context as well as the complex relationships between contexts. While acknowledging the diversity of accounts of the good, his account does not despair of an ultimate unity that connects them. Perhaps most importantly, it does so without sacrificing the distinctiveness of each context. With his unapologetic principle, Lovin moves past the either-or of choosing between a theology of integrity or an untheological politics. Each context pursues its distinctive goods in its distinctive way and should be free to articulate its purpose on its own terms without being reduced to the purposes of the others. Because we pursue multiple goods in multiple contexts, each of which affects the others, it is also in the interest of the common good for each context to communicate and collaborate with the others. Doing so actually facilitates an internal sharpening of each context's identity and mission. In short, Lovin's account makes clear that one need not choose between theology and politics, church and world, distinctiveness and relevance.

And yet for all of these advances, Lovin remains beholden to some of the same oversights present in Niebuhr's account, preventing the emergence of new developments within realism that witness theologians might more readily appreciate. It appears that his endorsement of an unapologetic principle moves Lovin's realism toward a witness emphasis on the distinctive integrity of the Christian tradition. It honors the witness insight that the church must be clear about its own identity in the world if it is to have an effective political witness. In fact, Lovin's account not only affirms the witness emphasis on unapologetic theology for the church but also declares the need for just such an unapologetic approach for all contexts. In this sense, Lovin both takes witness insights seriously and sees their relevance for all of the institutions and communities in which we live. But, as witness theologians are likely to point out, Lovin's discussion still focuses on politics rather than the church. His "unapologetic politics" may have moved beyond Niebuhr's focus on "apology," but it has not moved far enough beyond Niebuhr's overemphasis on extra-ecclesial "politics." From the witness theologian's perspective, then, Lovin makes the same old mistake in a new era.

Indeed, although Lovin incorporates witness insights about the need for unapologetic politics, he emphasizes the interaction of the various contexts and their forums at the expense of attention to *how* each context ensures its distinctive integrity. On the one hand, Lovin's embrace of an unapologetic principle emphasizes the importance of the witness emphasis on cultivating resources to sustain unapologetic politics. He identifies the need for "an unapologetic moment"[35] for each context—a needed opportunity for all the contexts in which we live our lives to articulate their claims "in their own terms," lest any one context "claim to represent the one context to which all other goods must be subordinated."[36] On the other hand, he gives no indication of how each context prepares for such moments. In other words, his argument for the importance of maintaining the integrity of each context comes with inadequate attention to the resources and practices that preserve this integrity. How does the business world articulate its identity and maintain it? How do religious traditions foster their sense of identity and mission in the world? How does the university ensure that its identity, values, and goods are not subordinated to those of the economic world? Addressing these questions seems especially important in light of both Lovin's call for an unapologetic moment and the difficulty of protecting the integrity of each context from the encroachment of others. How is the balance between contexts maintained? Lovin notes that forums develop without anyone controlling the debate, but it would seem that maintaining the balance of contexts requires that

35. Ibid., 150.
36. Ibid.

each context focus on cultivating its identity and mission in the very ways that witness theologians emphasize about the church.

Lovin's embrace of an unapologetic principle thus raises the witness critique of realism in an especially acute way. Now it is not merely churches, but also businesses, schools, and universities that need to be able to articulate and preserve a distinctive identity. But to whom does this responsibility fall? No doubt witness theologians would argue that leaders and participants within each context should take responsibility for articulating their distinctive identity and mission. It makes as little sense for theologians to ensure the integrity of the nation-state as it does for business leaders to articulate and cultivate the identity and mission of the church. Clearly, theologians bear responsibility for unapologetic theology. Despite seeming progress toward rapprochement with witness theologians on this point, in the end Lovin's account still does not address how the church preserves its distinctive identity. He affirms that the church will be better able to do so if it also "becomes more articulate about how a society would have to be organized to make unapologetic theology possible."[37] But his proposal stops short of the kind of attention to the church and its practices that witness theologians would surely appreciate—even if they continue to disagree with Lovin about which context is primary.

To this line of argument the realist will of course respond that we all exist in multiple contexts and speak many particularistic internal languages. Our existence in multiple contexts ensures that the unapologetic moment of each context cannot be isolated from that of the others. Christian business leaders will have much to say in the internal forums of business. Christian theologians are also citizens and parents and will need to contribute to the integrity of those contexts. On this point, the realist emphasis differs from that of the

---

37. Ibid., 151.

witness theologians. But both approaches invite the question of how these resources are cultivated, returning us to the witness emphasis on the resources and practices that foster identity and mission—only this time, the question is writ large, applicable to all contexts, not only the church. It seems imperative for Lovin's account to address the question of *how* each context prepares itself for the unapologetic moment. In fact, it would seem that this becomes the central task of Christian ethics. And this requires a witness insistence on attention to the narratives, language, and practices that constitute the identity and mission of each context.

Although witness and realist theologians will continue to maintain different foci when it comes to the church's proper role vis-à-vis politics, they can agree that the church as a context must prepare itself for the unapologetic moment. This is a place—especially given Lovin's attention to the importance of integrity and his identification of religious movements as one of the most powerful new realities—where witness and realist theologians might productively think together. After all, realists need not abandon their interest in politics to account for how the church might prepare for an unapologetic moment. Indeed, their distinctive articulation of the church's identity and mission might prove critical in the unapologetic moment. Chapter 2, with its aim of developing a Niebuhrian conception of the church as a self-critical and creative culture, is an attempt to explore just what distinctive insight realists might have to offer to the question of the church's unapologetic politics.

In sum, both Hauerwas and Lovin make invaluable contributions to the field. If Hauerwas's emphasis on the church as its own polis demonstrates the centrality of the church for sustaining the kind of politics for which Lovin calls, Lovin highlights the difficulty and drawbacks for the church of witness theologians' exclusive focus on it as a site of politics. But each one's failure to adequately address questions posed by the other constitutes a missed opportunity to bridge some of the needless gaps between witness and realist approaches.

### New Augustinian Approaches

In an effort to bridge the continuing divide between witness and realist approaches, a number of notable studies have appeared that appeal to Augustine, a figure foundational to, yet largely outside of, the discussion. But for all the advances of these proposals by "new Augustinians" including Charles Mathewes, Eric Gregory, and Luke Bretherton, they too reveal residual effects of the witness-realist polarization. Charles Mathewes, for example, provides a theologically robust account of how participation in public life constitutes an "ascetical process of spiritual formation" that cultivates the theological virtues of faith, hope, and love.[38] Mathewes's proposal shares with witness theologians convictions about the importance of speaking publicly in particularistically Christian language, an emphasis on the importance of virtues for the Christian moral life, and the grounding of both in their proper ecclesial context. But its reliance on Augustine's ontology enables a far more nuanced account of the relationship between "church" and "world," and therefore the importance of extra-ecclesial involvement, than that of witness proposals. Mathewes is thus able to conceive of Christian participation in public life as an ecclesial practice itself, one whose "worldly" activity forms Christians in the theological virtues of faith, hope, and love.

But despite his rhetoric of ecclesial affirmation, Mathewes's substantial account is ultimately too individualistic; it goes too far astray from a witness emphasis on the church, participating in the

---

38. Charles Mathewes, *A Theology of Public Life* (Cambridge: Cambridge University Press, 2007), 2.

same realist mistake made by Niebuhr and Lovin. Mathewes anticipates this criticism and does occasionally discuss what churches should be doing.[39] He offers a powerful reflection on the role of the Eucharist in preparing Christians for public life.[40] He also discusses the role of black church communities in both preparing for and sustaining the work of the civil rights movement.[41] But most of Mathewes's statements on the significance of the church stop at the level of simply asserting its importance without exploring how the church functions as an institution.[42] His account provides very little detail about how church practices actually shape and prepare Christian believers for public involvement. What ought churches to be doing, for example, to resist the very problems Mathewes names as the most acute of our time: consumerism, global capitalism, and our culture of entertainment?[43] How do their current liturgies and practices prepare them to resist the allure of these cultures? What new forms of resistance might they enact? For all of its affirmation of the church's importance on these matters, eschatology ultimately subsumes any robust role for ecclesiology in Mathewes's account, leaving Mathewes firmly in realist territory.

Similarly, Eric Gregory's *Politics and the Order of Love: An Augustinian Ethic of Democratic Citizenship* improves on, yet ultimately remains bound to, the terms of the witness–realist debate. Gregory develops an Augustinian civic liberalism that places love at the heart of democratic engagement. His account strikes middle ground with respect to a number of discussions that span liberal political theory and theological ethics, mediating between *"critics of*

---

39. Mathewes, *Theology of Public Life*, 208–9.
40. Ibid., 294.
41. Ibid., 217.
42. To his credit, Mathewes pays more attention to this topic in *The Republic of Grace: Augustinian Thoughts for Dark Times* (Grand Rapids: Eerdmans, 2010).
43. Mathewes, *Theology of Public Life*, 224.

Augustine who *defend* liberal democracy" and *"fans* of Augustine who *attack* liberal democracy."[44] Effectively identifying himself as a fan of Augustine who defends liberal democracy, Gregory makes distinctive contributions to political theory by offering an interpretation of modern liberalisms as variations of Augustinianism, where he identifies his own Augustinian civic liberalism as one of three major options along with Augustinian realism and Augustinian proceduralism. At the same time, Gregory contributes to recent debates in theological ethics where he aims to maintain a delicate balance between those who reject the Augustinian realism associated with Reinhold Niebuhr and those Augustinians like John Milbank and Stanley Hauerwas who substitute ecclesiology for participation in liberal democratic politics.[45] As he puts it, his account is motivated by a concern to mediate between "a prideful Augustinianism . . . content to repeat its mantras about sin and the realistic limits of politics and virtue," on the one hand, and "an equally prideful Augustinianism [that] celebrates its retreat into a postliberal withdrawal from political life altogether"[46] on the other. Gregory's account thus shares with realists an appreciation for liberal democracy and its ability to check human sin and shares with witness theologians an emphasis on the central role the theological virtue of love plays in the Christian moral life. If Mathewes's use of Augustine places eschatology front and center (rather than the doctrine of sin, as in realist accounts, or ecclesiology, as in witness accounts), Gregory's reliance on Augustinian *caritas* embraces Christology and the Trinity as the best theological tools for navigating the relationship between Christianity and politics.

---

44. Gregory, *Politics and the Order of Love*, 2.
45. Ibid., 17–18.
46. Ibid., 28.

In his attempt to resist an overemphasis on ecclesiology, Gregory also goes too far in the opposite direction. To be fair, he explicitly acknowledges that developing the ecclesiological implications of Augustine's account of love would require a much larger study.[47] But his use of Augustinian *caritas* and emphasis on Christology brings up the question of ecclesiology. How, after all, are Christians and other citizens to be shaped in the virtue of love? Augustine's answer to this question leads straight to the church. As Gregory himself notes, "Augustine's church is where this sentimental education and moral cultivation takes place. He likens the church to 'sacred lecture halls for the peoples of the world.'"[48] Gregory's focus on motives both contributes significantly to political theory and reaps the wisdom of the witness emphasis on the importance of virtues for Christian ethics, but these very features make it all the more strange that his account forfeits the opportunity to discuss how citizens are to be shaped in the virtue of love. In other words, an emphasis on Christology demands an accompanying ecclesiology, especially given the Augustinian nature of Gregory's account. Formation in love does not happen automatically. A retrieval of love is finally incomplete without attention to the practices, communities, or institutions that actually form people in the virtue of love. Ultimately, Gregory's account pushes ecclesiology too far out of the picture.

Finally, Luke Bretherton's *Christianity and Contemporary Politics: The Conditions and Possibilities of Faithful Witness* shares with Mathewes's and Gregory's works a common theological touchstone in the work of Augustine. Bretherton situates his study in relationship to the "ecclesial-turn" made by witness accounts that maintain that "the first task of the church is to be a church."[49] Bretherton values these proposals but finds them wanting because they do not account

47. Ibid., 255.
48. Ibid., 293.

for the Christian political activity that is already taking place. Thus, as his title suggests, he recalibrates his own ecclesiological account with a nod to realist concerns that Christians not limit their politics to the church, describing possibilities for churches' faithful witness amid the actual conditions determined by the state, civil society and the market. He focuses on practices of community organizing, the US Sanctuary movement, and fair trade as examples of how churches already negotiate their relationships with local, national, and global structures as they love their neighbors. Like Mathewes's and Gregory's political theologies, Bretherton's makes significant strides beyond prominent witness and realist accounts. With his emphasis on Augustine's concept of the *saeculum*, or "the time between Christ's ascension and his return," Bretherton improves on prominent witness conceptualizations of the church-world relationship,[50] enabling a more nuanced account of political life. His account gives ample attention to the complex interaction between churches and local, national, global, and market structures, appreciating both the opportunities for faithful witness that these structures afford and the limitations they impose on faithful discipleship. His descriptive ethnographies of "how Christians are already acting politically" to "negotiate a common life with the various non-Christian others in relation to the state and the market" put flesh and bones on prescriptive accounts that call for the church to be the church, offering an account of Christian politics that realists can appreciate.[51]

In contrast to Mathewes's and Gregory's proposals, Bretherton's account—despite its many gains—exhibits problems that tip the scales too heavily in the witness direction, especially in its overidealized ecclesiology. More specifically, his grounding of the publicness of

---

49. Luke Bretherton, *Christianity and Contemporary Politics: The Conditions and Possibilities of Faithful Witness* (Malden, MA: Wiley-Blackwell: 2010), 17.

50. Ibid., 81–82.

51. Ibid., 17.

the church in worship reveals a lingering idealism about how the church morally forms its members. Bretherton does well to attend to the conditions and possibilities of Christian witness as determined by local, national, and global structures, but what about "the conditions and possibilities" of faithful worship? When it comes to ecclesial practice, one notices the absence of the careful analysis that marked his discussion of local, state, and global structures. There is no mention of a need to examine the ways Christian worship is corrupted by sins such as racism and sexism and can therefore be (and historically is always partially) malformative of Christian communities. Consequently, his account fails to deal adequately with justice issues within churches related to their own exclusionary practices in worship, leadership, and theological reflection.

In the final analysis, each of these accounts constitutes significant gains but still privileges either ecclesiology or extra-ecclesial politics. They provide an indication of the kind of theological creativity possible when the witness-realist divide is traversed but also the difficulty of doing so. As the next section suggests, other resources exist in the theological landscape that span the witness-realist divide in ways that open new vistas in Christian ethics.

## Feminist Contributions

What about feminist theologies? What difference might it make if their contributions were more readily acknowledged among witness and realist theologians in public theology and if feminists better engaged the thought of Niebuhr, Yoder, and King? Not only do feminist theologies enable readings of Niebuhr, Yoder, and King that free their legacies from witness-realist captivity, these readings, in turn, benefit feminist projects. The wariness that feminist theologians have toward dualisms, including those that mark the witness-realist debates, provides helpful avenues around the witness-realist divide.

These include attention to the practical impact of Christian truth claims on marginalized persons (rather than questions about the public accessibility of Christian truth) and more expansive conceptions of politics and violence that enable them to more readily avoid the seemingly intractable witness-realist divide. In particular, the insights of feminist theologians into the inherently political nature of theology and the so-called private realm, along with their concern to combat the systemic violence of sexism, racism, and classism, mean that their accounts are not premised upon a choice between ecclesial and extra-ecclesial politics or between rejections of military violence and potential justifications of force. Feminists are not alone in these insights, but their sustained attention to them recommends their involvement in the discussion. Their insights broaden the field of vision such that what appear at first to be stark either-or choices are more appropriately seen on a larger spectrum, bringing more considerations into view than the witness and realist perspectives allow.

But at the same time, feminists often fail to do any better than witness and realist theologians at engaging theologians of other stances. In fact, feminists have not shown much interest in any of the three figures of this study; when they have done so, the assessment is often almost wholly negative. Feminist concern for the marginalized, while absolutely indispensable to Christian ethics, can also prevent feminist theologians from appreciating the potential for alliances with theologians like Niebuhr, Yoder, and King. I aim to show how feminist insights open new vistas for constructive engagement with Niebuhr, Yoder, and King, and how these readings challenge feminists to recognize these figures—despite significant obstacles—as potential feminist allies.

Of course, given the diversity of feminist theologies, it is difficult to generalize about how they relate as fields to the equally diverse approaches of witness and realist theologians. When it comes to theories of truth, some feminists join their witness colleagues in emphasizing the priority of revelation and the formation of religious experience through participation in the life of the church. Others subscribe, with their realist colleagues, to moral and theological realism, emphasizing the role of experience in validating Christian truth claims. But one thing is certain: feminist theologians prioritize the effect of Christian Scripture, doctrine, and practices on the most vulnerable. Feminist analysis of the power of theological language, doctrine, and practices to shape moral actors and influence cultural norms actually aligns them with witness theologians, who also emphasize the role of narrative and practices in shaping the church's life.[52] In a sense, feminist attention to the damaging effects of tradition carries the witness emphasis on the role of tradition in creating human experience one step further to consider how that tradition, when corrupted by the sin of sexism, can be malformative. Feminist experience on the margins of ecclesial power gives feminists special insight into the church's failure to conform to Christ and its negative effect on individual believers and society at large. This attention to the power of sin also puts them in good company with realists, revealing the church to be every bit as prone to corruptions of power as other institutions.

This experience with the political power of the church's practice often informs feminists' conceptions of politics. Unlike their witness and realist colleagues, feminists do not tend to construe politics as requiring a choice between a responsible action in extra-ecclesial arenas and a primary focus on the inherently political nature of the church's internal life. For many feminists, the political is not limited

52. As Amy Plantinga Pauw puts it, "The most constructive critiques of the church's language and practices by reformist feminists have been along broadly cultural-linguistic lines." See Plantinga Pauw, "The Word is Near You: A Feminist Conversation with Lindbeck," *Theology Today* 50, no. 1 (April 1993): 47.

to participation in state structures or even the "public realm," but includes the very task of theology itself and its relationship to broader practices of naming and organizing cultural and social meanings and structures. As Catherine Keller puts it, "Theology always means—whatever else it means—theopolitics. . . . God-talk begins and ends among the *res publica*, the 'public things.'"[53] Or as Kwok Pui-lan argues, "Feminist theologians understand 'politics' in a comprehensive and multifaceted sense not limited to state power, participation in government, and political representation and rights. 'Politics,' for them, concerns the collective welfare of the whole people in the *polis*."[54] Feminist, womanist, *mujerista*, and Latina theologians highlight the political nature of theology in a variety of ways. Some focus on the role of theological language, doctrines, and practices in shaping persons and influencing social norms.[55] Still others analyze gendered dualisms that assign gender roles and circumscribe female agency.[56] And a host of others draw attention to the inherent political dimension of their theological projects, which attend to differences not only of gender but also of race and class.[57] These theologies are inherently political in at least two senses: they

53. Catherine Keller, *God and Power: Counter-Apocalyptic Journeys* (Minneapolis: Fortress Press, 2005), 135.

54. Kwok Pui-lan, "Feminist Theology, Southern," in *The Blackwell Companion to Political Theology*, ed. Peter Scott and William T. Cavanaugh (Malden, MA: Blackwell, 2004), 194.

55. Post-Christian theologian Mary Daly's claim, "If God is male, then the male is God," or Elizabeth A. Johnson's, "The symbol of God functions," attend to the power of theological language to shape cultural norms. See Daly, *Beyond God the Father: Toward a Philosophy of Women's Liberation* (Boston: Beacon, 1973), 19; and Johnson, *She Who Is: The Mystery of God in Feminist Theological Discourse* (New York: Crossroad, 1992), 4.

56. Christian social ethicist Beverly Wildung Harrison points out, for example, that the liberal divide between public and private often results in gendered dualisms and roles that underwrite inequality. Much of Harrison's work combats dualisms that position women as less than fully autonomous human beings. In her words, the problem is, "We go from *duality* to *dualism*, from *difference* to *subordination* and *subjection*"; *Making the Connections: Essays in Feminist Social Ethics*, ed. Carol S. Robb (Boston: Beacon, 1985), 25.

57. See, for example, Delores S. Williams, *Sisters in the Wilderness: The Challenge of Womanist God-Talk* (Maryknoll, NY: Orbis, 1993); and Ada María Isasi-Díaz, *En La Lucha: Elaborating a Mujerista Theology* (Minneapolis: Fortress Press, 2004).

address issues related to life in community and their primary goal is to question and reform unjust societal structures. These theologians draw attention to the political nature of theology in ways not dissimilar to both witness and realist theologians. With realists, these feminists attend to how the Christian tradition bears on larger societal organization and meaning. With witness theologians, they highlight the inherently political nature of the church community's mission. But their specific attention to the practice of theology itself also resists the dualistic way the witness-realist debate poses the question.

Consequently, feminists rarely drive as firm a wedge between ecclesial and extra-ecclesial politics as their witness and realist colleagues do. Their accounts of Christian identity and mission emphasize both the importance of the church as a political entity and the necessity of extra-ecclesial political action. In addition to feminist work that calls attention to the inherently political nature of the theological task, early feminist work often features the witness appreciation for the inherently political nature of the church as a visible community that embodies an alternative politics from that of the larger society. This insight led early feminists to critique patriarchal corruption of liturgical practices and to develop alternative worship spaces, such as the Women-Church movement, to advance the cause of women's ordination and reformation of liturgical practices.[58] Forming countercultural communities to offer a redemptive witness over against the larger institutional church, these "feminist base communities" are grounded in insights about the inherently political nature of the church that witness theologians claim in their emphasis on the church as a political structure that embodies an alternative witness to the world.

---

58. See Rosemary Radford Ruether, *Women-Church: Theology and Practice of Feminist Liturgical Communities* (San Francisco: Harper & Row), 1985.

Recent feminist work also examines the way particular ecclesial practices hold potential for larger societal transformation beyond offering a visible, embodied alternative polis. For example, Mary McClintock Fulkerson's recent work resists a dualism that would separate the church's ecclesial politics from its relevance to extra-ecclesial politics. Fulkerson's analysis of the ecclesial practices at Good Samaritan Methodist Church in Durham, North Carolina reveals their capacity to create "a shared space of appearance" that brought people together across the boundaries of race, gender, class, and ability, enabling each to engage "the other."[59] Although these practices "are the everyday, lived world activities of average people,"[60] they "are redemptive and political"[61] because they "brought people together in a variety of settings that contravened many of their inherited racialized enculturations. . . . Complete obliviousness to the marked 'Other' was not an option."[62] With witness theologians, Fulkerson reveals the importance of this church community's practices in its ability to foster an alternative to the racism that marks the larger society. But she also attends to the impact of these practices on larger social structures as church members move out into their other communities. Her conception of the church allows for its role as witness, yet also shows how this witness directly affects the world.

Indeed, because the church often fails to actually embody such alternative social spaces, feminists have also pursued politics outside of church structures. Recognizing the interrelation between "church" and "world," feminists recognize that just as the church has its own politics, involvement in extra-ecclesial politics also bodes well for the ability of the church to fully embody its redemptive witness. Work

---

59. Mary McClintock Fulkerson, *Places of Redemption: Theology for a Worldly Church* (Oxford: Oxford University Press, 2007), 21.
60. Ibid., 154.
61. Ibid., 23.
62. Ibid., 154.

in feminist social ethics ranging from welfare to labor rights to issues in bioethics reveals this emphasis on the church's calling to both embody an alternative polity and engage in extra-ecclesial matters that bear directly on public policy.[63]

Finally, while the witness-realist divide is premised upon a narrowly construed understanding of violence that tends toward understandings of politics that either admit the justified force of the state or that eschew the violence of the state, feminists operate with more broadly construed understandings of violence. Feminist theologies tend not to regard political action primarily in terms of coercion and violence, and pay very little attention to issues of state violence. The major anthologies of Christian attitudes toward war feature few or no feminist authors.[64] Similarly, collections and anthologies of feminist theologies and ethics rarely address the issue.[65]

63. See, for example, Lisa Sowle Cahill, *Theological Bioethics: Participation, Justice, and Change* (Washington, DC: Georgetown University Press, 2005).

64. One major collection, *War and Christian Ethics: Classic and Contemporary Readings on the Morality of War*, ed. Arthur F. Holmes (Grand Rapids: Baker Academic, 2005), includes no feminist authors. Another major anthology, *War in the Twentieth Century: Sources in Theological Ethics*, ed. Richard B. Miller (Louisville: Westminster John Knox, 1992), includes only one feminist author: Jean Bethke Elshtain. Aside from Elshtain, who is author of *Women and War* (Chicago: University of Chicago Press, 1987) and coeditor with Sheila Tobias of *Women, Militarism, and War: Essays in History, Politics, and Social Theory* (Savage, MD: Rowman & Littlefield, 1990), the only other feminist who has engaged these issues is Catholic moral theologian Lisa Sowle Cahill, with her volume *Love Your Enemies: Discipleship, Pacifism, and Just War Theory* (Minneapolis: Fortress Press, 1994). But this volume does not offer a feminist theological perspective per se.

65. A survey of the edited volumes in feminist and womanist theology reveals little attention to the issue of war. Discussion of war in the most recent feminist collection, *The Oxford Handbook of Feminist Theology*, ed. Mary McClintock Fulkerson and Sheila Briggs (Oxford: Oxford University Press, 2012), is limited to a few references to terrorism. Each of the following include only one article on the topic: *Feminist Theological Ethics: A Reader*, ed. Lois K. Daly (Louisville: Westminster John Knox, 1994); *The Power of Naming: A Concilium Reader in Feminist Liberation Theology*, ed. Elisabeth Schüssler Fiorenza (Maryknoll, NY: Orbis, 1996); and Janet Martin Soskice and Diana Lipton, *Feminism and Theology* (Oxford: Oxford University Press, 2003). Beverly Wildung Harrison's collections on Protestant feminist social ethics, *Justice in the Making: Feminist Social Ethics* (Louisville: Westminster John Knox, 2004) and *Making the Connections*, contain no articles on war/pacifism. Nor do *A Troubling in My Soul: Womanist Perspectives on Evil and Suffering*, ed. Emilie M. Townes (Maryknoll, NY: Orbis, 1993); *The Cambridge Companion to Feminist Theology*, ed. Susan Frank Parsons (Cambridge: Cambridge

In general, feminist theologians and ethicists have avoided topics related to just war, nonviolence, and pacifism, directing their attention to other important issues. Rather than focusing on male conceptions of violence such as war, feminist, womanist, *mujerista*, and Latina theologians tend to understand violence in terms of the systemic violence that perpetuates women's oppression and/or internal forms of violence that destroy persons' sense of wholeness and dignity. Consequently, feminists tend to focus on moral issues ranging from domestic violence to ecological destruction to various forms of trauma. This broader conception of violence works hand in hand with their broader conceptions of what counts as political. In all of these ways, feminists manage to stake out a middle ground between witness and realist accounts.

This is not to say, however, that feminist theologies do not suffer from their own failures of vision. In fact, the very resources that enable feminists to avoid these witness-realist binaries often result in feminists' own form of blindness. The history of feminist theologies can be read as a reminder of the propensity to allow one's most significant strength to become one's weakness. Despite early liberal feminist interrogation of theologies that assumed the male as normative, thereby reflecting male-centered understandings of God, church doctrine, and liturgy,[66] these theologians were later rightly criticized by their womanist, *mujerista*, and Latina colleagues for participating in the same essentializing moves they sought to escape. If the first feminist theologians revealed the tradition's blindness to

University Press, 2002); or Daphne Hampson, *Theology and Feminism* (Oxford: Basil Blackwell, 1990).

66. I have in mind Elisabeth Schüssler Fiorenza, Rosemary Radford Ruether, Mary Daly, Letty M. Russell, Beverly Wildung Harrison, Sallie McFague, and Delores S. Williams, among others. For an excellent account of the origins and development of feminist theology, see Rosemary Radford Ruether, "The Emergence of Christian Feminist Theology," in *The Cambridge Companion to Feminist Theology*, ed. Susan Frank Parsons (Cambridge: Cambridge University Press, 2002), 3–22.

gender, the next generation of womanist, *mujerista,* Latina, and poststructuralist feminists continued and deepened it by calling into question the very categories used by the preceding generation.

From its origins, then, feminist theology has been concerned with challenging received binaries within the tradition, beginning with the male-female binary. But as this history of feminist attention to gender demonstrates, what begins as an important insight that opens the field can come to function as a blindfold, obscuring other options. Perhaps this very attention to gender is partially the reason why feminists have tended not to engage Niebuhr, Yoder, and King. Although the boundaries separating the various feminist theologies are important for maintaining the space necessary to do their work, I worry that the boundaries also limit the relevance of feminist insights to other important areas, like public theology.

My efforts in each of the chapters that follow are meant to show how the boundaries that separate witness, realist, and feminist approaches can be used as tools to identify sites for needed work in Christian ethics. Reading the thought of Niebuhr, Yoder, and King alongside that of various feminist theologians enables fresh readings of these figures and identifies opportunities for new projects that both enhance Niebuhr's, Yoder's, and King's legacies and strengthen the internal projects of witness, realist, and feminist theologians alike. These readings reveal, among other things, how witness and feminist emphasis on the moral potential of religious communities identifies ecclesiology as a new endeavor for realists; how feminist attention to the systemic violence of sexism and realist attention to extra-ecclesial politics identify feminism as a form of Christian politics for witness theologians; and how feminists' and womanists' accounts of Christian love highlight an underappreciated creative synthesis in King's thought, revealing feminist trajectories in even the most unfeminist of thinkers. Doing Christian ethics at these boundaries holds the potential to enliven the field of Christian ethics, rendering it more powerful in addressing moral challenges.

## 2

---

# Churches as Self-Critical and Creative Cultures

*A Witness- and Feminist-Inspired Appropriation of*
*Reinhold Niebuhr's Thought on the Church*

> "Judgment begins in the house of God."
> —Reinhold Niebuhr[1]

"I make no apology for being critical of what I love."[2] So ends the preface to Reinhold Niebuhr's collected reflections on his experience in church ministry.[3] I begin with this quote because it names an aspect of Niebuhr's identity that is often overlooked in contemporary discussion of Niebuhr: his calling as a minister of the church. This

---

1. Reinhold Niebuhr, *Essays in Applied Christianity: The Church and the New World,* ed. D. B. Robertson (New York: Meridian, 1959), 333.
2. Reinhold Niebuhr, *Leaves from the Notebook of a Tamed Cynic* (New York: Willett, Clark & Colby, 1929), xiv.
3. An earlier version of portions of this chapter appeared as "Churches as 'Self-Critical Cultures': Reinhold Niebuhr, Kathryn Tanner, and the Church's Politics," in *Gendering Christian Ethics,* ed. Jenny Daggers (Newcastle: Cambridge Scholars, 2012), 23–50.

vocation certainly called him beyond the church to active roles in public life and the life of the mind, but Niebuhr began his career as pastor at Bethel Evangelical Church in Detroit, preached continually in churches and university chapels across the country, and was a church activist his entire life. Despite other important roles, Niebuhr always thought of himself first and foremost as a preacher.[4]

But Niebuhr's statement about criticism is telling in more ways than one. It highlights his ecclesial role and reflects the theme of self-criticism that both pervades his thought on the church and provides resources not merely for development of a Niebuhrian ecclesiology, but one that challenges those of witness theologians. This is not to say that Niebuhr devoted his theology to ecclesiology. As his witness critics are quick to point out, Niebuhr dedicated most of his theological attention to the politics of nations. Indeed, of the three figures in this study, Niebuhr enjoys arguably the most enduring intellectual influence across the broadest spectrum of audiences. His thought still features prominently in both theological circles and public debate. In addition to his ecclesial vocation, his many contributions include active involvement in politics, cofounding the journal *Christianity and Crisis*, and teaching at Union Theological Seminary in New York City. His legacy is visible among groups and individuals across religious and political divides. From "atheists for Niebuhr" to theo-conservatives, from John McCain to President Barack Obama, a variety of groups and leaders still reference Niebuhr's key ideas about human sin, the need for justice and a balance of power, and the importance of democracy for solving problems.[5] Although this "social concern" derived from Niebuhr's

4. Reinhold Niebuhr, *Justice and Mercy*, ed. Ursula M. Niebuhr (New York: Harper & Row, 1974), 4.

5. For accounts of the revival of interest in and significance of Niebuhr's wide-ranging influence, see Richard Crouter, *Reinhold Niebuhr on Politics, Religion, and Christian Faith* (New York:

"religious context,"[6] critics view his political activism as an indication of a lack of interest in the church rather than love for it.

Niebuhr's interest in politics leads some prominent witness theologians to question his contributions to ecclesial reflection. These scholars see a Niebuhr more interested in the fate of Western civilization than the church, more concerned with political responsibility than faithful Christian discipleship, and more preoccupied with justice than a Christian witness of peace. Although Niebuhr understood himself as a Christian apologist, arguing that Christianity offers the only adequate understanding of human beings and their relationship to nature, history, and the divine, these scholars regard "apology" as more of an epithet reserved for those who lift Christian insights out of their proper context—churches and the life of Christian discipleship—and apply them to an arena not of primary concern to Christians—democratic politics and the quest for justice. For these scholars, the proper medium for conveying truth is not an "apology" that demonstrates the relevance of Christian faith to the social, political, and economic realities of the day, but an ecclesially embodied countercultural "witness" over against those realities. But, as Niebuhr's prefatory remark indicates, there was a time he refused to apologize—when talking about the church.

Nevertheless, critics often claim that Niebuhr's theology lacks an ecclesiology. Niebuhr's primary commitment, so the argument goes, is to politics rather than the church. In its most extreme form, this criticism contends that Niebuhr scarcely acknowledges the church's existence. Niebuhr's contemporaries made this claim, as do contemporary theologians such as John Howard Yoder, Stanley Hauerwas, William T. Cavanaugh, Samuel Wells, and Luke

Oxford University Press, 2010); and Paul Elie, "A Man for All Reasons," *The Atlantic Monthly* 300, no. 4 (November 1, 2007): 82–96.

6. Ursula Niebuhr, *Justice and Mercy*, x.

Bretherton. More often than not, they make the claim in stark terms. Hauerwas, for example, writes, "For Niebuhr and the social gospelers the subject of Christian ethics was America."[7] Or as Cavanaugh puts it: "Ecclesiology is simply absent from Niebuhr's political theology."[8] The boldness of such claims demands scrutiny. How can scholars portray Niebuhr—a child of the church who was ordained to Christian ministry, served as a pastor for 13 years, and educated generations of pastors at a prominent Protestant seminary—as ignoring the church? More importantly, how have such negative characterizations impoverished contemporary ecclesiological reflection?

This witness portrayal of a "liberal" Niebuhr is one product of the witness-realist debate dominating Christian ethics in recent decades, and it still serves as fodder for witness theologians in the current debate. For their part, realists often highlight the theological nature of Niebuhr's work. For every witness study that decries Niebuhr's lack of theological prowess, there is a realist volume that highlights the theological contributions of Niebuhr's thought. Langdon Gilkey reclaims those credentials in his "theological study" of Niebuhr's life and work.[9] Larry Rasmussen's edited volume describes Niebuhr as a "theologian of public life."[10] Robin W. Lovin underscores Niebuhr's theological realism alongside his moral and political realism.[11] And Scott R. Erwin explores the "theological vision" that pervades Niebuhr's work.[12] But none of these studies address Niebuhr's

7. Stanley Hauerwas, *The Hauerwas Reader*, ed. John Berkman and Michael Cartwright (Durham, NC: Duke University Press, 2001), 60.

8. William T. Cavanaugh, "Church," in *The Blackwell Companion to Political Theology*, ed. Peter Scott and William T. Cavanaugh (Malden, MA: Blackwell, 2004), 401.

9. Langdon Gilkey, *On Niebuhr: A Theological Study* (Chicago: University of Chicago Press, 2001).

10. Larry Rasmussen, ed. *Reinhold Niebuhr: Theologian of Public Life* (San Francisco: Harper & Row, 1989).

11. Robin W. Lovin, *Reinhold Niebuhr and Christian Realism* (Cambridge: Cambridge University Press, 1995).

thought on the church. Not since *Essays in Applied Christianity* has there been substantial focus on the topic.[13] Unfortunately, the debate between witness and realist theologians over Niebuhr's theological credentials neglects his ecclesial contributions.

### Reinhold Niebuhr as Christian Witness

This chapter responds to that neglect by engaging both witness and feminist criticism of Niebuhr's theology and Niebuhr's thought on the church. It appreciates realist work that highlights Niebuhr's theological contributions, but regrets that realists have failed to develop Niebuhr's ecclesiological reflection. It also appreciates the genuine insight in witness claims that Niebuhr's theology lacks an ecclesiology but regrets hyperbolic formulations that obscure his valuable discussion of the church. The polarization between these two perspectives detracts from Niebuhr's reflection on the church and important feminist work that—when juxtaposed with Niebuhr's—reveals new trajectories for Christian ethics that both enhances the constructive reach of Niebuhr's work and contributes to the internal projects of his witness and feminist critics.

I begin by exploring witness and feminist criticisms of Niebuhr. Despite their differences, witness and feminist criticisms of Niebuhr feature surprising structural similarities. When it comes to the moral potential of religious communities, the criticisms overlap substantively. Witness and feminist theologians share formally similar concerns about Niebuhr's use of experience as a theological source and his focus on public and political life as his moral context of

---

12. Scott R. Erwin, *The Theological Vision of Reinhold Niebuhr's The Irony of American History: "In the Battle and Above It"* (Oxford: Oxford University Press, 2013).

13. One recent exception includes Wendy Dackson's discussion of Niebuhr's "outsider ecclesiology." See "Reinhold Niebuhr's Outsider Ecclesiology," in *Reinhold Niebuhr and Contemporary Politics: God and Power*, ed. Richard Harries and Stephen Platten (Oxford: Oxford University Press, 2010), 87–101.

choice. In addition, witness claims that Niebuhr lacks an ecclesiology map directly onto feminist criticisms that Niebuhr underestimates the moral potential of religious communities. These criticisms identify rich sites for construction in Niebuhr's theology.

Treating these criticisms as invitations to explore the potential of Niebuhr's thought, I provide a charitable, close reading of Niebuhr that renders his theology more amenable to witness and feminist agendas. Might Niebuhr's thought possess resources for an account of the church and its moral capacities that would honor the insights of both witness and feminist theologians? What would the character of such a community be? What virtues would its members embody? What kinds of ethical action would they pursue? Highlighting thematic similarities between Niebuhr's discussion of churches and theologian Kathryn Tanner's[14] exploration of Christianity's capacity to create "self-critical cultures," I develop Niebuhr's reflection on the nature and role of the church into a Niebuhrian account of churches as self-critical cultures engaging in formative practices of contrition that cultivate the virtues of humility and hope, giving rise to creative ethical action.

This account not only identifies new directions for those committed to Niebuhr's legacy, it also contributes to the projects of both witness and feminist theologians. Realist Robin W. Lovin, for example, perceptively notes that Niebuhr's realism, in its concern for avoiding cultural accommodation and in its emphasis on cultivating habits of criticism and responsibility, actually resembles certain witness approaches.[15] My account might be construed as an attempt

---

14. Although Kathryn Tanner does not explicitly identify as a feminist theologian, I treat her as one in this chapter because of her interest, shared most prominently with feminists, in the relationship between theology and social justice, specifically the value of theology in challenging "(1) fixed hierarchies of superiors and subordinates, (2) oppressive relations of domination or exploitation, and (3) intolerance toward others." See *The Politics of God: Christian Theologies and Social Justice* (Minneapolis: Fortress Press, 1992), 130.

to develop this insight of Lovin's into a realist ecclesiology—one that responds to witness criticism but nevertheless maintains its integrity as a realist project. But while I embrace witness convictions that the church's distinctive identity and practices of moral formation are central for Christian ethics, my account also contributes needed corrections to witness theologies. It demonstrates how witness theologians might develop an ecclesiology that better heeds realist concerns that churches not ground their distinctiveness in an overestimation of their moral abilities or maintain an over-rigid church-world boundary that undermines the relevance of Christian involvement in public life.

My account also contributes to feminist projects. Feminist Rebekah L. Miles, for example, draws on what she describes as feminist Sharon Welch's notion of "horizontal transcendence"[16] to appropriate Niebuhr's best insights about human capacities for self-transcendence while also incorporating corrections to Niebuhr's neglect of the moral potential of communities. But, in keeping with her stance as a realist, Miles does not develop her appropriation along explicitly ecclesiological lines. The account in this chapter might also be construed as an attempt to further develop her proposal in ways that more deliberately heed witness focus on the church.

Most importantly, my work attempts to engage in the "mutual hearing and criticism among those who disagree" and to display the "common commitment to mutual correction and uplift" that are "in keeping with the shared hope of good discipleship, proper faithfulness, and purity of witness"[17] that obtain among members

---

15. Robin W. Lovin, *Christian Realism and the New Realities* (Cambridge: Cambridge University Press, 2008), 95–96.

16. See Rebekah L. Miles, *The Bonds of Freedom: Feminist Theology and Christian Realism* (Oxford: Oxford University Press, 2001), 121–23, 132–33, 135–36, 152; and Welch, *A Feminist Ethic of Risk*, 179–80.

17. Kathryn Tanner, *Theories of Culture: A New Agenda for Theology* (Minneapolis: Fortress Press, 1997), 123–24.

of the genuine community of argument. In short, it attempts to think constructively at the boundary of witness, realist, and feminist approaches about the church's identity and mission.

## Niebuhr and Witness and Feminist Traditions

What are witness and feminist theologians to make of Reinhold Niebuhr's theological and political legacy? Insofar as witness theologians claim that Niebuhr omits ecclesiology, the answer is clear: nothing. The divide between realists and witness theologians on this question is long entrenched. Witness theologians claim that realists ignore the church,[18] and realists chastise witness theologians for idealizing the church's moral capacities.[19] Witness theologians argue that realists reduce Christianity to a set of "insights" to be applied to economic, political, and social problems, forsaking the church's distinctive politics as an alternative society.[20] Realists criticize witness theologians for failing to make discriminating judgments between good and evil[21] and for espousing an "irresponsible" or even "sectarian" politics.[22] Witness theologians argue that realist accounts ignore the church's special or paradigmatic role in history,[23] and realists worry that witness accounts of the church as a "holy" community produce dangerous religious pretensions.[24] Driving these witness criticisms of realism are presuppositions about the nature of

---

18. See, for example, John Howard Yoder, "Reinhold Niebuhr and Christian Pacifism," *Mennonite Quarterly Review*, 29, no. 2 (April 1955): 115.
19. Reinhold Niebuhr, *Beyond Tragedy: Essays on the Christian Interpretation of History* (New York: Charles Scribner's Sons, 1937), 62.
20. Stanley Hauerwas, *With the Grain of the Universe: The Church's Witness and Natural Theology* (Grand Rapids: Baker Academic, 2013), 111.
21. Reinhold Niebuhr, "We Are Men and Not God," in *Essays in Applied Christianity*, 172.
22. Lovin, *Reinhold Niebuhr and Christian Realism*, 99.
23. Hauerwas, *With the Grain*, 117.
24. Reinhold Niebuhr, "Reply to Interpretation and Criticism," in *Reinhold Niebuhr: His Religious, Social, and Political Thought*, ed. Charles W. Kegley and Robert W. Bretall (New York: Macmillan, 1956), 437.

truth, the significance of the church as a political community versus participation in extra-ecclesial politics, and the relationship between church and world—specifically, whether this relationship requires a witness of peace or allows for the use of force for the sake of justice.

Feminist treatment of Niebuhr is more varied. Early feminist reception of Niebuhr resembled the lack of enthusiasm, even outright disdain, exhibited by many witness theologians. These criticisms attacked Niebuhr for espousing a male-centered conception of human experience,[25] positing a dichotomy between public and private that relegates justice to the public realm and love to the private realm,[26] and harboring a pessimism about the moral potential of groups that eventually capitulates to political conservatism.[27] More recently, however, several feminists offer more qualified responses, with one asking, "What's so bad about Reinhold Niebuhr?"[28] These theologians suggest that Niebuhr's thought is not as incompatible with feminist theologies as early feminist criticism suggested. Miles demonstrates how prominent feminist theologians, such as Rosemary Radford Ruether and Sharon Welch, offer versions of feminist Christian realism. Other realists claim the work of feminists Jean Bethke Elshtain and Catherine Keller as forms of realism.[29]

But why even ask about witness and feminist reception of Niebuhr at once? It seems unlikely that witness and feminist theologians would agree in their assessments of Niebuhr's theology, let alone possess a common stake in his legacy. Because of the prominence of theological liberalism within early feminist theologies, witness theologians often reduce feminism to one more brand of liberalism,

---

25. See, for example, Valerie Saiving Goldstein, "The Human Situation: A Feminine View," *The Journal of Religion* 40, no. 2 (April 1960): 100–12.

26. Daphne Hampson, *Theology and Feminism* (Oxford: Basil Blackwell, 1990), 126.

27. Sharon D. Welch, *A Feminist Ethic of Risk*, rev. ed. (Minneapolis: Fortress Press, 2000), 37.

28. Miles, *Bonds of Freedom*.

29. Lovin, *Christian Realism and the New Realities*, 28–37.

dismissing it altogether.[30] Similarly, very few feminists engage witness approaches; when they do, the response from witness theologians has been less than productive.[31] But this lack of engagement hides remarkable similarities of both content and tone in witness and feminist critiques of Niebuhr.

Like witness critiques, feminist responses both illuminate significant contributions and obscure others. On one hand, feminists identify problems in Niebuhr's thought that demand attention. On the other, their critiques sometimes prevent an accurate assessment of Niebuhr's contributions to reflection on the church's public role. Like prominent witness critiques, some feminist claims are exaggerated enough to suggest that deeper compatibilities may be fueling the disagreement.[32] Structurally, feminist criticisms map on to those of witness theologians about the status of revelation and experience, the proper locus of moral activity, and the church's vocation vis-à-vis the world. When it comes to the moral potential of religious communities, their criticisms align in both structure and substance.

### The Status of Revelation and Experience

The most prominent witness strategy for dismissing Niebuhr is to characterize him as a theological liberal who fails to prioritize revelation over experience as a source for theological reflection, narrative over myths and symbols as the conveyer of Christian truth, and "witness" over "apology" as the authentic Christian mission in the world. Because witness theologians pride themselves on having advanced beyond the errors of theological liberalism, anyone whose work falls into this category is often dismissed out of hand.

30. See, for example, Stanley Hauerwas, "Failure of Communication *or* A Case of Uncomprehending Feminism," *Scottish Journal of Theology* 50, no. 2 (1997): 234.
31. Ibid., 228–39.
32. See Miles's *Bonds of Freedom* for an excellent discussion and assessment of feminist criticism of Niebuhr.

Niebuhr, of course, acknowledged the enduring influence of his liberal Protestant heritage, but he also understood himself to be parting company with the liberals of his day. Witness theologians of various bents argue that Niebuhr nevertheless retains key elements of a liberal stance that are detrimental to his theology. Yoder argues, for example, that Niebuhr's theology is actually anthropology—that his theological starting point is neither God nor revelation but human beings and their experience.[33] Hauerwas argues that Niebuhr places too much emphasis on the role of myth in communicating Christian truth and the role of experience in validating it.[34] And John Milbank contends that, despite his emphasis on human limitations and on sin, Niebuhr smuggles a notion of progress into his ethics by positing a spiritual element that gradually and instrumentally remedies an inherently conflict-ridden natural realm.[35] However the claim is made, these theologians agree: Niebuhr's theology neither starts from the right place—the revelation of God—nor takes the appropriate stance toward Christian truth. His thought places too much emphasis on human experience, myths and symbols, and the potential for progress in our dealings with the world and not enough on the priority of God's revelation, the narrative structure of Christian truth, and the need to relinquish "control" over human destiny. In short, despite Niebuhr's emphasis on sin, he remains beholden to theological liberalism.

Although feminists do not share witness concerns about the prioritizing of human experience over revelation, they also raise questions about Niebuhr's reliance on experience. Their worries center on the question, "Whose experience?" The earliest feminist

33. Yoder, "Reinhold Niebuhr and Christian Pacifism," 102.
34. Hauerwas, *With the Grain*. See especially chapter 4, "The Liberalism of Reinhold Niebuhr," 87–111.
35. John Milbank, "The Poverty of Niebuhrianism," in *The Word Made Strange: Theology, Language, Culture* (Oxford: Blackwell, 1997), 236.

critiques argue that Niebuhr's model of the self is too individualized and autonomous to account adequately for its relational nature[36] and that Niebuhr construes sin too narrowly to account for women's experience.[37] Valerie Saiving Goldstein was the first to suggest that Niebuhr's account of sin as pride is perhaps not as accurate or theologically sound for women, whose problem may be less pride than a lack of self-esteem.[38] But a host of others followed, including Judith Plaskow and Daphne Hampson.[39] More recently, Traci C. West challenges Niebuhr's failure to attend to women's experience in a slightly different way. She argues that putting Niebuhr into conversation with the black women activists in Harlem (who were addressing some of the same ethical issues, at the same time, in the same neighborhood) has the power to expand our ethical frameworks beyond the "disembodied intellectual tradition whereby thought is passed down from one man . . . to another man."[40] Although both Niebuhr and feminist theologians affirm the importance of human experience in ways that witness theologians would likely challenge, feminist concerns about the role of human experience in Niebuhr's theology nevertheless formally connect their criticisms to those of their witness colleagues.

### The Proper Locus of Christian Moral Activity

The second critique of Niebuhr that witness and feminist theologians share is that his realism overlooks important realms of moral

36. See, for example, Catherine Keller, *From a Broken Web: Separation, Sexism, and Self* (Boston: Beacon, 1986).

37. See Miles, *Bonds of Freedom*, 29–36, for discussion of these criticisms.

38. Goldstein, "The Human Situation: A Feminine View."

39. Judith Plaskow, *Sex, Sin, and Grace: Women's Experience and the Theologies of Reinhold Niebuhr and Paul Tillich* (Washington, DC: University Press of America), 1980; Daphne Hampson, "Reinhold Niebuhr on Sin: A Critique," in *Reinhold Niebuhr and the Issues of Our Time*, ed. Richard Harries, 46–60 (Grand Rapids: Eerdmans, 1986).

40. Traci C. West, "Constructing Ethics: Reinhold Niebuhr and Harlem Women Activists," *Journal of the Society of Christian Ethics* 24, no. 1 (2004): 29–49.

formation and activity. For witness theologians, Niebuhr pays too much attention to politics and not enough to the church. As Hauerwas puts it, in his spin on Ursula Niebuhr's recollection that Niebuhr thought of himself first and foremost as a preacher: "Niebuhr always regarded himself first and foremost a preacher, but a preacher whose congregation was constituted by a church called America."[41] Similarly, Yoder argues that Niebuhr's focus is so misplaced that he has no doctrine of the church at all. "The concept of the church is quite absent from his thought," he writes. "When he mentions the word 'church' it is only to criticize the medieval synthesis of Catholicism."[42] And, as Bretherton puts it, in Niebuhr's thought "the church becomes an adjunct to the prevailing social order in the name of maintaining a proximate justice."[43] Each of these theologians contends that the orientation—the very locus—of Niebuhr's theology is fundamentally off-target, resulting in a failure to recognize both how the church shapes its members in moral virtue and how it offers its own distinctive political witness. Without this emphasis, Niebuhr is forced to communicate Christian "insights" with mere "symbols" and "myths."

Feminists also criticize Niebuhr for focusing on politics. In their rendering, the claim is that Niebuhr focuses on the public realm as a moral sphere at the expense of the private realm. One line of criticism focuses on what a number of feminists see as a problematic division between love as the appropriate moral norm for private life and justice for the public realm. Beverly W. Harrison, for example, argues that Niebuhr "never questioned the dualism embedded in liberal political ideology between the 'private' sphere, that is, the arena of those interpersonal, humane relations of the family, and

---

41. Hauerwas, *With the Grain*, 92.
42. Yoder, "Reinhold Niebuhr and Christian Pacifism," 115.
43. Luke Bretherton, *Christianity and Contemporary Politics: The Conditions and Possibilities of Faithful Witness* (Malden, MA: Wiley-Blackwell, 2010), 90.

the 'public' sphere, those 'impersonal relations' of institutions and collectivities."[44] Daphne Hampson makes a similar claim, arguing that sacrificial love is "a moral norm relevant to interpersonal (particularly family) relations, and significant for parents (particularly mothers, heroes, and saints), but scarcely applicable to the power relations of modern industry."[45] But Harrison and Hampson are not alone. Plenty of other feminists, including Rosemary Radford Ruether, make similar claims.[46] These feminists worry that Niebuhr's dialectic between love and justice ossifies into a rigid dichotomy between public and private that establishes rival moral norms for private and public life. Although not explicitly a concern about lack of attention to the church, this criticism is formally similar to witness critiques in its contention that Niebuhr focuses on the wrong moral arena.

### The Church's Mission in the World

A third critique follows from the second: both witness and feminist theologians argue that Niebuhr despairs of the moral capacities of religious communities. Witness theologians contend that Niebuhr conceives of no special role for, or distinctive function of, the church vis-à-vis the world. In Hauerwas's words, "Augustine and Milbank assume that the church is the true bearer of history, whereas Niebuhr assumes that the church, at best, may have a role in history that is but the unfolding of the human condition."[47] Similarly, Yoder argues that Niebuhr fails to acknowledge that through Christ the church

---

44. Beverly Wildung Harrison, *Making the Connections: Essays in Feminist Social Ethics*, ed. Carol S. Robb (Boston: Beacon, 1985), 27–28.

45. Hampson, *Theology and Feminism*, 126.

46. Rosemary Radford Ruether, *New Woman, New Earth: Sexist Ideologies and Human Liberation* (New York: Seabury, 1975), 199. Ruether argues that, according to Niebuhr, "Love morality is 'unrealistic' in the public sphere. Here the only possible morality is that of a 'justice' defined as a balancing of competitive egoism. . . . Morality is privatized, sentimentalized, and identified with the 'feminine' in a way that both conceals the essential immorality of sexism and rationalizes a value-free public world."

47. Hauerwas, *With the Grain*, 117.

possesses special moral resources for love—that the church's doctrines of resurrection, regeneration, and the Holy Spirit not only enable love but dictate that love is more in keeping with the nature of reality than any thesis positing limits to human moral action.[48] Instead of emphasizing the redemptive reality of Christ, Niebuhr's realism substitutes responsibility as an alternative ethical norm for Christ.[49] Milbank makes the same claim, arguing that Niebuhr ultimately concerns himself with the wrong realities. In his words: "Because the Cross and resurrection reveal to us that this pattern is recovered precisely at the point of suffering and despair, no 'ethical limitations' can ever be ultimate for the Christian."[50] Whereas Niebuhr assumes a neutral reality to which Christians bring their insights, Milbank contends that "creative charity" is "more fundamental to the ways things truly are."[51] What is missing from Niebuhr's theology, according to these theologians, is any account of the church's moral capacities to provide a witness of peace in a violent world. Despairing of this possibility, Niebuhr assumes the responsibility to intervene—with violence if necessary—as though the outcome could be controlled.

Feminists also take Niebuhr to task for a complacency that underestimates the moral potential of religious communities. Sharon Welch argues that Niebuhr's distinction between the "moral" individual and "immoral society" underestimates the moral potential of religious communities. She develops an "ethic of risk," contrasting it with what she calls Niebuhr's ethic of control. Instead of Niebuhr's "comfortable" serenity prayer (which asks "for courage to change what I can, the serenity to accept what I cannot change, and the wisdom to know the difference"), Welch suggests an alternative:

48. Yoder, "Reinhold Niebuhr and Christian Pacifism," 116.
49. Ibid., 114.
50. Milbank, "The Poverty of Niebuhrianism," 251.
51. Ibid., 249.

"What improbable task, with which unpredictable results, shall we undertake today?"[52] Others, including Sheila D. Collins and Harrison, argue that Niebuhr's appeal to an impossible transcendent ideal refuses the possibility of real change within history.[53]

Despite their differences, then, witness and feminist theologians share the same set of concerns about Niebuhr's estimation of religious communities and their moral potential. If Niebuhr's theology is to ground an account of the church's public role, it needs to admit the possibility that the church, as a moral community, is capable of moral action that transcends human sin.

This last criticism—shared by witness and feminist theologians in structure and substance—is most significant. It helpfully identifies a problem in Niebuhr's theology that realists could address without risking faithfulness to their own convictions: namely, realists should pay more attention to the centrality of the church for their accounts of Christian ethics. But it does so in a way that also contributes to witness and feminist projects. Appropriating Niebuhr's thought for a realist ecclesiology that incorporates witness emphasis on the church as an arena of moral formation, as well as Welch's "horizontal transcendence" as a necessary community-oriented corollary to Niebuhr's emphasis on self-transcendence, contributes to Niebuhr's legacy. It also strengthens witness and feminist theologians' own accounts. After all, the most prominent witness accounts fail to account for either extra-ecclesial politics or the corruption of church tradition and its potential to malform. The feminist accounts under consideration stop short of developing their appropriations of Niebuhr's thought in explicitly ecclesiological directions, leaving witness concerns about the church unaddressed.

52. Welch, *A Feminist Ethic of Risk*, 37.
53. Sheila D. Collins, *A Different Heaven and Earth* (Valley Forge, PA: Judson, 1974), 157–58; Harrison, *Making the Connections*, 59.

## A Niebuhrian Ecclesiology on Witness and Feminist Terms

Where are we, then, in relation to witness and feminist criticisms that Niebuhr neglects the church? These theologians claim that: 1) his theology is not grounded in revelation or attentive to women's experience; 2) he devotes his moral energies to the public and political sphere rather than the church or the private sphere; and 3) although he assumes the responsibility to advance civilization, he exhibits little hope in the moral capacities of religious communities. There are genuine insights here, but these claims also overshadow important aspects of Niebuhr's thought that might be developed into a Niebuhrian account of the church that responds to witness and feminist criticism. What are the witness and feminist requirements for a Niebuhrian account of the church's identity and public mission?

For witness theologians, revelation and Scripture provide the story that structures this community's life of distinctive practices, which in turn shape it into a certain kind of culture that has something to say to the rest of the world. The problem with Niebuhr's thought, as these theologians see it, is that he does not have an adequate understanding of the church as its own distinctive counterculture that witnesses to Christ over against the world. But a closer reading reveals that Niebuhr shares witness convictions. His account emphasizes the role of divine revelation, distinctive Christian practices, and the church's mission vis-à-vis the world. Both Niebuhr and witness theologians affirm Christian truth as grounding a countercultural witness; both suggest formative practices that enable this witness; and both view the church as having a unique vocation in the world.

For feminist theologians, Niebuhr ignores female experience and emphasizes divine transcendence, leading to support of the status quo and a failure to fully account for the innovative moral capacities of religious communities. But, as was the case with witness accounts, these feminist criticisms are overstated. A closer look at Niebuhr's thought reveals the real problem to be not a lack of concern with women's experience, espousal of male conceptions of sin, or inattention to the importance of communities, but Niebuhr's failure to maintain the dialectics within his theology that better account for these realities. Because Miles has already taken up these feminist criticisms, I focus in what follows on the witness criticisms of Niebuhr.

## The Role and Status of Revelation

Both witness and feminist theologians question the role and status of revelation and experience in Niebuhr's theology, but neither set of claims fares well under scrutiny. Witness claims that Niebuhr prioritizes experience at the expense of revelation are better at portraying Niebuhr as a theological liberal than describing the role Scripture plays in his theology. It is true that witness theologians and Niebuhr espouse different theories of truth: witness theologians subscribe to a narrative theory of truth, whereas Niebuhr adheres to a moral and theological realism.[54] But this difference does not sustain the witness claim that Niebuhr privileges human experience over divine revelation as a source of theology. Similarly, feminist claims that Niebuhr undervalues female experience function better when restated as a critique of Niebuhr's failure to maintain the dialectic between his accounts of sin as pride and sin as sensuality that, when held together, cover a fuller range of human experience.[55] The lack of precision in these criticisms misconstrues the central role of revelation in Niebuhr's thought and its amenability to a diverse range of human experience.

54. For a discussion of Niebuhr's moral and theological realism, see Lovin, *Reinhold Niebuhr and Christian Realism*, 11–24.
55. For discussion of this point, see Miles, *Bonds of Freedom*, 35–36.

Contrary to witness claims, Niebuhr's theology does not start with an account of human beings per se; it starts with the *biblical* account. In other words, Niebuhr starts with human experience because the Bible does. Hauerwas often characterizes Niebuhr's view as stipulating that the truth of Christianity must be validated by experience in order for it to be true, but this is to misunderstand the role of experience in Niebuhr's theology. Experience does not render Christian claims true or false; Christian claims simply are true. In Niebuhr's words, "Yet there is in the Christian religion an insight into this matter which does not depend upon the corroboration of history. ... The Christian knows that the cross is the truth."[56] Or as he puts it elsewhere, "The atoning death of Christ is the revelation of ultimate reality which may become the principle of interpretation for all human experience. It is not a principle yielded by experience, but it is applicable to experience and validated by it."[57] When Niebuhr claims experiential corroboration for Christian doctrines, it is not an assertion of the priority of experience over revelation. It is a demonstration that experience corresponds to the truth of revelation.[58]

While Niebuhr uses the language of drama, rather than narrative or "story" as in witness accounts, he also places importance on the formative role of revelation and Scripture in establishing the church's identity. True to witness form, Niebuhr speaks of the church as providing the medium in which Christians are to "think and live":

> All who have become Christian will find their own convictions formed by the witness of the whole Christian Church through the ages, beginning with the witness of Scripture, including, of course, the Scripture which gives us the witness of the Church before the Church;

56. Niebuhr, *Beyond Tragedy*, 212–13.
57. Ibid., 19–20.
58. For an account of Niebuhr as an ethical naturalist, see Lovin, *Reinhold Niebuhr and Christian Realism*, 97–118.

namely Israel. A responsible theologian as distinguished from an irresponsible speculator, will think and live within the discipline of this Church, though he will feel free to correct what seem to him to be errors of the past.[59]

Far from abandoning Scripture, Niebuhr makes here what sounds like a statement straight out of a witness account of the church's identity as a particular community, with a particular history, formed by the particular narrative of Scripture, which narrates its particular ongoing role in history. While witness and realist theologians subscribe to different theories of truth that lead to disagreement over the public accessibility of Christian truth claims, Niebuhr's biblical perspective belies witness claims that he reduces Christian truth to that which is verified by experience or that he does not admit the morally formative nature of Christian narrative.

## Site of Moral Formation

Witness and feminist theologians also misconstrue the role of the church in Niebuhr's theology. Because Niebuhr devotes most of his attention to the realm of politics, witness theologians claim that he has no place for the church in his theology. Feminists argue that Niebuhr's theology posits a dualism between public and private life that risks idealizing the private realm and ignoring the need for justice in family and personal relationships and the possibilities of love in the public realm. But again, these claims are better stated, respectively, as disagreements over how the church best communicates its message rather than as proof that Niebuhr disregards the church, and as criticism that Niebuhr does not emphasize as much as he should the potential for sin in the "private realm" or the possibilities of love in the "public realm."[60]

---

59. Niebuhr, "Reply to Interpretation and Criticism," 445.

Contrary to witness claims that Niebuhr's theology omits the church, Niebuhr views Christian worship as embodying the biblical drama, drawing attention to the central role of worship in shaping Christian disciples. In his words, "The whole drama of faith [is] portrayed in the liturgy."[61] The liturgy, including preaching, prayer, and sacraments, cultivates contrition in its participants. "The expression of contrition is a natural consequence of the soul's self-discovery in the sight of God," Niebuhr writes. "In worship, we become conscious of our violation of the law and the will of God. We confess that we have done the things we ought not to have done and left undone the things which we ought to have done."[62] Far from devaluing the church and its worship, Niebuhr describes worship as a means of entering into the drama of Christian life. His discussion echoes witness-sounding descriptions of the formative effect of church practices in shaping Christian believers. Take, for example, his description of preaching: "Christian preaching is not so much teaching about what Christians ought to do," he argues, "but it is the induction and the enrichment of people in the Christian faith through sermons, through pastoral experience, through private prayer, and the common prayers and worship of the church."[63] This is not the mere "application" of Christian "insights" to political, social, and economic problems. Rather, it is a robust understanding of the powerful role of worship—in all its facets—in the moral formation of Christian believers.

The need for human beings to submit themselves to God's judgment and avail themselves of God's mercy also saturates Niebuhr's discussion of prayer, which focuses on the role of

---

60. See Miles, *Bonds of Freedom*, 40–47. I agree with Miles's argument here that feminist critics "overdraw Niebuhr's distinction between public and private life."
61. Niebuhr, *Justice and Mercy*, 1.
62. Ibid., 2.
63. Ibid., 132.

contrition in cultivating the virtues of humility and hope. "Our estimate of the meaning of the human drama . . . can only be solved by religious contrition. . . . In the moment of prayer in which we become more fully conscious of the dishonesty of our judgments, we also achieve a fuller measure of honesty."[64] This honesty provides a realistic assessment not only of the limits inherent to human freedom but also the possibilities inherent to human capacities for transcendence. "The only moments in which the self-righteousness is broken are moments of genuine prayer. Yet something of that broken spirit and contrite heart can be carried into the contests of life."[65] Prayer as a practice of contrition provides, then, a full assessment of the human condition. It enables one to recognize one's limits, but it also enables one to embrace one's creativity and its transformative power.

Niebuhr's prayers are often direct pleas to God for help in being contrite such that Christians might better embody the virtue of humility. Consider the following: "Father Almighty, who are not served by men's hands as though you need anything, but who delights in the worship of a contrite heart, grant us grace in this hour of worship to forswear the pride to which our hearts are prone, to remember that you have made us and not we ourselves, that you are the beginning and the end of our life."[66] And again: "O God, whom the heavens cannot contain, yet who visits the humble with your presence, and loves a contrite heart, give us eyes to see our share in the common sins of mankind, so that we will not walk in pride and deceive ourselves."[67] And again: "Grant us grace that our pride may be humbled and we may know him who can be known only

---

64. Reinhold Niebuhr, *Discerning the Signs of the Times: Sermons for Today and Tomorrow* (New York: Charles Scribner's Sons, 1946), 13–15.

65. Ibid., 18.

66. Niebuhr, *Justice and Mercy*, 11–12.

67. Ibid., 75.

in contrition."[68] And again: "Keep us humble in your sight."[69] And again: "Grant us the grace of honest self-knowledge, that we may not think of ourselves more highly than we ought to think."[70] Over and over, Niebuhr prays that God will enable the church to embody the virtue of humility.

These practices of prayer indicate the church's particular calling: to invite honest self-criticism among its members so that they might be formed in the virtues of humility and hope. "The cross of Christ" is nothing "less demanding than an invitation to honest self-analysis. . . . The final mystery of good and evil in life and history is in fact that love . . . cannot be achieved by strenuous striving; rather, it is achieved by an honest self-scrutiny and self-awareness."[71] While Niebuhr parts company with witness theologians in their holding up "peaceableness" as the church's central vocation, he nevertheless agrees with witness theologians about the centrality of the church in the moral formation of its members. In his words, "Richer resources of faith will be required than those which the liberal culture of the past two centuries has lived by. . . . The one is a form of hope which gives meaning to life not only by what is accomplished in history. . . . The other resource required for our day is a sense of humility which recognizes the lack of strength to bring forth as a common form of human weakness in which all share."[72] Hauerwas may argue that Niebuhr's emphasis on contrition and humility pales in comparison to what the church is actually called to do in the world, that "changed self-understanding or attitude is no substitute

68. Ibid., 27.
69. Ibid., 25.
70. Ibid., 95.
71. Ibid., 94.
72. Niebuhr, *Discerning the Signs*, 54–55. Or, as he puts it elsewhere, "The new generation which has come to power in our nation seems to understand somewhat the necessity of this modesty and moderation. But it is for the generation represented in the pews of this church to develop the posture, the stance, the style adequate for bearing the burdens of this era without illusion or hysteria." *Justice and Mercy*, 81.

for the existence of a church capable of offering an alternative to the world."[73] But perhaps with some development, Niebuhr's insights about the role of churches in cultivating humility actually present an alternative: a people and a community that is self-critical in light of God's judgment and creative through the empowerment of God's mercy.

## The Church's Vocation in the World

Witness claims that Niebuhr provides no alternative to the world are further grounded in the argument that Niebuhr's ethic assumes responsibility for controlling human history. Witness theologians claim that he ignores the church at the expense of the nation, failing to articulate a special role for the church in history. But these arguments ignore both Niebuhr's emphasis on the transcendence of God and on the reality of human limits. Niebuhr repeatedly asserts that human beings do not control history. Only God can give ultimate meaning to the fragments of history. Niebuhr argues not that humans can determine the course of history, but that God's control and fulfillment of history frees human beings to act within history. These criticisms ultimately mistake Niebuhr's attention to history for an assumption of its control.

Likewise, feminist claims that Niebuhr's emphasis on transcendence prevents transformation fall flat in light of his frequent attention to human moral possibilities.[74] The real problem is not transcendence per se, but Niebuhr's failure to adequately account for the moral possibilities of group transcendence.

---

73. Hauerwas, *With the Grain*, 138.
74. For Miles's refutation of this point, see *Bonds of Freedom*, 43. She also argues that Niebuhr's emphasis on the transformative possibilities of a transcendent norm belies feminist claims that it "leads to a pessimistic support of the status quo."

Emphasis on God's control and completion of history dominates Niebuhr's sermons. Contrary to Yoder's claim that Niebuhr abandons the truth of the gospel to take responsibility for human history, Niebuhr's sermons repeatedly proclaim that while human beings must act in history, only God can provide the ultimate meaning that completes it. This theme resounds throughout Niebuhr's sermons, where listeners are often reminded that "from the standpoint of our faith we should take our humble and contrite place in God's plan of the whole, and leave it to him to complete the fragmentation of our life."[75] Far from any assertion of the need to direct the course of human history, Niebuhr's sermons constantly warn against the folly of such endeavors, sounding frequent appeals for Christians and others to recognize the dangers inherent in any pretension to be masters of our own destinies.

Not surprisingly, Niebuhr's prayers feature the same theme of trust in God's control of history and the need for human beings to abandon pretensions of control. His prayers frequently appeal to God to be reminded of human limitations and human beings' ultimate lack of control over history. "Give us grace," Niebuhr prays, "to know we do not share your foresight into the future or your power over it. So we may humbly ransom our own time because our days are evil."[76] Niebuhr's frequent refutations of the notion of progress also belie Yoder's claim. Niebuhr never pretends that we can control the outcome of history, only that we must venture to find "proximate solutions of insolvable problems."[77] In his words, "This drama of human history is indeed partly our construct, but it stands under a sovereignty much greater than ours. . . . We have discerned a mystery and a meaning beyond our smallness and our greatness, and a

75. Niebuhr, *Justice and Mercy*, 22.
76. Ibid., 84.
77. Ibid., 82.

justice and a love which completes our incompletions, which corrects our judgments, and which brings the whole story to a fulfillment beyond our power to fulfill any story."[78] Niebuhr's reflection here suggests that witness characterizations of him as some kind of historical control freak might be less about Niebuhr's actual views of human agency in relation to God's agency and more about what type of moral action Christians ought to pursue. On this count, real differences exist between Niebuhr and witness theologians. But a productive assessment of Niebuhr's contributions depends on accurately describing the differences that do exist rather than creating differences that do not. Niebuhr's affirmation of responsibility is not an invitation to illusions of total and complete control over history but rather a modest assessment of the importance of human action within history under God's providence. It is ultimately a statement of hope.

For Niebuhr, judgment is necessarily connected to hope.[79] His emphasis on hope means that the church is not only the bearer of judgment but also a community of the transformed, a people of hope:

> The Christian church is a community of hopeful believers, who are not afraid of life or death, of present or future history, being persuaded that the whole of life and all historical vicissitudes stand under the sovereignty of a holy, yet merciful, God whose will was supremely revealed in Christ. It is a community which does not fear the final judgement, not because it is composed of sinless saints but because it is a community of forgiven sinners, who know that judgement is merciful if it is not evaded. If the divine judgement is not resisted by pretensions of virtue but is contritely accepted, it reveals in and beyond itself the mercy which restores life on a new and healthier basis.[80]

---

78. Ibid., 53; 59.
79. As Christopher Lasch puts it, hope for Niebuhr is "the nerve of moral action" and springs from "gratitude and contrition"—"gratitude for Creation and contrition before Judgment." See *The True and Only Heaven: Progress and its Critics* (New York: W. W. Norton & Company, 1991), 371.

In this passage, Niebuhr connects judgment with courage and hope. He makes clear that the ability to receive judgment and repent creates in the church the character of contrition. Niebuhr connects the humility born of this contrition with the purpose of creative human action. "The remorse and repentance which are consequent upon such contemplation," writes Niebuhr, "are similar in their acknowledgment of freedom and responsibility and their implied assertion of it."[81] Sounding remarkably similar to Yoder, Niebuhr argues that "the faith and hope by which the church lives ... are the condition for a courageous witness against 'principalities and powers.'"[82] When the church repents of its sin and self-interest, it is enabled by God's grace to be creative in its resistance to injustice.[83]

Indeed, Niebuhr also often prays that God will grant the church the confidence to lay claim to its potential for transcendence. The church is, as Niebuhr puts it, a "community of grace."[84] Part of its vocation is to witness to the power of God's grace in the pursuit of justice. "Give us grace," Niebuhr prays, "to build our communities after the fashion of your kingdom."[85] In fact, Niebuhr's discussion of the sacraments navigates between the ability of the church to embody the love to which it is called and its failure to do so. "A community of grace, which lives by faith and hope, must be sacramental," he writes. "It must have sacraments to symbolize the having and not having of the final virtue and truth."[86] In a characteristic dialectic, Niebuhr

---

80. Reinhold Niebuhr, *Faith and History: A Comparison of Christian and Modern Views of History* (New York: Charles Scribner's Sons, 1949), 238.

81. Reinhold Niebuhr, *The Nature and Destiny of Man: A Christian Interpretation, Vol. 1: Human Nature* (Louisville: Westminster John Knox, 1996 [originally published 1943]), 255.

82. Niebuhr, *Faith and History*, 238.

83. For an account of the church's public witness that appropriates similar themes from the theology of Dietrich Bonhoeffer, see Jennifer M. McBride, *The Church for the World: A Theology of Public Witness* (New York: Oxford University Press, 2012).

84. Niebuhr, *Faith and History*, 240.

85. Niebuhr, *Justice and Mercy*, 49.

86. Niebuhr, *Faith and History*, 240.

here acknowledges the moral potential of the church to embody the love of its Savior, but not without also acknowledging the failure of the church to do so as fully as Christ does. Although Niebuhr certainly stops short of the degree of confidence witness theologians frequently exhibit in their assessments of the church's moral abilities, he does nevertheless affirm the church's vocation as a community of grace. The problem here is not, as witness theologians contend, that Niebuhr has no regard for the role of the church in Christian discipleship, or, as feminist theologians contend, that his emphasis on divine transcendence prevents innovative change in history. Rather, the problem is that his account of the church's identity and mission in these regards could be more fully developed and that he denies the possibilities of group transcendence.

Nor does this affirmation of the importance of responsible action in the world preclude Niebuhr from articulating a special role for the church. If taken at face value, witness claims that Niebuhr is not interested in the church overlook Niebuhr's reflection on the church and its similarity to witness emphasis on Scripture, worship, preaching and prayer. In his sermons and prayers, Niebuhr offers a view of how the church ought to form its members to hear the divine word of judgment and mercy, to practice contrition, and to embody humility and hope. The church community distinguishes itself only by its willingness to submit itself to God's judgment, not for its superhuman moral ability. "The church," Niebuhr writes, "is not a congregation of people who can pride themselves upon their unique goodness."[87] Rather, "the sanctity of the church does not consist in the goodness of its members but in the holiness of its Lord."[88] "The Church can disturb the society of sinners only if it is not itself too secure in its belief that it has the word of God."[89] In fact, Niebuhr

---

87. Niebuhr, *Beyond Tragedy*, 60–61.
88. Niebuhr, "Can the Church Give a Moral Lead?" in *Essays in Applied Christianity*, 92.

frequently describes the calling of the church in terms of this "moral insight."[90] Although he acknowledges the possibility that political leaders are capable of proceeding with necessary humility, Niebuhr sees the church as the place where this virtue is best cultivated. In these places in his work, he not only makes witness-sounding contentions that the church offers an alternative witness to the nation, but he also makes witness-sounding affirmations that the church has special resources to enable it to provide this witness.

Moreover, Niebuhr shares the witness concern about the church's cultural accommodation. While he views arrogance and pride as the general temptations here, rather than the use of force more narrowly construed, he nevertheless is concerned that the church act in ways over against the larger culture:

> The church is the body of Christ: and Christ is the revelation of the living God, the creator, judge and redeemer of all nations. Such a fellowship can never be completely at home in any nation or perfectly conform to national purposes and ambitions. ... In America, for instance, there are still many prophets of God who imagine that Christianity and the religion of "the American dream" are one and the same thing. ... The final resistance must come from the community which knows and worships a God, to whom all nations are subject. ... The Christian Church must be and remain a fellowship of Christ; and Christ is the judge of the self-will and self-righteousness of every social group.[91]

There is no doubt that a central part of Niebuhr's theological project consists in the application of Christian beliefs, including God's transcendence, to the national and political realm. Each of Niebuhr's major works offers an apology for the Christian view of human beings as the only one adequate for the challenges facing Western

89. Niebuhr, *Beyond Tragedy*, 110.
90. Ibid., 92.
91. Ibid., 84–87.

civilization. Niebuhr's central ethical formulation posits the transcendent norm of self-sacrificing love as a divine standard hovering over and informing conceptions of justice. One also thinks of Niebuhr's turn to Christian beliefs to criticize America's idealism. Each of these examples demonstrates Niebuhr's method of invoking the Christian tradition to encourage America, as a nation, to be a self-critical culture. What scholars often fail to appreciate, however, is that Niebuhr identifies the church itself as the locus for this self-critical activity. "The kind of humility which is required of the nations to meet the possession of the new powers in their possession may be partly achieved by a shrewd political intelligence. . . . But ultimately this humility is a religious achievement. Rather it is not so much an achievement as it is a gift of grace, a by-product of faith which discerns life in its total dimension and senses the divine judgment which stands above and against all human judgments."[92] From this perspective, it is not just that the Christian tradition possesses the resources to create national self-critical cultures—that Christianity possesses resources relevant to the nation, as witness theologians often construe Niebuhr's project—but that the church itself might just be the paradigmatic self-critical culture.

### Churches as Self-Critical Cultures

Does Niebuhr's thought possess the resources to develop a realist ecclesiology that responds to witness and feminist concerns? Their criticisms dictate that any Niebuhrian account of the church: 1) needs to acknowledge the role of revelation in shaping moral communities comprised of persons of diverse experiences; and 2) needs to be the kind of community whose culture inculcates countercultural virtues. Although Niebuhr did not construct his theology in terms of a

92. Niebuhr, *Discerning the Signs*, 71–72.

narrative theory of truth that puts the church's embodiment of a countercultural witness front and center, his theology does provide the necessary resources for developing just such an account of the church.

Juxtaposing Niebuhr's theology with that of Kathryn Tanner in *The Politics of God* reveals significant points of connection between Niebuhr's reflection on the identity and mission of the church and Tanner's description of Christian self-critical cultures.[93] According to her account, self-critical cultures are reflective cultures, not customary cultures. Whereas in customary cultures "transformations . . . happen by way of unreflective habits," in reflective cultures "transformations are promoted by reflection on principles or standards of procedure, and in that way produce a self-critical culture."[94] Because reflective cultures are marked by "deliberative reproduction," they are "not simply self-transformative; they are self-critical."[95] Tanner's work shares certain prominent features with Niebuhr's—including emphasis on divine transcendence and a strong conception of divine providence—but her theology also operates in terms more familiar to both witness and feminist theologians, including emphasis on Christianity as a distinctive culture and the potential of Christian beliefs to challenge oppressive social and political structures. Making the connections between Niebuhr's discussion of the church and her description of self-critical Christian cultures yields new possibilities for constructive projects that contribute to realist, witness, and feminist agendas alike.

---

93. Tanner opens her investigation in *The Politics of God* by noting that her study shares a concern with the early Niebuhr: it seeks to discern "whether Christian action might not combine 'a more radical political orientation and more conservative religious convictions than are comprehended in the culture of our age'" (see *Politics of God*, viii). Tanner is quoting Niebuhr's *Reflections on the End of an Era* (New York: Charles Scribner's Sons, 1934), ix.

94. Tanner, *Politics of God*, 42.

95. Ibid., 46.

In fact, as my reading demonstrates, the themes that dominate Niebuhr's reflection on the church are the exact features of self-critical cultures in Tanner's account. Both emphasize "(1) the limited and finite nature of human ideas, proposals, and norms; (2) their historical and socially circumscribed bases; and (3) their essentially fallible and defeasible character."[96] I highlight these similarities in order to develop a Niebuhrian conception of the church as a self-critical culture whose members, in relation to God's judgment and mercy, engage in practices of contrition that form them in virtues of humility and hope, prompting their engagement in creative ethical action.[97]

Tanner's account takes up the concern feminist theologians express about Niebuhr's emphasis on divine transcendence, asking whether divine transcendence—rather than being consigned to underwriting the status quo—can actually be the source of innovative social change. She argues for the importance of a transcendent creator God for creating the possibility of self-critical cultures. One importance of belief in divine transcendence, according to Tanner, is that it creates "a view from a distance," which encourages reflective cultures to hold themselves accountable to a divine norm that serves as the basis of critique for current social and political organization.[98] Rather than endorsing current arrangements, belief in divine transcendence can create a distinction between divine and human realms that encourages criticism of natural and social orders. This view from a distance "potentially involves their criticism,"[99] leading Tanner to

---

96. Ibid., 69.
97. For elaboration on this point, see my discussion in "Churches as 'Self-Critical Cultures,'" in *Gendering Christian Ethics*, where I argue that these similarities between Niebuhr's discussion of the church and Tanner's concept of self-critical cultures continue in their identification of justice, the combating of complacency, and the cultivation of humility and hope as the accompanying goals for political action (38–43).
98. Tanner, *Politics of God*, 67.
99. Ibid.

conclude that "a belief in divine transcendence generally fosters the structural features of self-critical cultures."[100]

## "The Limited and Finite Nature of Human Ideas"

The first feature of self-critical cultures, according to Tanner, is that their belief in divine transcendence compels recognition of "the limited and finite nature of human ideas" in contrast with the divine realm. Despite witness claims that Niebuhr's theology fails to give priority to revelation, and feminist criticisms that Niebuhr's emphasis on divine transcendence reinforces the status quo, Niebuhr's discussion of the church features this same distinction between divine and human realms and the power of divine transcendence to enable ethical action. For Niebuhr, belief in divine transcendence posits God as divine other and ultimate judge, compelling human beings to submit themselves to God's judgment and receive God's mercy. These convictions, in turn, ground his view of the church.

> The church is that place in human society where men are disturbed by the word of the eternal God, which stands as judgment upon human aspirations. But it is also the place where the word of mercy, reconciliation and consolation is heard. . . . The Church is the place in human society where the Kingdom of God impinges upon all human enterprises through the divine word, and where the grace of God is made available to those who have accepted His judgment.[101]

The sharp distinctions between divine and human that suffuse this passage are striking. They belie the witness criticism that Niebuhr starts with human experience and not divine revelation. Niebuhr contrasts "human society" with the word of the "eternal God," "human enterprises" with the "Kingdom of God," and "men" with "God." The entire passage trades heavily on the distinction between

100. Ibid.
101. Niebuhr, *Beyond Tragedy*, 62.

divine and human, clearly indicating the priority of God's word over any limited human understanding of it.

The passage does not merely distinguish God from humans, God's realm from the natural and social realm; it also emphasizes the character of this relationship as one of judgment, affirming the authority of God's revelation over human experience. Niebuhr speaks of the church as the place where humans are "disturbed" by the word of God. It is the place where the word of God "stands as judgment" upon human aspirations. The kingdom of God "impinges" upon human enterprises. The emphasis on judgment in the passage recalls Tanner's claim that belief in a transcendent God creates a standard of critique against which all human action is measured. The church is that community of people who listen for the divine word of judgment. The church as a body of believers willingly submits itself to God's judgment and mercy, availing itself of the moral resources they provide.

These same emphases appear repeatedly in Niebuhr's prayers. His prayers convey deep reverence for God as the Transcendent One, whose ways are beyond human understanding but whose judgment and mercy enable moral action.

> Eternal God, Father Almighty, maker of heaven and earth, we worship you. Your wisdom is beyond our understanding, your power is greater than we can measure, your thoughts are above our thoughts; as high as the heaven is above the earth, your majesty judges all human majesties. . . . Give us grace to apprehend by faith the power and wisdom which lie beyond our understanding; and in worship to feel that which we do not know, and to praise even what we do not understand; so that in the presence of your glory we may be humble, and in the knowledge of your judgment we may repent; and so in the assurance of your mercy, we may rejoice and be glad.[102]

102. Niebuhr, *Justice and Mercy*, 37.

It is important to note Niebuhr's emphasis here not only on judgment but also on mercy, as mercy forestalls the kind of despair and evisceration of human agency that feminists identify in their critiques of divine transcendence.

By emphasizing divine mercy alongside divine judgment, Niebuhr guards against despair. The church is the place where God's word of "mercy, reconciliation and consolation is heard."[103] It is the place "where the grace of God is made available."[104] In this way, Niebuhr defends against the possibility that belief in God's transcendence might undercut its transformative potential: "The Christian," he writes, "is freed by that grace to act in history."[105] Judgment need not immobilize Christians. Rather, it is a catalyst. It prompts believers to embrace their own capacities for self-transcendence.

Far, then, from rejecting the priority of God's word, Niebuhr's emphasis on divine judgment maintains a radical distinction between God and human beings. His account certainly attends to human beings' experience of God's judgment and God's mercy, but this attention to the human experience is a far cry from witness claims that Niebuhr's theology is first and foremost anthropology, or that Niebuhr fails to prioritize revelation. Feminist worries about the role of transcendence in contributing to ethical inertia also prove unconvincing in light of Niebuhr's emphasis on the role of God's mercy in enabling human action and the pursuit of justice.

### "The Historical and Socially Circumscribed Basis" of the Church

A second theme of Niebuhr's discussion of the church mirrors Tanner's argument that self-critical cultures foster recognition of the

103. Niebuhr, *Beyond Tragedy*, 62.
104. Ibid.
105. Niebuhr, "Why the Christian Church is Not Pacifist," in *War in the Twentieth Century: Sources in Theological Ethics,* ed. Richard B. Miller (Louisville: Westminster John Knox, 1992), 45.

historically and socially circumscribed basis of human institutions. This characteristic of the church allows Niebuhr to adequately acknowledge its historical and socially constructed nature. Niebuhr not only affirms that all human communities are historically and socially constructed; he also affirms that they play an important role in human moral formation.[106]

This acknowledgment allows Niebuhr to emphasize the ways the church as a human institution shares certain features with all other institutions as historically and socially circumscribed entities. "The church . . . is a very human institution," he writes. "It is subject to the aberrations of particular generations and the faulty insights and sinful ambitions of special groups and classes. The 'heavenly city' of the church happens to exist on earth and to draw its sustenance from very earthly sources."[107] This conviction, informed by Niebuhr's early work in *Moral Man and Immoral Society*, grounds his claim that religious communities are subject to the same dynamics as all other groups.

> The church, as well as the state, can become the vehicle of collective egotism. Every truth can be made the servant of sinful arrogance, including the prophetic truth that all men fall short of the truth. This particular truth can come to mean that, since all men fall short of the truth and since the church is a repository of a revelation which transcends the finiteness and sinfulness of men, it therefore has the absolute truth which other men lack.[108]

Or as he puts it elsewhere, "No church can lift man out of the partial and finite history in which all human life stands. Every interpretation of the church which promises an 'efficient grace,' by which man ceases to be man and enters prematurely into the Kingdom of God,

---

106. For Miles' discussion on this point, see *Bonds of Freedom*, 67–68.
107. Niebuhr, *Beyond Tragedy*, 121.
108. Niebuhr, *The Nature and Destiny of Man: Human Nature*, 217.

is a snare and a delusion. The church is not the Kingdom of God."[109] Niebuhr clearly indicates that the church as a culture does not manage to escape the historical and social realities that shape other cultures. It, too, is subject to historical and social influence. It, too, is a human institution subject to sin.

But attending to the particular nature of the church as historically and socially constructed also enabled Niebuhr, in the later stages of his career, to acknowledge—in the witness sense—what makes the church a particular kind of community set apart from other communities. "I have increasingly recognized the value of the Church as a community of grace which, despite historic corruptions, has the 'oracles of God,' as St. Paul said about Israel. The Church is the one place in history where life is kept open for the final word of God's judgment to break the pride of men and for the word of God's mercy to lift up the brokenhearted."[110] It is in this light that one should understand Niebuhr's warnings about religious pretension. His affirmation of the church's particularity as a community not only allows him to acknowledge what makes the church a particular kind of community apart from others; it also allows him to provide an account of the particular sins to which the church is prone.

Consequently, just after Niebuhr expresses his appreciation for the church as a community of grace, he notes a more dubious particularity: religious arrogance and moral complacency. "When I see how much new evil comes into life through the pretension of the religious community, through its conventional and graceless legalism and through religious fanaticism," he writes, "I am concerned that my growing appreciation of the Church should not betray me into this complacency."[111] The very thing that makes the church distinctive

---

109. Niebuhr, *Beyond Tragedy,* 62.
110. Niebuhr, "Reply to Interpretation and Criticism," 437.
111. Ibid.

vis-à-vis other communities—its identity as "the one place in history where life is kept open for the final word of God's judgment . . . and for the word of God's mercy to lift up the brokenhearted"—is the very identity that renders it particularly prone to the sin of religious pretension. In Niebuhr's words, "The explicit religious element, at the center of the religious community, also lends itself to the most explicit forms of the pretensions of finality. That is why the Christian Church must be more humble and not suggest so complacently that is has achieved, in its own life, a form of universal love which it would bestow upon the nations."[112] Rather than interpreting such comments as indicating a betrayal of the church and its distinctive role, Niebuhr's concerns are better understood as issuing from the same convictions that lead witness theologians to emphasize the particularity of the church as a community shaped by a particular narrative, formed in particular practices, for a particular vocation.

In this sense, Niebuhr takes the distinctive particularity of the church twice as seriously as witness accounts. Whereas witness accounts focus on the particularity of the Christian tradition and how this particularity translates into its special vocation in the world, Niebuhr's discussion goes one step further to consider not only the distinctive calling of the church but its distinctive failing. Niebuhr's emphasis on the historical and social construction of the church as an institution provides a powerful tool, for example, to address feminist concerns about the church's complicity in sexism or claims that Niebuhr fails to adequately account for female experience. It names sexism and other violations of human dignity as aberrations of church practice and doctrine that arise from the church's historical and social construction rather than ignoring their malformative effect on church practices.

112. Niebuhr, *Discerning the Signs*, 85–86.

## The "Essentially Fallible and Defeasible Character" of the Church

A third feature of Niebuhr's descriptions of the church is its capacity for error. Here again there is a point of connection with Tanner's account of self-critical cultures, which acknowledges the "essentially fallible and defeasible character" of human ideas, plans, and organizations. Niebuhr identifies this propensity across the spectrum of Christian traditions, noting, for example, that both Catholics and Protestants are prone to such fallibility.[113] Because of the particular tendency of religious groups to make such errors, Niebuhr focuses on the importance of contrition as a central religious practice. The call for contrition is a constant throughout Niebuhr's career; the theme pervades his work.

> The church is created not by the righteousness of the pharisee but the contrition of the publican; not by the achievement of pure goodness but by the recognition of the sinfulness of all human goodness. This contrition is the fruit of faith in the transcendent God who cannot be identified with any human goodness. ... The church is not a congregation of people who can pride themselves upon their unique goodness. It is rather a congregation of people to whom the eternal God has spoken and who answer the eternal word in terms of Job's contrition: "I have uttered things too wonderful for me, which I understood not. Wherefore I abhor myself and repent in dust and ashes." Man's contrition is the human foundation of the church. But God's grace is its completion.[114]

113. As Niebuhr puts it, "Protestantism is right in insisting that Catholicism identifies the church too simply with the Kingdom of God. This identification, which allows a religious institution, involved in all the relativities of history, to claim unconditioned truth for its doctrines and unconditioned moral authority for its standards, makes it just another tool of human pride. . . . But as soon as the Protestant assumes that his more prophetic statement and interpretation of the Christian gospel guarantees him a superior virtue, he is also lost in the sin of self-righteousness. The fact is that the Protestant doctrine of the priesthood of all believers may result in an individual self-deification against which Catholic doctrine has more adequate checks. . . . There is no final guarantee against the spiritual pride of man. . . . If that final mystery of the sin of pride is not recognized the meaning of the Christian gospel cannot be understood." *Nature and Destiny: Human Nature*, 201-2.

114. Niebuhr, *Beyond Tragedy*, 60–61.

Witness theologians may construe such acknowledgments as undermining the church's calling to live now in accordance with the true reality of love or to provide a foretaste of the kingdom of God, but Niebuhr's awareness of sin in this passage actually resembles their own recognition of the church's complicity in the sins of the world that prevents it from providing a countercultural witness. Feminists will note that this practice of contrition assumes pride as the central sin; as such it may not be as powerful for some whose sin more closely resembles what Niebuhr calls the "sin of sensuality," but nevertheless it provides a powerful tool for feminists in calling for the church to confess and repent of its sexism.

Lest Niebuhr's comments on the fallible nature of the church give way to a picture of the church that can only acknowledge its limits, it is also important to remember that Niebuhr's conception of sin is dialectical. The essentially defeasible and fallible nature of human existence, as well as the church's existence, is not only defined in terms of the sin of pride but also the sin of sensuality. Niebuhr's theological anthropology describes humans as both finite and free, and his conception of sin reflects both aspects of this dialectical identity. At times, humans are prone to deny their finitude by pretending to be more than they are. This is the sin of pride. But at other times, humans fail to do justice to their capacities for freedom, committing the sin of sensuality. This conception of sin has the benefit of capturing a wider range of human experience and propensity to sin—in ways feminists can appreciate—but it also has the benefit of drawing attention to the responsibility of the Christian realist in calling for an expansion of the imagination when human possibilities for creative moral action are not taken seriously. Niebuhr's conception of sin as sensuality provides a critical tool for identifying occasions when individuals and communities fail to embrace their God-given capacities for transcendence and creative action.

Feminist emphasis on the "horizontal transcendence" of church communities better maintains Niebuhr's own dialectic in that it dictates that the church engage not only in practices of contrition, but also practices of creativity. When persons think too little of themselves and their capabilities, Niebuhr would have them claim their God-given freedom for transcendence. Contrary to the worry that self-criticism leads to a immobilizing and crippling suspension of our creative capacities and desire to work for change, Lovin, for example, argues that in contexts where freedom becomes trivialized, "The role of Christian Realism is not to talk about realistic limits, but to expand political imagination. . . . When no one any longer dares to be utopian, however, the role of the Realist may be to recall that the human reality also includes the capacity for such dreams."[115] Lovin concludes that "properly understood, the Christian Realist claim that there are no limits to our moral achievements within history is not an invitation to pride, but to politics."[116] Maintaining the dialectic between sin as pride and sin as sensuality, between human finitude with the limits it imposes and human freedom with the creativity it entails, makes clear that the defeasible and fallible nature of the church does not only apply when it commits the sin of pride. It also applies when the church fails to embrace its freedom and engage in creative action.

## Conclusion

These points of connection between Niebuhr's reflections on the church and Tanner's discussion of self-critical cultures highlight the constructive potential for developing a Niebuhrian ecclesiology that

115. Lovin, *Reinhold Niebuhr and Christian Realism*, 246.
116. Ibid., 157.

integrates witness and feminist concerns. It does not erase the significant differences that will continue to abide between witness and realist theologians, especially those pertaining to their theories of truth and judgments about the compatibility between Christian truth claims and the resort to violent force. But it does suggest that some of their other differences are not finally differences of kind but of degree. Witness accounts imply that Niebuhr fails to prioritize revelation and Scripture, when in fact the difference might be more aptly stated as a difference of emphasis. Witness theologians highlight the publicly inaccessible nature of Christian narrative, whereas Niebuhr emphasizes the verification of the drama of God's judgment and mercy in experience. Witness criticisms imply that Niebuhr ignores the role of the church in moral formation, when in fact the difference might be better described as a difference in focus. Witness accounts emphasize practices of peaceableness, whereas Niebuhr focuses on practices of contrition. Witness accounts suggest that Niebuhr abandons the church's distinctive witness to presume responsibility for human affairs, when in fact the difference resides in contrasting approaches to avoiding cultural accommodation. Witness accounts focus on the church's need to embody a witness of peace in a violent world, whereas Niebuhr emphasizes the need for humility and hope in an overconfident, unreflective culture.

The Niebuhrian account of the church I have developed in this chapter contributes to ecclesial gaps in both Niebuhr's and contemporary realists' projects and to witness and feminist accounts. It is robust enough to satisfy witness theologians who understand the church as its own particular culture without ignoring realist concerns that such an account not overestimate the moral capacities of the church or misconstrue the interrelationship between "church" and "world." It also addresses witness concerns about the church's vocation in history and its ability to shape its members in proper

Christian moral formation while addressing feminist concerns that churches challenge oppressive social structures.

Developing a Niebuhrian ecclesiology contributes not only to Niebuhr's legacy but also to the accounts of his realist successors. Both Lovin and Miles develop important realist accounts that extend Niebuhr's own account beyond his focus on the politics of nations, but they do not articulate their accounts in an explicitly ecclesiological framework. My comparison of Niebuhr with Tanner gives rise to a vision of the church as a community of self-criticism that engages in practices of contrition and creativity to engender virtues of humility and hope. Niebuhr's understanding of the church's distinctive vocation to recognize and receive God's judgment and mercy by engaging in practices of contrition and creativity enables a realist ecclesiology that meets witness theologians on their terms without sacrificing realist commitments.

For their part, witness theologians might find in this Niebuhrian ecclesiology a way for the church to narrate not only its own history but also that of the world. The failure to do this is the very problem some have pointed to in prominent witness accounts of the church-world relationship. Robert Jenson, for example, speculates that accusations of sectarianism and claims that Hauerwas does not believe in the doctrine of creation result from the failure of Hauerwas's account to clarify how the distinctive role of the church relates to the world's destiny, to explicitly state that "the world is narratively enveloped in the church."[117] It may just be that Niebuhr's biblical perspective on the drama of history provides what Jenson's critique identifies as the missing component of prominent witness accounts like Hauerwas's—an account of how the church narrates the true history of the world. While scholars often point to Niebuhr's concern

---

117. Robert Jenson, "The Hauerwas Project," *Modern Theology* 8, no. 3 (July 1992): 293.

for politics and the fate of Western civilization as evidence for his lack of concern with the church, a closer look reveals that Niebuhr's concern for the nations derives from this very perspective in Scripture. Niebuhr's emphasis on politics and history might be construed, in other words, not as an evasion of ecclesiology but an extension of it. Niebuhr's focus on both the church's history and on human history, on the sin of the world and the sin of the church, acknowledges the incarnational or worldly character of the church, but also suggests what I would call the "churchliness of the world."

In this way, witness theologians might manage at once to engage what realists have called the "new realities" and make manifest the distinctive mission of the reality of most concern to them: the church. Rather than maintaining a distinctiveness that jeopardizes the church's ability to make clear its shared destiny with the world, Niebuhr's thought allows for a distinctiveness that appears not in the church's unique ability to embody love but in its willingness to confess its complicity with the world in failing to embody this love as fully as its Lord. Put differently, Niebuhr does allow for the church's distinctive role; it is just that this distinctiveness lies in its awareness of its own tendency to sin by claiming its distinction from the world. Contrary to Hauerwas's claim that the church has no special role in Niebuhr's theology, Niebuhr's focus on judgment, contrition, humility, and hope can be seen as a particularly Niebuhrian contribution to church practice and formation—one that might even be construed as an elaboration of "peaceableness." After all, at the heart of the witness vision of the church's peaceableness is a critique of the church's failure to embody God's peace.

This account also contributes to feminist accounts. Although Welch, Miles, and Tanner cast their accounts, respectively, as corrections to, appropriations of, or attempts to continue the abandoned projects of Niebuhr's theology, they do not formulate their accounts in explicitly ecclesiological terms. Contrary to other feminist criticisms that Niebuhr does not account for female experience, ignores the need for justice in the private realm, and espouses a belief in divine transcendence that underwrites the status quo, the Niebuhrian account of the church developed here coheres well with calls from feminist theologians like Kwok Pui-lan for the church to confess its complicity in women's oppression. In her words, "While male liberation theologians have exhorted the church to bring about social change, female theologians are more realistic about ecclesial power and their optimism more guarded. The church, steeped in male hierarchy and tradition, has to repent for its sexism before it can be a beacon of hope and an agent for change."[118] Niebuhr's thought issues just such a demand for the church to submit to God's judgment and embrace the moral transformation it initiates.

While the witness and feminist criticisms considered in this chapter pinpoint problems in Niebuhr's thought that need to be addressed, too often these criticisms are overstated. Reading Niebuhr's thought and that of his realist, witness, and feminist interlocutors at the boundary, however, locates sites for construction that could give rise to collaborative projects that strengthen the internal agendas of all involved.

118. Kwok Pui-lan, "Feminist Theology, Southern" in *Blackwell Companion to Political Theology*, 207.

# 3

## Feminism as Christian Politics

*A Realist- and Feminist-Inspired Appropriation of
John Howard Yoder's Pacifism*

"Christian identity itself calls for feminist engagement."
—John Howard Yoder[1]

In November 1973, Mennonite theologian John Howard Yoder
delivered a lecture to a meeting of Evangelicals for Social Action.[2]
"We would not be gathered here," he said, "if we did not believe
that the love of a sovereign God drives us into concern for the social
order. . . . God does not simply tell *us* to accept the existing order; he

1. John Howard Yoder, "Feminist Theology Miscellany #1: Salvation Through Mothering?"
(October 1990), 5. I am grateful to Mark Thiessen Nation and Gayle Gerber Koontz, as well
as Eileen K. Saner, librarian at Anabaptist Mennonite Biblical Seminary in Elkhart, Indiana,
for helping me locate these unpublished memos before they were digitized. They can now
be found in the "John Howard Yoder Digital Collection" at http://replica.palni.edu/cdm/
landingpage/collection/p15705coll18.
2. Portions of this chapter appeared in "The Feminist-Christian Schism Revisited," *The Journal
of Scriptural Reasoning* 13, no. 2 (November 2014): http://jsr.shanti.virginia.edu/
volume-13-number-2-november-2014-navigating-john-howard-yoders-the-jewish-
christian-schism-revisited/the-feminist-christian-schism-revisited/.

tells us also that it must change."[3] Neither the lecture nor its message was unusual. Yoder spent much of his life either engaged in or advocating for active Christian engagement in social, economic, and political life. After serving with the Mennonite Board of Missions and Charities and directing the Mennonite Central Committee's postwar relief effort in France, Yoder taught Christian ethics at Associated Mennonite Biblical Seminary and the University of Notre Dame. Much of his scholarly output consists of essays drawn from lectures on Christian political responsibility, yet this is the very aspect of his theology critics often overlook.

Most Christian ethicists would identify Yoder's contributions to the field primarily in terms of his apology for Christian pacifism. Yoder argues that Christian discipleship demands nonviolence, primarily (although not exclusively) construed as nonparticipation in the military apparatus of the state. He devoted most of his scholarly energies to reclaiming Christ as normative for Christian ethics and proclaiming the radical reformation vision as normative for all Christians. Nevertheless, scholars routinely underappreciate Yoder's insistence on the social, economic, and political involvement this pacifist politics entails.

Yoder's focus on Christian pacifism leads realists and "new Augustinians" alike to question whether Yoder's theology contributes to extra-ecclesial politics. These scholars see a Yoder who is more interested in the purity of Christian witness than the dirty hands of politics, more interested in the church's own politics than responsible action within larger political structures, and more interested in a witness of nonresistant love than the pursuit of justice. Despite Yoder's claim that the "incarnation is by definition

---

3. John Howard Yoder, *For the Nations: Essays Evangelical and Public* (Eugene, OR: Wipf & Stock, 2002), 182.

*involvement*,"[4] these scholars construe Yoder's account as a renunciation of secular politics, not a rallying call for political action.

Both realists and new Augustinians appreciate aspects of Yoder's position but ultimately regard it as politically irresponsible.[5] Robin W. Lovin, for example, notes that Yoder and other witness theologians "appear to find the choice between criticism and responsibility an easy one. It is for them a 'Constantinian' distortion of Christianity's role to take responsibility for working out solutions to society's problems."[6] The realist-leaning new Augustinians follow suit. Charles Mathewes writes, "For Yoder, politics as an immanent project must simply be renounced, for we have a better vision of politics modeled for us by Jesus, and this politics is not really about organizing life in this world, but is instead a matter of already living, albeit adventally, in the kingdom."[7] And while he is far from describing Yoder's project as antipolitical, new Augustinian Eric Gregory nevertheless aligns it with Stanley Hauerwas's antiliberalism.[8]

Realists' concerns about the rejection of political responsibility are important, but their criticisms overlook the political activity Yoder's theology demands. As Yoder himself argues, such characterizations of his position as abdicating "responsibility," forgoing "politics," and being "unrealistic" define these terms too narrowly. Describing Yoder as antiliberal also obscures his receptivity to what he calls "tactical alliances"[9] between Christianity and political liberalism.

---

4. John Howard Yoder, *The Christian Witness to the State* (Scottdale, PA: Herald, 1964), 57.
5. Reinhold Niebuhr took the same position toward the perfectionist pacifists of his day. See "Why the Christian Church is Not Pacifist," in *War in the Twentieth Century: Sources in Theological Ethics*, ed. Richard B. Miller (Louisville: Westminster John Knox, 1992), 30.
6. Robin W. Lovin, *Reinhold Niebuhr and Christian Realism* (Cambridge: Cambridge University Press, 1995), 99.
7. Charles Mathewes, *A Theology of Public Life* (Cambridge: Cambridge University Press, 2007), 240–41.
8. Eric Gregory, *Politics and the Order of Love: An Augustinian Ethic of Democratic Citizenship* (Chicago: The University of Chicago Press, 2008), 125.

These accounts not only underappreciate the inherently political nature of Yoder's proposal; they also undervalue the extra-ecclesial politics it requires.

The appropriation of Yoder's thought by prominent witness theologians exacerbates the problem. While witness interpretation underscores the ecclesial politics of Yoder's radical reformation vision, witness successors to Yoder's legacy often construe it in more antiliberal directions than Yoder's own project. As Yoder himself notes, Hauerwas contributes to characterizations of Yoder's stance as sectarian by "maximiz[ing] the provocative edge of the dissenting posture with titles like *Against the Nations* . . . or *Resident Aliens*."[10] Hauerwas cites Yoder as a major influence but does not detail as clearly as Yoder did either the myriad ways ecclesial politics demands extra-ecclesial political action or the feminism Yoder claims as integral to Christian identity. If realists and new Augustinians misconstrue Yoder's account by claiming it renounces politics, witness theologians both neglect the full range of Yoder's ecclesial politics and obscure his contributions to extra-ecclesial politics.

Feminist interpretation falls along the same lines. Some feminists follow realists in overstating their criticism of Yoder. Elisabeth Schüssler Fiorenza, for example, argues that Yoder's interpretation of the New Testament *Haustafeln* "maintains that we must advocate [the New Testament pattern of patriarchal submission] today,"[11] implying the irreconcilability of feminist theologies with Yoder's. Others, like Cynthia Hess, follow witness theologians in appropriating Yoder's thought—in her case, to address the internal violence of trauma—but focus on ecclesial politics to the exclusion of politics beyond the

9. John Howard Yoder, *The Priestly Kingdom: Social Ethics as Gospel* (Notre Dame, IN: University of Notre Dame Press, 1984), 61.
10. Yoder, *For the Nations*, 3.
11. Elisabeth Schüssler Fiorenza, *Bread Not Stone: The Challenge of Feminist Biblical Interpretation* (Boston: Beacon, 1984), 83.

church. While these feminist engagements focus rightly on gender justice and related issues, they either neglect the role of social egalitarianism in Yoder's account of ecclesial politics or fail to explore its relevance to extra-ecclesial politics.

This "irresponsible," "apolitical," "antiliberal," "antifeminist" Yoder is another product of the polarized debate between witness and realist theologians in Christian ethics. Focused on a narrow construal of violence as the evil-restraining means of the state, it forces Yoder's ethics to be framed in either-or terms: one must either adopt Yoder's pacifist politics, eschewing extra-ecclesial political responsibility, or one must reject it, embracing "realistic" politics. Despite Yoder's claims that his account is both more "realistic about sin and more hopeful about reconciliation,"[12] neither option allows for a conception of Yoder as Christian realist. Just as importantly, feminist criticism of Yoder hides his embrace of social egalitarianism as part of Christian politics, leaving unexplored Yoder's claim that "Christian identity itself calls for feminist engagement."[13]

As with witness and feminist assessments of Niebuhr's ecclesiology, these criticisms contain important but partial truths. They rightly identify Yoder's emphasis on the church as an alternative polis and his refusal of force as a political option, but they are wrong to imply that he therefore rejects politics or is antiliberal. Similarly, witness and feminist appropriations of Yoder are right to emphasize his ecclesial

---

12. John Howard Yoder, *Body Politics: Five Practices of the Christian Community Before the Watching World* (Scottdale, PA: Herald, 1992), 76.

13. Reclaiming, developing, and implementing this insight of Yoder's project is even more pressing in light of his pervasive sexual violence against women. I highlight the underdeveloped feminist component of Yoder's understanding of the church not to exonerate Yoder but to argue that contemporary witness theologians who claim Yoder's legacy cannot fully articulate their own projects without attending to the work of feminist and womanist theologians. I further address the difficulties Yoder's complex legacy raises in my forthcoming article, "Doing Justice to the Complex Legacy of John Howard Yoder: Restorative Justice Resources in Witness and Feminist Ethics," *Journal of the Society of Christian Ethics* 35, no. 2 (Fall/Winter 2015).

politics, but they are wrong to ignore the role of social egalitarianism, including feminism, within his account of Christian politics.

## John Howard Yoder's Account of the Church's Postliberal Feminist Politics

This chapter challenges realist and feminist responses to as well as witness appropriations of Yoder's theology. I argue that these accounts conceal the postliberal, feminist vision of Yoder's theology and its call for Christian political involvement. The realist caricature of a Yoder who renounces politics hides Yoder's insistence that Christians are called to change the world. Witness appropriations of Yoder's theology that run in antiliberal directions wrongly suggest that because Yoder is postliberal, he is also antiliberal. And feminist dismissals of Yoder's theology as hopelessly patriarchal overlook the centrality of social egalitarianism, of which feminism is an essential part, to his account of Christian politics.

My reading reveals a Yoder who is more interested in extra-ecclesial political action than realists can see, but one who—unlike realists—does not neglect the church and its role in forming Christian political actors. It reveals a Yoder who emphasizes the church's politics but who—unlike witness theologians—does not espouse postliberal concerns for Christianity's cultural purity over against political liberalism or dismiss the diversity of feminist theologies as mere versions of theological liberalism. It reveals a Yoder who—despite his own profound personal failure to live out the commitment in his own life—authored a theology that posits feminism as intrinsic to Christian identity. This analysis challenges both realist caricatures of Yoder as renouncing politics and prominent witness theologians' claims to Yoder's legacy. I argue that it is, in fact, contemporary feminists who may unintentionally be providing the most powerful articulation of parts of Yoder's free church vision, and that witness theologians not only have a moral obligation to engage these theologians but that doing so strengthens their own accounts of the church's identity and mission.

I begin this argument by analyzing realist, feminist, and witness criticism and appropriation of Yoder. I first show that—contrary to realist concerns—Yoder's theology does not reject politics. Second, I show that—contrary to feminist claims—Yoder's theology does not advocate the oppression of women. Third, I show that—contrary to witness claims—Yoder's theology is not antiliberal and regards feminism as constitutive of the ecclesial politics of the church. Challenging witness appropriation of Yoder while highlighting the realist and feminist aspects of Yoder's discussion of ecclesial politics both calls into question witness claims to Yoder's legacy and identifies the importance of feminist and womanist work for the future of witness theologies. Analyzing Yoder's relationship to feminism highlights surprising points of connection between his postliberal account and that of various feminist theologians, including shared conceptions of Christianity as a culture, shared conceptions of their respective theologies as Christian projects of retrieval, and shared understandings of the church's vocation as a countercultural witness of peace. This comparison reveals that the work of many feminist theologians, while certainly not attempting to do so in any intentional way, contributes meaningfully to Yoder's own radical reformation project.[14]

14. My account of "feminism as Christian politics" resonates at points with Nathan R. Kerr's account of an "apocalyptic politics of mission," (173) which also draws on Yoder's theology and "operates in a mode akin to what the theologies of liberation have taught us to call 'the preferential option for the poor'" (191). Although Kerr does not focus, as I do, on Yoder's treatment of and connections with feminist theologies, his claim that "'the poor' names . . . not the *object* of the church's outgoing, but rather the very 'non-site' of the church's gathering" (192) illuminates Yoder's claim that "Christian identity itself calls for feminist engagement." See *Christ, History and Apocalyptic: The Politics of Christian Mission* (Eugene, OR: Cascade, 2009).

## Yoder and Realist, Feminist, and Witness Traditions

What are realists, feminists and witness theologians to make of Yoder's theological and political legacy? Realist consideration of Yoder's legacy turns quickly to his account of ecclesial politics and his church-world dualism. Yoder's emphasis on the distinctive politics of the church leads realists to question whether Yoder's theology provides for politics this side of the kingdom. They criticize witness theologians for failing to make discriminating judgments between good and evil and for affirming the moral imperative of love with little attention to justice. From a realist point of view, theologians like Yoder do their theology with too much confidence in the power of Christians to live now as in the kingdom of God and too little willingness to take responsibility—including the use of force—for dealing with human sin. Despite human capacities for self-transcendence and mutual love, perfect realizations of love are, for realists, rare occurrences rather than the regular stuff of day-to-day ethics.

One prominent realist criticism of Yoder is that his account focuses on discipleship within the church as the church's political witness to the exclusion of participation in the wider liberal political order. These theologians identify Yoder's church-world distinction and critique of Constantinianism as key to his renunciation of extra-ecclesial politics. Lovin, for example, describes Yoder as refusing the "'Constantinian' distortion."[15] Similarly, Mathewes argues that Yoder's account "ultimately . . . recapitulates the 'church versus world' dichotomy that we should transcend."[16] Rather than offer a viable proposal for how to live in this world, Yoder's account "does not confront the conditions of our lives during the world so much

15. Lovin, *Reinhold Niebuhr and Christian Realism*, 99.
16. Mathewes, *Theology of Public Life*, 241.

as suggest that Jesus offers us a way to avoid those conditions."[17] While Gregory's account gives less attention to Yoder's theology than Mathewes's and describes it in more charitable terms, he nevertheless aligns Yoder with Hauerwas in "the refusal to ally Christian social ethics with liberalism because of its hegemonic commitment to secularism."[18] Because Yoder's church-world distinction is identified as foundational to his "antiliberal" failure to take extra-ecclesial politics seriously, it deserves careful attention. Are these realist and new Augustinian criticisms warranted?

A close reading of Yoder reveals that the problem is not so much his church-world dualism but his overidentification of the state with the "world."[19] And while realist accounts identify the church-world dualism as a barrier to Christian engagement in the world, Yoder makes clear that his church-world dualism does not valorize the church and denigrate the world. Rather, it is a statement about calling. There is no ontological dualism that undermines the ultimate unity of the cosmos under the lordship of Christ. "Church" and "world" possess separate mandates, but they "are not two compartments under separate legislation or two institutions with contradictory assignments, but two levels of the pertinence of the same Lordship."[20] Christians and non-Christians share the same destiny; they differ only in what they believe about that destiny: "The calling of the people of God is thus no different from the calling of all humanity. The difference between the human community as a whole . . . and the faith community . . . is a matter of awareness or knowledge or commitment or celebration but not of ultimate

---

17. Ibid.
18. Gregory, *Politics and the Order of Love*, 125.
19. As Hauerwas once put it: "One must ask if Yoder's theological predisposition has not prevented him from considering a more positive understanding of the nature of political community." See "The Nonresistant Church," in *Vision and Virtue: Essays in Christian Ethical Reflection* (Notre Dame, IN: Fides, 1974), 218.
20. Yoder, *Body Politics*, ix.

destiny."[21] In other words, the church's mandate to proclaim and celebrate this destiny—not the destiny itself—is what distinguishes the church from the world.

Nor does the distinction assign righteousness to the church and sinfulness to the world. Yoder argues that *all* of culture is a blend of order and revolt. This means not only that churches take part in the rebellion of "the world," but also that the world manifests some degree of order and therefore exists as a site of God's grace. Rather, the distinction is a descriptive one. It is a "distinction of confession"[22]—the church self-consciously confesses Christ as Lord; the world does not. It identifies the church as a believing community while respecting the world's unbelief. As Yoder puts it, "The fundamental duality with which the Christian speaking to the environing society must reckon is not the difference between church and state as social institutions . . . but the difference between faith and unbelief as the presuppositions of his ethical message."[23] In other words, Yoder's church-world dualism is "not the kind of *dualism* that would imagine that the church could separate itself entirely from the world, but rather a *duality* based on faith and unbelief, allegiances in opposite directions."[24] The world may not profess belief in Christ's rule, but its unbelief neither prevents it from witnessing unawares to the redemptive reality of Christ nor prevents the church's engagement in politics.

Indeed, Yoder explicitly rejects the idea that his ethic eschews political participation beyond the church. Again and again he calls

21. Yoder, *For the Nations*, 24.
22. Craig A. Carter, *The Politics of the Cross: The Theology and Social Ethics of John Howard Yoder* (Grand Rapids: Brazos, 2001), 148.
23. Yoder, *Christian Witness*, 29.
24. Gerald W. Schlabach, "The Christian Witness in the Earthly City: John H. Yoder as Augustinian Interlocutor," in *A Mind Patient and Untamed: Assessing John Howard Yoder's Contributions to Theology, Ethics, and Peacemaking*, ed. Ben C. Ollenburger and Gayle Gerber Koontz (Telford, PA: Cascadia, 2004), 232.

attention to the inherently public nature of the church's mission and the extra-ecclesial involvement Christian politics demands. Yoder's insistence that "the incarnation is by definition *involvement*"[25] belies realist contentions that he renounces politics for fear of compromising moral purity or watering down the church's distinctive message. Contrary to realist suggestion, his church-world dualism does not constitute a physical barrier obstructing Christian participation in politics. The question is not *whether* Christians should attempt to effect social, economic, and political change, but *how*.

Despite its lack of precision, this realist criticism nevertheless helpfully identifies one of the real disagreements between realist and witness theologians. Realists reserve the right to use force. Witness theologians refuse force as a political option. Realist criticism is therefore right insofar as it identifies Yoder's emphasis on the church as polis and its refusal to use force. But it is wrong to suggest this refusal dictates the eschewal of all forms of political activity.

What about feminists? Where do they stand when it comes to Yoder? Whereas Niebuhr's theology garners substantial feminist engagement, there is very little feminist response to Yoder's work. Most of the existing criticism addresses Yoder's discussion of "revolutionary subordination." Both feminist Schüssler Fiorenza and womanist Rosetta Ross identify problems here.[26] Schüssler Fiorenza interprets Yoder's reading of revolutionary subordination as "defend[ing] the New Testament pattern of patriarchal submission

---

25. Yoder, *Christian Witness*, 57.
26. See Schüssler Fiorenza, *Bread Not Stone*, 83; Rosetta Ross, "John Howard Yoder on Pacifism," in *Beyond the Pale: Reading Ethics from the Margins*, ed. Stacey M. Floyd-Thomas and Miguel A. De La Torre (Louisville: Westminster John Knox, 2011), 199–207. Yoder notes in the epilogue to chapter 9 on revolutionary subordination in the second edition of *The Politics of Jesus* that Schüssler Fiorenza misinterprets "accept things as they are" to refer to the inferior status assigned to women by society, when in fact he meant the redemptive reality of equality in Christ. See *The Politics of Jesus: Behold the Man! Our Victorious Lamb* (Grand Rapids: Eerdmans, 1972), 192.

because it motivates Christian slaves and women to accept 'things as they are.'"[27] Ross also finds Yoder's interpretation in tension with womanist aims: "Although he says the call of the *Haustafeln* is to overcome one-sided subordination, Yoder interprets the *Haustafeln* as calling for acceptance of subordination—which, from the perspective of womanism, offers no improvement in temporal quality of life."[28] To make matters more complicated, Yoder's sexual violations against women only bolster the perception that Yoder's politics is anathema to feminist aims.

Feminist Cynthia Hess acknowledges that although Yoder did not always embody the best insights of his theology in his own life,[29] his account of nonviolence remains useful for addressing the internal violence of trauma. She argues that the voluntary and egalitarian characteristics of Yoder's account of ecclesial relations, as well as its emphasis on "hopeful participation,"[30] enable victims to lay claim to "a communal future that differs from their traumatic past."[31] Embodying and internalizing the narrative of Jesus, which acknowledges the reality of trauma but also frames it within a redemptive story,[32] and enacting and proclaiming the redemptive reality inaugurated through Christ's cross and resurrection are ecclesial practices that contribute to healing for those members of the church who suffer the internal violence of trauma.

27. Schüssler Fiorenza, *Bread Not Stone*, 83.
28. Ross, "John Howard Yoder on Pacifism," 203. Womanist Nekeisha Alexis-Baker offers a more sympathetic take on revolutionary subordination. See "Freedom of the Cross: John Howard Yoder and Womanist Theologies in Conversation," in *Power and Practices: Engaging the Work of John Howard Yoder*, ed. Jeremy M. Bergen and Anthony G. Siegrist (Scottdale, PA: Herald, 2009), 83–97.
29. Cynthia Hess, *Sites of Violence, Sites of Grace: Christian Nonviolence and the Traumatized Self* (Lanham, MD: Lexington, 2009), 9.
30. Ibid., 89–107.
31. Ibid., 129–47.
32. Ibid., 109–27.

Despite their diverging assessments of the value of Yoder's theology, these feminist engagements also obscure Yoder's account. Schüssler Fiorenza and Ross mistake Yoder's argument that the church "accepts living under an unjust social order"[33] for an argument that Christians need not be concerned with injustice. But accepting its existence under an unjust order does not mean condoning it. Yoder does, after all, describe the order as unjust. This statement says less about Yoder's attitudes toward gender equality and more about the means available to faithful Christians to subvert that injustice. Put differently, Yoder's interpretation does not betray complacency about gender injustice but reveals his understanding of the most obedient means of challenging it. He makes clear here, as he does with respect to other social injustices, that it is not that the church "ceases to be concerned for the *relative* improvement of the society under which it lives, improvements which certainly must go in the direction of a broader franchise, the elimination of discriminatory legislation, and everything else that causes men to suffer,"[34] but that the church cannot pursue these improvements in ways that deny its confession that Christ is Lord. The problem, properly understood, is not that Yoder's theology condones the oppression of women—a state of affairs his theology explicitly rejects as unjust—but that his theology refuses to privilege Constantinian responses to such injustice. In short, Yoder's arguments about revolutionary subordination are not an affirmation of the oppression of women but an articulation of the church's distinctive challenge to that state of affairs.

While Hess's appropriation of Yoder's theology better acknowledges the congeniality between it and feminism, it too has shortcomings. Unlike Schüssler Fiorenza and Ross, Hess recognizes

33. Yoder, *For the Nations*, 117.
34. Ibid., 18.

the role of egalitarianism in Yoder's ecclesial politics. But her project is limited to reconceptualizing Yoder's account of nonviolence for the ecclesial response to trauma, leaving realist concerns about extra-ecclesial politics unaddressed.

These feminist/womanist accounts only get us halfway. None appreciate both the social egalitarianism of Yoder's theology and its relevance to extra-ecclesial politics. Nevertheless, together they illuminate central but underdeveloped elements of Yoder's theology. Schüssler Fiorenza's and Ross's criticisms reveal that the means of addressing women's equality is key for Yoder's account—not that it fails to identify the oppression of women as a social problem demanding Christian response. The distinctions between military, internal, and systemic violence in Hess's account pinpoint Yoder's tendency to focus on military violence, highlighting the need to further develop Yoder's relatively undeveloped reflection on social egalitarianism as an integral part of Christian politics.

The use to which prominent witness theologians and witness-leaning new Augustinians put Yoder's thought makes matters worse. While Yoder shares the witness critique of Niebuhr and emphasizes the importance of the church as its own political community with distinctive practices and a special role in history, his theology does not exhibit the same concern, among witness theologians, for protecting the purity of the Christian tradition over against political liberalism.[35] Whereas Hauerwas equates the Enlightenment with Constantinianism, Yoder often refers to the Enlightenment as an ally.[36] Whereas Hauerwas emphasizes the particularity of Christian

35. As Kerr argues, although Hauerwas shares Yoder's project of developing an anti-Constantinian politics, he "rush[es] so quickly to articulate the 'politics of Jesus' as also the 'politics of the church,'" leaving him "with an account of the ecclesial community that unintentionally abstracts from the historicity of Jesus and of all of the contingencies and complexities of historical reality, which Yoder's apocalypticism is meant especially to affirm." See *Christ, History, and Apocalyptic*, 130.
36. See, for example, Yoder, *For the Nations*, 81–82.

truth claims, Yoder emphasizes their translatability. Whereas Hauerwas dismisses feminist theologies as liberalism in a "different key,"[37] Yoder argues that feminism is one of the cultures Christianity created. In comparison, the account of new Augustinian Luke Bretherton seems a departure from the witness hostility toward politics; indeed, Bretherton describes his proposal as congenial at points with Yoder's.[38] But while his account overcomes Hauerwas's hostility toward Christian engagement in extra-ecclesial politics, it too fails to adequately consider feminism's place in Christian politics.

### The Postliberal Feminist Politics of Yoder's Theology

Where are we then in relation to realist and feminist criticism and witness appropriations of Yoder's theology that suggest it does not provide the necessary resources for a gender-justice-oriented account of extra-ecclesial politics? Realists accuse Yoder of rejecting "secular" politics in favor of ecclesial politics; feminists criticize Yoder for an account of Christian ethics that promotes gender injustice; and witness theologians take Yoder's legacy in antiliberal directions. These criticisms contain genuine insights, but each also overshadows other important views in Yoder's account vis-à-vis the worldly engagement Christian politics requires—views that place his theology in good company with certain realists and feminists.

When it comes to realist and witness theologians, the real issue is not a question of politics or no politics, but of force or no force in the pursuit of justice. There are definite differences here when it comes to the issue of state force, but the emphasis on military violence has driven a wedge between what can be interpreted as two

---

37. Stanley Hauerwas, "Failure of Communication *or* A Case of Uncomprehending Feminism," *Scottish Journal of Theology* 50, no. 2 (1997): 234.
38. Luke Bretherton, *Christianity and Contemporary Politics: The Conditions and Possibilities of Faithful Witness* (Malden, MA: Blackwell, 2010), 24.

different conceptions of extra-ecclesial politics. Feminists, in turn, offer a new way to conceptualize Yoder's pacifism in a broader sense, suggesting a broader conception of politics—not just in the Yoderian sense of claiming the church has its own politics, but also for politics beyond the church. Noting Yoder's own identification of feminism as part and parcel of Christian culture as well as the themes in Yoder's theology that call for alliances between ecclesial and non-ecclesial practices, I develop from within Yoder's thought an account of extra-ecclesial politics that views feminism as intrinsic to Christian politics.

Yoder's own sympathies with both witness and feminist stances suggest the possibility for a more productive relationship between these strands of the tradition—one that ultimately sheds new light on the feminist dimension of Yoder's politics, challenging realist contentions that Yoder abandons politics and witness claims that Yoder's postliberalism requires antiliberalism. Despite realist efforts to reject Yoder's approach and witness efforts to align their projects with Yoder's, Yoder makes key claims vis-à-vis both extra-ecclesial politics and feminism that reveal the postliberal feminist politics of his theology. Yoder's witness account possesses several features that distance it from the antiliberalism that characterizes some of those who self-consciously claim to carry Yoder's mantle. These include confidence in the public accessibility of Christian truth claims, identification of non-Christian analogues to Christian practices, encouragement of alliances between Christians and non-Christians, and an openness to learning from liberalism when it better embodies Christian truth than the church itself.

While other witness accounts emphasize the distinctiveness of the church in ways that suggest its claims are untranslatable to those outside the church, Yoder emphasizes the public nature of the church's witness. In his words, churches "do ordinary social things differently."[39] The ordinary nature of church practices ensures their communicability. Referring to the "body politics" that mark Christian communities, Yoder writes: "They are not 'ritual' or 'religious' in any otherworldly sense. . . . They . . . can be spoken of in social process terms, which can easily be transposed into non-religious equivalents that a sociologist could watch. People who do not share the faith or join the community can learn from them."[40] Yoder makes clear that the particularity of Christian truth claims does not detract from their universality. "The ordinariness of the humanness of Jesus is the warrant for the generalizability of his reconciliation."[41]

It is this communicable nature of Christian practices that ensures that they will be understood outside the church community and even become models for similar extra-ecclesial practices. Yoder frequently identifies such occurrences where church practices serve as models or paradigms for secular practices. In particular, the five practices that constitute the body politics of the church provide models for corresponding secular political practices. The Eucharist, or sharing bread, for example, "is a model not only for soup kitchens and hospitality houses, but also for Social Security and negative income tax."[42] "'Binding and loosing' can provide models for conflict resolution, alternatives to litigation, and alternative perspectives on 'corrections,'"[43] and "dialogue under the Holy Spirit is the ground floor of the notion of democracy."[44] All five practices are not merely ordinary social activities that all share; each possesses the potential for secular versions or expressions. The very public nature of the church

39. Yoder, *Body Politics*, 75. Further discussion of such overlapping practices can be found in Yoder's articles, "The Christian Case for Democracy," and "Civil Religion in America," in *For the Nations,* where Yoder details Christian contributions to democracy.
40. Yoder, *Body Politics*, 77.
41. Yoder, *Priestly Kingdom*, 62.
42. Yoder, *Body Politics*, 77.
43. Ibid.
44. Ibid., 78.

depends on the ability of those outside its walls to understand the church's practices. Yoder writes:

> For us to approach social ethics in this light will not lead us to differ at every point from what others have been saying on other grounds as to the immediate dictates for our contemporary caring. What will differ . . . is its shape as a whole; namely, the conception that the Christian social ethical witness must be defined not by its independence from the witness of the faith community but by its derivation therefrom.[45]

In other words, the difference is not the practices themselves but the reason for doing them and their place in a larger embodied way of life that professes belief in Christ.

These commonalities allow for churches to have "tactical allies"[46] in those who may not speak the same language or have the same "cosmic vision."[47] Yoder suggests, for example, that "we may . . . find tactical alliances with the Enlightenment, as did Quakers and Baptists in the century after their expulsion from the Puritan colonies, or with the Gandhian vision, as did Martin Luther King, Jr."[48] Early in his career, Yoder talked about these resonances in terms of middle axioms.[49] In later work, he described church practices as "prototypes"[50] providing "a kind of mediation, a 'bridging-over' . . . from the faith community to the other social structures."[51] He also described overlaps in nonchurch practice as "reflections,"[52] "spin-offs,"[53] and "non-religious equivalents"[54] of church practices.

---

45. Ibid.
46. Yoder, *Priestly Kingdom*, 61.
47. Ibid., 53.
48. Ibid., 61–62.
49. Yoder, *Christian Witness*, 35.
50. Yoder, *Body Politics*, 46.
51. Ibid., 74–75.
52. Ibid., 58.
53. Ibid.
54. Ibid., 77.

This recognition of points of connection between ecclesial and non-ecclesial practices engenders his generously receptive attitude to political liberalism. He often suggests that ideas and practices that appear "external" to the Christian tradition usually possess "internal" precursors that are original to the tradition. He speaks, for example, of freedom of assembly, speech, and press as "*external* implications" of the "*internal* vision" of Puritan Christianity's congregationalism and belief in the sovereignty of God's word.[55] Elsewhere, he discusses egalitarianism in similar ways, arguing that although social egalitarianism appears to be a product of the Enlightenment, the origins of its practice are to be found much earlier among Christians, who possess their own internal resources for the practice.[56] Even when Yoder criticizes the work of "liberal" theologians or discusses secular liberalism, he either considers the value, potential, and resonance of those traditions' ideas and practices with those of the Christian tradition or welcomes the opportunities that the secular analogues of Christian practices offer the churches to re-articulate their own reasons for their practice. In short, Yoder embraces similarities in practice as opportunities for collaboration rather than tools of exclusion.

It is, in part, this aspect of Yoder's work—his receptivity to alliances with liberal and "secular" versions of Christian practices—that leads some theologians to claim Yoder reduces theology to ethics, or even more pointedly, that Yoder is "heterodox."[57] Given Yoder's conviction that the gospel is good news for the nations and his incisive perception of non-ecclesial practices as participating unknowingly in the redemptive realities of Christ's lordship, it seems

---

55. John Howard Yoder, *The Jewish-Christian Schism Revisited*, ed. Michael G. Cartwright and Peter Ochs (Scottdale, PA: Herald, 2008), 172–73.
56. Yoder, *Body Politics*, 40.
57. See Paul Martens, *The Heterodox Yoder* (Eugene, OR: Cascade, 2012).

to me that Yoder would embrace any and all engagement in such practices regardless of whether they are attended by self-conscious Christian confessions. The more practices "outside" the church resemble the ecclesial practices Yoder details as the church's "body politics," the more visibly does all of creation witness to Christ's lordship. I suspect that rather than bristle at being called heterodox, Yoder would question why his encouragement of "secular" immersion in non-ecclesial "analogues"[58] of ecclesial practices renders him "heterodox," rather than rendering the cosmos more visibly under the lordship of Christ.[59]

Yoder's receptivity to liberalism is not the only difference between his account and that of other prominent witness theologians. He also embraces feminism as part of Christian pacifism. This difference between Yoder and witness appropriations of his legacy suggests the potential for developing an extra-ecclesial account of politics from within his thought that, without abandoning the ecclesial politics of pacifism, embraces political collaboration with non-ecclesial political actors where their practices overlap. The correspondence of these practices is perhaps strongest when they address issues of nonmilitary violence. Yoder's conception of pacifism—in its resistance to gender injustice and in its embrace of non-ecclesial practices of peace—might be construed as a form of responsibility that ventures out into the world in the form of political collaboration and partnership with others who resist the violence of racism, sexism, and classism. Taking Yoder's connection with both witness and feminist stances seriously

---

58. See Yoder, *Body Politics*, 41.

59. Kerr's perceptive analysis identifies such convictions as being grounded in Yoder's understanding of apocalyptic, which "names the particular operation of God's 'transcendence' and of God's 'Kingdom' *within* history, on the basis of its having *broken into* history *from beyond*. . . . 'Apocalyptic' is but an alternative way of portraying history's eschatological orientation, and of portraying the finite and contingent realities of the world as operative of divine 'transcendence,' now conceived as the priority of God's free and interruptive action in Christ." See *Christ, History and Apocalyptic*, 135–36.

highlights important similarities between postliberalism and feminism that have important implications for an account of Yoder's extra-ecclesial politics that addresses systemic violence.

It may seem counterintuitive to compare witness and feminist theologians. The current state of dialogue between them often leaves much to be desired. No doubt the paucity of engagement is due partly to these theologians' often-contrasting theological agendas.[60] But the relationship also owes much to the larger tension between postliberal and liberal theologies (a tradition to which some feminist theologies belong).[61] Witness theologians often define their work over against a theological liberalism they see as implicated in modern Western forms of secular reasoning and argue in favor of a return to tradition-based forms of reasoning. Following George Lindbeck's attention to Christianity as a cultural-linguistic system,[62] much postliberal work features a concern for exploring and preserving the distinctive integrity of Christian narratives, practices, and doctrines. Although the term *postliberal* encompasses a broad range of theological work,[63] postliberal theologies often take the work of Lindbeck, Hans Frei, and Karl Barth as points of departure and feature engagement with not only traditional Christian doctrines and practices, but also ecumenical issues and non–historical-critical forms of biblical interpretation.[64] While postliberal influence can be seen in

60. See Mary McClintock Fulkerson, "Feminist Theology," in *The Cambridge Companion to Postmodern Theology*, ed. Kevin J. Vanhoozer (Cambridge: Cambridge University Press, 2003), 110.

61. For an account of the often antagonistic relationship between postmodern theology and liberalism, see Gavin Hyman, "Postmodern Theology and Modern Liberalism: Reconsidering the Relationship," *Modern Theology* 65 (2009): 462–74.

62. George A. Lindbeck, *The Nature of Doctrine: Religion and Theology in a Postliberal Age* (Philadelphia: Westminster, 1984).

63. As John Webster notes, postliberalism is less a "school" or a "position" than a "set of projects." See "Theology after Liberalism?" in *Theology After Liberalism: A Reader*, ed. John Webster and George P. Schner (Oxford: Blackwell, 2000), 54.

64. Paul J. DeHart, *The Trial of the Witnesses: The Rise and Decline of Postliberal Theology* (Malden, MA: Wiley-Blackwell, 2006), 46–51.

projects that range from those of the various theologians of the so-called Yale School to Radical Orthodoxy and Scriptural Reasoning, I focus on witness theologians within Christian ethics who claim Yoder's legacy.

As with postliberal theologies, it is difficult to do justice to the sheer diversity of approaches that comprise feminist theology. It would be inaccurate to say that feminist theologians do not share with their postliberal colleagues an interest in Christian Scripture, practices, and doctrine, but feminist theologians (only some of whom identify as theological liberals) tend to focus less on maintaining Christian distinctiveness and more on critical-constructive retrievals of the tradition in light of redemptive possibilities for women and others on the margins. Their shared emphasis on God's preferential option for the marginalized and a prophetic concern for justice often takes precedence over efforts to preserve traditional formulations of Christian doctrine. Generally speaking, feminist theologians also take more appreciative and collaborative stances toward feminist theory and other secular disciplines for their critical value in naming and challenging injustice (both within and outside the Christian tradition) and in understanding the complex interworkings of religion, politics, and culture. Their attention to the role of power in the construction of tradition and interest in the ways theology is informed by a multiplicity of cultural identities, subjectivities, and social locations constitute some of their significant contributions. This is not to say that feminist and postliberal theologies have nothing in common, or that one cannot be both feminist and postliberal. But it remains the case that few postliberals committed to

Yoder's legacy have given feminism the attention it deserves,[65] and few feminists have engaged Yoder's work.

Because of feminist theology's origins in liberal theology, contemporary postliberal theologians tend to gloss over the diversity of feminist theologies, identifying them narrowly with theological liberalism.[66] As one witness theologian puts it: "My difficulty with much feminist theology is, in short, not that it is feminist, but that it is so often liberal Protestant theology in a different key."[67] While such claims rightly acknowledge the status of some feminist theologies as varieties of theological liberalism, they also tend to underappreciate the diversity of feminist approaches. Often, one must look to footnotes of these accounts to find any acknowledgment that nonliberal feminist theologies exist, and even then these theologies are often dismissed as versions of modernism.[68] To their credit, these accounts note exceptions, but unfortunately the exceptions go unexplored. Apart from the failure of these accounts to consider the potential merits of liberal Christian feminism (or theological liberalism more generally), they ultimately give the impression that little diversity exists within Christian feminism, and that any diversity that does exist finally collapses into the only similarity that matters.

It is striking how such approaches differ from Yoder's own—not only in relation to feminism but also to liberalism. In what follows, I detail three core assumptions about Christianity and its relationship to the world shared by Yoder, prominent witness theologians, and certain feminists, detailing in each section where Yoder diverges

---

65. Two important exceptions include J. Denny Weaver, *John Howard Yoder: Radical Theologian* (Eugene, OR: Cascade, 2014); and Weaver, *The Nonviolent Atonement* (Grand Rapids: Eerdmans, 2011).

66. See, for example, R. R. Reno, "Feminist Theology as Modern Project," *Pro Ecclesia* 5, no. 4 (Fall 1996): 405–26. Linda Woodhead makes a similar argument in "Spiritualising the Sacred: A Critique of Feminist Theology," *Modern Theology* 13, no. 2 (April 1997): 191–212.

67. Hauerwas, "Failure of Communication," 234.

68. Reno, "Feminist Theology as Modern Project," 405n2.

from witness conceptions and aligns more closely with the feminist ones: first, that Christianity is a culture with its own particular language, practices, and ethics; second, that errors in the development of the tradition require projects of retrieval; and third, that the church's vocation is to provide a countercultural witness of peace over against the world. Each of these points of similarity suggests a more productive relationship between witness and feminist theologians and clarifies Yoder's account of extra-ecclesial politics.

## Christianity as a Distinctive Culture

Witness theologians' understanding of Christianity as a distinctive cultural-linguistic system emphasizes the importance of the church as the locus of the particular language, practices, and modes of reasoning within Christianity over against the larger cultures in which it exists. Yoder himself agrees to as much in his emphasis on revelation and in his affirmation of the revelation of Christ as normative for Christian ethics. The identity and mission of the church, for Yoder, derives from Jesus' mission to establish a new community that operates according to a different set of convictions than those of the surrounding culture. The church constitutes its own society, a new political order whose existence challenges the ways of the dominant order:

> When He called His society together Jesus gave its members a new way of life to live. He gave them a new way to deal with offenders—by forgiving them. He gave them a new way to deal with violence—by suffering. He gave them a new way to deal with money—by sharing it. He gave them a new way to deal with problems of leadership—by drawing upon the gift of every member, even the most humble. He gave them a new way to deal with a corrupt society—by building a new order, not smashing the old. He gave them a new pattern of relationships between man and woman, between parent and child, between master and slave, in which was made concrete a radical new vision of what it

means to be a human person. He gave them a new attitude toward the state and toward the "enemy nation."[69]

This passage offers perhaps Yoder's most detailed description of the church as a distinctive culture over against the world. He makes clear that for every typical "worldly" response, the church has its own alternative, which witnesses not only to the realities realists emphasize but also to the redemptive reality of Christ.

But unlike witness theologians who dismiss feminism, Yoder insists that feminism is part of this distinctive Christian culture. He describes as "feminist" a major component of what he regards as the church's pacifist identity: the social egalitarianism of the early church.[70] He mentions "feminism" along with hospitals, service of the poor, generalized education, egalitarianism, and abolitionism as examples of cultures that Christians created.[71] And he himself authored two unpublished memos on "feminist theology" in which he both argues for the centrality of gender egalitarianism to Jesus' ministry and identifies Jesus as a feminist.[72] A close reading of these memos reveals the significance of feminism to Yoder's account of Christian politics.

---

69. John Howard Yoder, *The Original Revolution: Essays on Christian Pacifism* (Scottdale, PA: Herald, 2003), 29.

70. Yoder, *Priestly Kingdom*, 73. Yoder also treats "feminist" as a synonym for "Christian" in *The War of the Lamb: The Ethics of Nonviolence and Peacemaking*, ed. Glen Stassen, Mark Thiessen Nation, and Matt Hamsher (Grand Rapids: Brazos, 2009), 132–33.

71. John Howard Yoder, "How H. Richard Niebuhr Reasoned: A Critique of *Christ and Culture*," in *Authentic Transformation: A New Vision of Christ and Culture*, ed. Glen H. Stassen, D. M. Yeager, and John Howard Yoder (Nashville: Abingdon, 1996), 69.

72. Yoder also refers to the feminism of Jesus in "Paul's Vision of Universal Ministry," in *The Fullness of Christ* (Elgin, IL: Brethren, 1987), 52–53. Jewish feminist Judith Plaskow identifies "Jesus was a feminist" claims as one of three major forms of anti-Judaism present in Christian feminisms. She argues that feminist efforts to claim Jesus for their cause often require a negative depiction of the Judaism of Jesus' time. Given Yoder's own approach to the Jewish-Christian schism, it is safe to say that Yoder would agree with Plaskow when she says that "whatever Jesus's attitudes towards women, they represent not a victory *over* Judaism but a possibility *within* early Judaism." See "Feminist Anti-Judaism and the Christian God," *Journal of Feminist Studies in Religion* 7 (Fall 1991): 105.

In the first memo, "Feminist Theology Miscellany #1: Salvation Through Mothering?"[73] Yoder challenges literal interpretation of 1 Timothy 2:15 ("Yet woman will be saved through bearing children, if she continues in faith and love and holiness, with modesty," RSV) Rejecting the individualist conception of salvation assumed in this interpretation, Yoder identifies the fall as a "fall into patriarchy" and then argues that the restoration of matriarchy constitutes the meaning of salvation.[74] "It is that fallenness," he writes, "which is in the process of being set right when we are told that restored wholeness (salvation) will come about through mothering."[75] By "mothering" Yoder means not biological childbirth and/or the nurturing of children, but a certain mode of being in the world marked by "feminine" qualities:

> When measured by the understandings of human dignity propagated by our dominant cultures, the traits we are taught to call "feminine" are closer to the way of life that Jesus taught and exemplified than are those which we are taught to consider "masculine." The God of whom Jesus speaks in the gospels, although called "papa," is no patriarch. . . . Take any contemporary schema of gender style stereotypes: authority versus compassion, rationality versus relatedness, manipulation versus interaction, distancing versus identification . . . regularly you will find that Jesus himself, and what he asks of his followers (including the males among them), and the style of mutual love which Peter and Paul and James ask for in the later church, are qualities which stand in the "feminine" column of the list.[76]

73. Yoder, "Feminist Theology Miscellany #1," 1–7. John C. Nugent also discusses this memo in *The Politics of Yahweh: John Howard Yoder, the Old Testament, and the People of God* (Eugene, OR: Wipf & Stock, 2011), 26–29. It is important to consider whether these memos, like Yoder's memos on sexual ethics, may have also functioned for Yoder as a form of self-exoneration and/ or self-rationalization.
74. Ibid., 6.
75. Ibid.
76. Ibid.

In this passage Yoder identifies "mothering" as central to the church's calling. Followers of Jesus are to be compassionate, relational, interactive, sympathetic, and engaged in mutual love. In short, they are to be what convention defines as essentially "feminine."[77] Yoder elaborates on the idea of "mothering" as an alternative mode of living and discusses Jesus' own embodiment of these "feminine" qualities in the second memo.

In "Feminist Theology Miscellany #2: What Kind of Feminist Was Jesus?"—note that the title already describes Jesus as feminist and proceeds to determine which kind—Yoder examines several key Gospel passages that describe Jesus' interactions with women.[78] These readings reveal that "Jesus did not merely accept women as full human beings in his dealings with them, without discriminating against them as the normal practices of the time would have called him to do,"[79] but that "both women and men received his independent attention as objects of ministry. Women were no less worthy than men of being dealt with, spoken with, healed, taught."[80] Yoder concludes from his study of the Gospels, "not simply that Jesus does not discriminate, that he considers women and men equally to be persons worthy of his esteem. He goes beyond that and is specifically accessible and generous beyond the line of duty to women at points of specific sex-related discrimination. To use

---

77. As Mark Thiessen Nation notes, Yoder's arguments on this subject cohere with those of feminist ethicist and political philosopher Jean Bethke Elshtain, who makes a similar argument regarding the moral revolution of early Christianity in *Public Man, Private Woman*. See "Feminism, Political Philosophy, and the Narrative Ethics of Jean Bethke Elshtain," in *Virtues and Practices in the Christian Tradition: Christian Ethics After MacIntyre,* ed. Nancey Murphy, Brad J. Kallenberg, and Mark Thiessen Nation (Harrisburg, PA: Trinity Press International, 1997), 294.
78. John Howard Yoder, "Feminist Theology Miscellany #2: What Kind of Feminist Was Jesus?" (October 1990), 1–4.
79. Ibid., 1.
80. Ibid.

modern language: he is not simply nondiscriminatory. He takes affirmative action."[81]

Here again, Yoder interprets Jesus' mission as a turning of the cultural—specifically, gendered—tables. Not only does the Christian calling require the embodiment of a certain "feminine" way of life, as we saw in Yoder's reading of 1 Timothy, so too does it involve practices that disrupt the dominant culture's treatment of women. Jesus' practice of affirming women's full dignity as persons challenges the unjust practices of the wider culture and, in doing so, reveals part of the church's mission.

Despite witness lack of interest in or even antagonism toward Christian feminism, Yoder's own feminist theological reflections and references to feminism suggest an important relationship between feminist theologies and Yoder's radical reformation vision. His feminist theology memos provide a fuller description of Yoder's "feminist free church vision" and reveal that, in Yoder's account, feminism and Christianity are "intrinsically interlocked rather than merely mutually compatible."[82] His approach differs from that of his witness successors, bringing into view similarities between his account and what some feminist theologians identify as the "cultural-linguistic presuppositions" often shared between postliberals and feminists.[83]

## Witness and Feminist Theologies as Projects of Retrieval

Many witness theologians—Yoder included—and feminists identify their theologies as projects of retrieval. Witness theologians understand themselves to be engaged in a post-Enlightenment

81. Ibid., 2–3 (underlining original).
82. Yoder, "Feminist Theology Miscellany #1," 5.
83. Amy Plantinga Pauw, "The Word is Near You: A Feminist Conversation with Lindbeck," *Theology Today* 50, no. 1 (April 1993): 45–55.

attempt to rescue Christian theology from Enlightenment captivity (as seen in liberal theology's assumption of Enlightenment norms and values). This is at the heart of prominent witness claims that feminist theology is but one more form of "modern theology" to "be rejected" for its use of methods foreign to the Christian tradition.[84] Yoder, however, sees feminist theologies as efforts to recover an original Christian witness, not an abandonment of traditional Christian belief and practice.

Yoder's understanding of Christianity's project of retrieval is not about the Enlightenment but about Constantinianism. And part of what was lost in the Constantinian error was the social egalitarianism of the early Christian community grounded in Jesus' espousal of gender equality. Contrary to contemporary witness theologians who claim that most feminist theologies employ quintessentially modern categories and criteria, Yoder himself understands such work as originating from the tradition. He agrees, for example, with the "basic stance" of Schüssler Fiorenza regarding the patriarchal corruption of early church tradition.[85] Schüssler Fiorenza and a host of other pioneering feminist theologians join Yoder in identifying Jesus as the revelation of what is ethically normative for Christian communities. It is this very conviction that funds their assessment that "within a short time the emancipatory vision [of Jesus and the early church] was lost"[86] and that shapes their understanding of the theological task as involving a retrieval of Christian origins. The comparisons between Yoder's critique of Constantinianism and early feminist critiques of patriarchy are striking. Yoder's frequent comparisons of "the classic 'radical reformation'" with "current 'liberative'" forms of Christianity suggest that, far from being a threat

---

84. Reno, "Feminist Theology as Modern Project," 406.
85. Yoder, *Politics of Jesus*, 190.
86. Ibid.

to the integrity of the tradition, Yoder sees feminist theologies as sharing in his own project of reaching back to the root.[87] Both radical reformation and liberation movements are, in his words, "criticism[s] of Christendom from within."[88]

Yoder's stance here corresponds with many feminists' understanding of their own work. Feminists have expended a great deal of energy to defend themselves from claims that they smuggle non-Christian methods into their theology, some by drawing attention to the variety of "internal" approaches various feminists take to their theological work.[89] Others have demonstrated that feminist concerns construed as "external," such as justice, actually derive from the tradition itself and that, contrary to common accounts, feminist theologians regularly engage orthodox Christian themes.[90]

When it comes to non-Christian feminisms, or even Christian feminisms judged by witness theologians to be too dependent on methods foreign to the Christian tradition, Yoder departs from his witness successors. The evidence suggests that Yoder would explore the role these feminisms might nevertheless play in refocusing the church's attention on its own feminist commitments.[91] To construe all feminist theologies as "external" threats to the integrity of a distinctive Christian tradition, as many witness theologians do, is to overlook feminists' confidence in the redemptive power of their

---

87. Yoder, *Jewish-Christian Schism*, 45.
88. Ibid.
89. Joy Ann McDougall, "Keeping Feminist Faith with Christian Traditions: A Look at Christian Feminist Theology Today," *Modern Theology* 24, no. 1 (January 2008): 103–24.
90. See Jenny Daggers, "The Prodigal Daughter: Orthodoxy Revisited," *Feminist Theology* 15, no. 2 (2007): 186–201.
91. As Yoder notes, the Enlightenment's case for egalitarianism "only reinforces the importance of our clarifying that the New Testament has its own grounds for its own egalitarian witness, differently shaped from that of the Enlightenment, older and more deeply rooted, even though it has been lost and betrayed for centuries" (*Body Politics*, 40). For a similar argument about the importance of liberalism to postmodern theology, see Hyman, "Postmodern Theology and Modern Liberalism," 470.

religious tradition, the complex processes of culture, and the very nature of the theologian's task.

## Christianity as Countercultural Witness

Witness theologians, Yoder, and feminists also often share a view of Christianity's normative role as providing a countercultural witness. For witness theologians, this means embracing a witness of peace, and Yoder's pacifism is often the point of departure for these theologians. But Yoder's conception of what this countercultural witness entails brings his position closer to feminism than other prominent witness accounts. In fact, there are significant "overlapping circles"[92] between Yoder's theology and the work of a number of feminist theologians when it comes to articulating the church's mission in and relationship to the world. The critiques of hierarchical leadership in Rosemary Radford Ruether's pioneering feminist work, for example, mirror Yoder's call for a return to the anticlericalism[93] and decentralized authority structure of early Jewish and Christian communities. Her rejection of clericalism in favor of *diaconia,* or service,[94] resembles Yoder's contention that leadership in these communities should be marked by "consensual decision-making" and "a non-clerical ministry."[95] Similarly, her discussion of the Woman-Church movement and "feminist base communities"[96] calls to mind Yoder's convictions about the church as a countercultural community. Ruether sees feminist base communities as places where Christians who are committed to Jesus' original emancipatory vision embody that vision and bring it "to bear on the

---

92. Yoder, *Jewish-Christian Schism,* 69.
93. Ibid., 108.
94. Rosemary Radford Ruether, *Sexism and God-Talk: Toward a Feminist Theology* (Boston: Beacon, 1983), 207.
95. Yoder, *Jewish-Christian Schism,* 137.
96. Ruether, *Sexism and God-Talk,* 205.

institutionalized Church."[97] Yoder himself draws a direct comparison between Jews, radical reformation Christians, and contemporary base communities.[98] Like these communities, Ruether regards the feminist base communities as alternative communities of the Word that exist apart from larger church structures and provide a witness to the dominant tradition in the hope of its repentance and reform.

Attention to Yoder's "feminist free church vision" also points to similarities with other feminist ecclesiologies. In fact, Yoder's "missionary openness"[99] often looks more akin to certain feminist accounts of the church and Christian tradition than some prominent witness ecclesiologies. Serene Jones's image of the church as "a space of bounded openness"[100] provides one such example. This image captures both the church's identity as a community "distinguished by the specificity of its adorning practices and disciplines" and its identity as a community whose openness is "forever transgressing those boundaries in order to greet what is different from it," whose practices "make the church's sanctified borders fluid."[101]

It is not only Yoder's description of the church but his account of its practices that bears significant similarities with certain feminists' work on religious practices. For example, his discussion of the "body politics" of the church, of Christian practices as "ordinary social activities done differently," resembles Mary McClintock Fulkerson's ethnographic study of Christian practices at Good Samaritan Methodist Church,[102] whose practice is "distinctively Christian" yet

97. Ibid.
98. Yoder, *Jewish-Christian Schism*, 124.
99. Ibid., 126.
100. Serene Jones, *Feminist Theory and Christian Theology: Cartographies of Grace* (Minneapolis: Fortress Press, 2000), 170.
101. Ibid., 171; 174. This description bears similarity to Chris K. Huebner's discussion of Yoder's conception of church as "the scattered body of Christ." See *A Precarious Peace: Yoderian Explorations on Theology, Knowledge, and Identity* (Scottdale, PA: Herald, 2006), 124–26.
102. Mary McClintock Fulkerson, *Places of Redemption: Theology for a Worldly Church* (Oxford: Oxford University Press, 2007).

utterly "worldly." But it is not only that both Fulkerson and Yoder emphasize the simultaneously ordinary and redemptive nature of Christian practices; they also describe their purpose in similar ways. Both accounts emphasize the way the church is called to resist forms of marginalization that deny the redemptive reality of Christ. For Yoder, the public nature of the church necessarily entails addressing difference across "cultural boundaries." For example, he speaks of the social egalitarianism of Jesus as entailing new relationships between men and women and a rejection of ethnic provincialism. The good news Jesus proclaims is for all the nations. The gospel of Christ declares a radical equality for all people, regardless of ethnic or other differences. His description of Jesus' mission as rejecting ethnic provincialism demonstrates this facet of the church's identity and mission:

> Another besetting sin of the political realm is provincialism: the limitation of one's love to one's own kind of people. . . . The alternative vision which it is our business to proclaim is more than cross-cultural education; it is a spiritual mandate. "If anyone is in Christ—there is a whole new world!" . . . But unless the wider vision be spiritually rooted, it will not hold in the crunch against the instincts of group enmity. . . . Unless the *positive love of the enemy* stands behind the affirmation of the dignity of other groups, unless divisions are transcended by a dynamic rooted in the divine nature . . . and in the reconciling work of Christ . . . it cannot tame our demonic native ethnocentrism.[103]

Love of enemy, not rejection of outsiders, is the Christian mandate. Yoder argues that the Christian community is obligated to love its enemies, that the outsider is central to the biblical vision of human dignity:

> The beginning difference between the nationally defined vision of human dignity and the biblical one is the place of the outsider. The

103. Yoder, *For the Nations*, 191–92.

Abrahamic covenant begins with the promise that all the peoples of the earth are to be blessed. . . . It seems clear that in the *ordinary* meaning of "civil religion," the American experience has always needed the polar outsider to precipitate a common self-awareness: the savage, the slave, the infidel, the "hun," the "Jap," the godless Communist. . . . It may be that our own ethnically mixed society demanded the foil of a racially polar bad guy nation to reflect upon ourselves a borrowed sense of natural unity.[104]

While Yoder speaks specifically here of demonizing those who differ from Americans ethnically or nationally, his concern for human dignity across other differences appears elsewhere in his work. His discussion of baptism as transcending "all prior given or chosen identity definitions," as producing "breakthroughs . . . where the barrier is slavery, gender, or class," and as constituting "a new kind of social relationship, a unity that overarches the differences . . . that previously had separated people,"[105] speaks to the continuing need for churches to challenge barriers to Christian unity.

Yoder's identification of social egalitarianism as an indispensable facet of the Christian mission resembles Fulkerson's conception of the church as providing a place for "the Other" to appear. Her account sees part of the church's mission as bringing people of different backgrounds together. In her study of Good Samaritan, Fulkerson describes this community's "homemaking practices" as bringing diverse groups of people (with respect especially to ethnicity, race, and ability) together around shared goals. These practices created "a shared space of appearance" where members engaged the Other.[106] Sounding an awful lot like Yoder's discussion of ecclesial practices, Fulkerson notes that although these practices "are the everyday, lived world activities of average people,"[107] they "are redemptive and

104. Yoder, *Priestly Kingdom*, 189.
105. Yoder, *Body Politics*, 28–30.
106. Fulkerson, *Places of Redemption*, 21.
107. Ibid., 154.

political"[108] because they "brought people together in a variety of settings that contravened many of their inherited racialized enculturations. . . . Complete obliviousness to the marked 'Other' was not an option."[109] Fulkerson speaks of these practices as offering a very public and political challenge by revealing obliviousness to race and other forms of difference. These striking similarities suggest that realists ultimately underestimate the worldly involvement Yoder's ethic requires and that witness theologians cannot afford to ignore feminist theologies if their goal is the continuation and development of Yoder's theological legacy.

Prominent witness accounts of the church as a pacifist witness offer rich contributions to Yoder's vision, but tend to follow Yoder in focusing on the Christian counter-witness to the violence of the state.[110] A number of feminist theologians suggest, however, that an overly narrow focus on the violence of war neglects other types of violence that demand attention. Feminists like Gloria Albrecht have called attention to the need for the church to address systemic violence related to race, gender, and class.[111] Recent feminist work by Jones and Hess on the internal violence of trauma broadens our conceptions of the forms violence takes in the everyday lives of many.[112]

---

108. Ibid., 23.

109. Ibid., 154.

110. A number of feminist theologians make this claim in relation to the work of Stanley Hauerwas, arguably the most prominent expositor of Yoder's project. See Debra Dean Murphy, "Community, Character, and Gender: Women and the Work of Stanley Hauerwas," *Scottish Journal of Theology* 55, no. 3 (2002): 341; and Linda Woodhead, "Can Women Love Stanley Hauerwas? Pursuing an Embodied Theology," in *Faithfulness and Fortitude: In Conversation with the Theological Ethics of Stanley Hauerwas*, ed. Mark Thiessen Nation and Samuel Wells (Edinburgh: T&T Clark, 2000), 172.

111. Gloria Albrecht, *The Character of our Communities: Toward an Ethic of Liberation for the Church* (Nashville: Abingdon, 1995): 117.

112. Serene Jones, *Trauma and Grace: Theology in a Ruptured World* (Louisville: Westminster John Knox, 2009); Hess, *Sites of Violence, Sites of Grace*.

Much womanist theology also contributes to the kind of pacifist vision Yoder developed. Marcia Y. Riggs, for example, articulates trenchant critiques of the sexism in black churches. Why, she asks, do black churches so often lead the way in movements for justice but fail to address gender justice?[113] Nearly every womanist account of the black church discusses what Riggs calls the church's failure "to connect the dots between the quest for racial and economic justice with sexual-gender justice."[114] And other womanist work, such as that of Emilie M. Townes, offers powerful analyses of "the cultural production of evil" that demands resistance.[115] The work of these and other feminists and womanists makes clear that a Christian witness of peace cannot be limited to resisting the violence of war.

Nevertheless, Yoder's references to the social egalitarianism of Jesus do provide a fuller account of what the pacifist politics of the church entails. In addition to forgiveness, suffering, the sharing of economic resources, and the other new ways Jesus calls his disciples to live, he also "gave them a new pattern of relationships between man and woman . . . in which was made concrete a radical new vision of what it means to be a human person."[116] As Yoder's own feminist theological reflections indicate, the content of social egalitarianism looks something like "mothering," a way of life marked by certain "feminine" qualities of relating to others. And, as Yoder's discussion of women's ordination indicates, social egalitarianism goes beyond the mere empowerment of women. The push for women's ordination in contemporary Christian communities, while a step in the right direction, nevertheless misses the larger point: every

---

113. Marcia Y. Riggs, *Plenty Good Room: Women Versus Male Power in the Black Church* (Cleveland, OH: Pilgrim, 2003).
114. Ibid., 80.
115. Emilie M. Townes, *Womanist Ethics and the Cultural Production of Evil* (New York: Palgrave Macmillan, 2006).
116. Yoder, *Original Revolution*, 29.

person in the community should play a leadership role. Properly speaking, no one should be ordained. Or, more precisely, all are already ordained through baptism.[117]

Yoder's elaboration of pacifism through his discussion of social egalitarianism suggests some of the potential directions for a further development of his pacifist vision. In this light, many feminists and womanists are pursuing an agenda Yoder would regard as consonant with his theology. It seems to me that Yoder would characterize this work as contributing in indispensable ways to the pacifism he identifies at the heart of Christian identity and mission.

## Conclusion

What has this engagement with realist and feminist criticism and witness appropriation of Yoder revealed? What new Yoderian account appears? For sure, certain features of Yoder's account have not changed. It is still the case that Yoder sees the church's own political witness as the starting point for Christian politics. It is still the case that Yoder rejects the use of violence as a political option.

But apart from these two characteristics, the picture of Yoder's theology that has come into view is quite different from what realist, feminist, and witness criticisms suggest at face value. My reading reveals a Yoderian account that, in its attention to confluences between Christian and American ideals, challenges witness theologians whose concern to maintain the purity of Christianity as a culture over against political liberalism prevents them from appreciating how these traditions inform and interact with each other. It also reveals a feminist account that emphasizes the egalitarian nature of relationships between men and women and that shares with other feminist theologies an understanding of the church's vocation

---

117. Yoder, *Body Politics*, 60.

vis-à-vis larger cultural trends. And it reveals a theology whose interest in tactical alliances challenges the realist stereotype that Yoder's ecclesial politics requires aversion to its extra-ecclesial variety. Yoder may overidentify the state with "the world" and focus on the church's rejection of military violence at the expense of other key components—especially feminism—of the church's pacifist politics, but reading his thought charitably reveals that his account of Christian pacifism eschews neither politics nor gender justice.

By using realist and feminist criticisms along with witness appropriation of Yoder as a guide, my reading identifies the places of true disagreement between these scholars so that their common convictions may become clear. I have identified the contours of a Yoderian account of an extra-ecclesial politics of peace that addresses systemic violence. The church actualizes such a politics by embodying Jesus' own politics—of which feminism is a central part—and by identifying and collaborating with nonchurch partners who engage in what Yoder refers to as "spin-offs"[118] of ecclesial practices.

Such an account benefits the projects of theologians in each stance. Attention to Yoder's feminist politics would enable witness theologians to enrich and more fully articulate what it means for "the church to be the church." It would expand realist accounts of what it means for Christians to engage in politics and more effectively highlight the relationship between the church's own inherently political existence and "secular" politics, as well as better acknowledge the ways the church and its practices sustain Christian engagement in extra-ecclesial politics. And it would provide a tool (that witness theologians should find particularly convincing) for feminists not only for defending their projects against witness dismissal as

---

118. Yoder, *Body Politics*, 58.

"external" to the tradition, but also for demonstrating their indispensability to witness developments of Yoder's legacy.

Finally, this account challenges feminists to see in Yoder's theology a feminist ally—despite his profound failures to personally embody feminist ideals. Indeed, given the renewed attention to Yoder's violence toward women, it is perhaps even more pressing to recognize the ways feminist and womanist responses to systemic violence contribute to the kind of ecclesial witness of peace Yoder called for in his theology and to articulate how to implement such a politics in ways that prevent the kind of violence Yoder himself perpetrated against women. Feminist engagement with Yoder's work would enable a needed internal critique of Yoder's wrongful behavior and ensure that the emphasis in his theology on a gender-justice-oriented ecclesial politics is not abandoned by contemporary witness theologians. Collaboration between realists, feminists, and witness theologians in further developing an account of feminism as Christian politics certainly would be consonant with what Yoder describes as the early church's "reconciling message."[119]

---

119. Yoder, *Jewish-Christian Schism*, 150.

4

---

# Christian Ethics for the Creatively Maladjusted

*Martin Luther King Jr.'s "Feminist" and*
*"Womanist" Politics of Love*

"Human salvation lies in the hands of the creatively maladjusted."
—Martin Luther King Jr.[1]

In his 1958 account of the Montgomery bus boycott, Martin Luther King Jr. describes his philosophy of nonviolence.[2] "The nonviolent resister," he writes, "is willing to accept violence if necessary, but never to inflict it. He does not seek to dodge jail. If going to jail is necessary, he enters it 'as a bridegroom enters the bride's chamber.'"[3]

---

1. Martin Luther King Jr., *Strength to Love* (Philadelphia: Fortress Press, 1981), 27.
2. This chapter incorporates a revised version of an article originally published as "Reconstructing Nonviolence: The Political Theology of Martin Luther King Jr. after Feminism and Womanism," *Journal of the Society of Christian Ethics* 32, no. 1 (Spring/Summer 2012): 75–92.
3. Martin Luther King Jr., "An Experiment in Love," in *A Testament of Hope: The Essential Writings and Speeches of Martin Luther King, Jr.*, ed. James M. Washington (New York: HarperCollins, 1986), 18.

Most people familiar with King's work would not be surprised to hear him address the topic of nonviolence in this passage. King is, after all, the winner of the 1964 Nobel Peace Prize and identified the world over as one of the most important figures in United States history for his leadership in the nonviolent civil rights movement. His status as a national and international hero is enshrined in government holidays, public monuments, and civic memory. Historical studies of King's life and leadership abound, as does philosophical analysis of nonviolent resistance. Even scholars of religion sometimes treat King more as a political figure than a Christian theologian. So what is to be made of King's invocation of this age-old description of Christian martyrdom as an analogy for the attitude with which nonviolent resisters are to approach their political action?

It would be difficult to find a passage in King's work that better captures the complexity of his legacy. On one hand, the quote identifies King as he is most often recognized: an American hero who led a massive campaign for social change through the power of nonviolence. On the other, it sets this campaign within the theological framework through which King himself understood it. The quote also assumes a male agent, reflecting King's struggle to properly acknowledge the leadership of women in the movement.[4] And its reference to erotic love names the centrality of love to King's conception of Christian nonviolence—albeit not in the form most associate with nonviolence—and perhaps even calls to mind King's well-documented extramarital affairs.

---

4. See David J. Garrow, *Bearing the Cross: Martin Luther King, Jr., and the Southern Christian Leadership Conference* (New York: Vintage Books, 1988), 141, 375–76, 655; and Rosetta E. Ross, *Witnessing and Testifying: Black Women, Religion, and Civil Rights* (Minneapolis: Fortress Press, 2003), 85–86, 191–92. For an exploration of problems related to gender in the legacy of the civil rights movement, see Traci C. West "Gendered Legacies of Martin Luther King Jr.'s Leadership," *Theology Today* 65 (2008): 41–56.

But I will argue that King's reference to erotic love carries significance for another reason: it reveals striking developments in his account of agape over the course of the civil rights movement that render King's conception of agape akin to that of feminists and womanists. Uncovering this "feminist" trajectory in a decidedly nonfeminist thinker is instructive for witness, realist, and feminist theologians alike—all of whom neglect King despite having good reasons to engage him.

The breadth of King's influence and the wide range of theological resources he utilized suggest that King would be a major figure in current accounts of ecclesial politics. His work spans the full spectrum of stances in contemporary Christian ethics: he was a master synergist who not only employed categories like natural law, but also weaved together various theological and political threads to mobilize diverse constituencies in the civil rights struggle. His embeddedness in the black church and embodiment of nonviolence render him the quintessential Christian witness. His well-known use of Reinhold Niebuhr's analysis of sin and thesis on the immorality of groups reveals his debt to Christian realism. And in his attention to the oppression of race and class, King anticipates liberationist themes. One would expect King to be the "go-to" figure for scholars articulating the church's public vocation.

But this is not the case. Black liberation theologians and other scholars interested in race give King the attention he deserves.[5] Those teaching in ministry- and church-oriented settings also offer important studies.[6] And there are increasing numbers of other

---

5. Prominent examples include James Cone and Cornel West. See, for example, Cone, *Martin & Malcolm & America: A Dream or a Nightmare* (Maryknoll, NY: Orbis, 1991); and Cornel West, "Prophetic Christian as Organic Intellectual: Martin Luther King, Jr.," in *The Cornel West Reader* (New York: Basic Books, 1999), 425–34.

6. For example, Richard Lischer, *The Preacher King: Martin Luther King Jr. and the Word that Moved America* (New York: Oxford University Press, 1995); and Preston N. Williams, "An Analysis of

analyses of King's theology.[7] But the majority of scholarship on King continues to take the form of historical treatments of his role in the civil rights movement. This is not to say that King is completely ignored by witness and realist theologians; he is frequently praised in passing or cited as an example of the rare but remarkable individual who initiated major societal transformation. But finding a contemporary account of the church's role in politics that pays sustained attention to King may be just as rare. How is it that this Baptist preacher—son and grandson of Baptist preachers, leader of the black church struggle for civil rights and reconciliation, and martyr for the gospel—does not feature more prominently in these debates within Christian ethics?

Perhaps it is King's versatility that renders him little more than a footnote in most contemporary accounts of the church's political vocation. The debate between witness and realist theologians certainly does not admit much room for figures like King, whose theological hybridity prevents him from standing too firmly in any one camp. Despite his profound Christian witness, King's embeddedness in the black church and his indebtedness to the social gospel and realism renders him an uneasy choice for witness theologians, whose work tends to neglect racism and who define their theologies over against social gospel and realist commitments to extra-ecclesial politics. Similarly, despite King's involvement in extra-ecclesial politics and his use of Niebuhrian analysis, his embrace of nonviolent love as a political practice puts him at odds with

---

the Conception of Love and Its Influence on Justice in the Thought of Martin Luther King, Jr.," *Journal of Religious Ethics* 18, no. 2 (Fall 1990): 15–31.

7. For example, Hak Joon Lee, *The Great World House: Martin Luther King Jr. and Global Ethics* (Cleveland, OH: Pilgrim, 2011); Lewis V. Baldwin, *The Voice of Conscience: The Church in the Mind of Martin Luther King, Jr.* (Oxford: Oxford University Press, 2010); Richard Wayne Wills Sr., *Martin Luther King, Jr. and the Image of God* (Oxford: Oxford University Press, 2009); and Garth Baker-Fletcher, *Somebodyness: Martin Luther King, Jr., and the Theory of Dignity* (Minneapolis: Fortress Press, 1993).

Niebuhr's view that love is relevant to politics only indirectly. This is not to mention the realist concession that force may sometimes be a necessary and justified political option. The new Augustinians mention King, but usually in cursory fashion. The one account that does engage King at length—that of Eric Gregory—neglects the explicitly theological character of his political practice. Feminists and womanists pay King the most attention, but mostly to critique his conception of redemptive suffering.[8] Despite anticipating liberationist themes, King's failure to address gender injustice and his personal struggle to treat women as equals put him at odds with most feminist and womanist agendas. In the final analysis, King belongs to everyone and to no one at once.

## Martin Luther King Jr.'s "Feminist and Womanist" Politics of Love

This chapter responds to this oddity through an engagement with feminist and womanist critiques of King and an exploration of King's thought on love. It appreciates witness and realist praise of King, but regrets that King does not occupy a more central role in these theologians' work. It especially appreciates Gregory's discussion of resonances between King's theopolitical thought and that of feminist ethicists of care, but regrets that this discussion overlooks substantial connections between King's and feminist and womanist theologians' discussions of love. It appreciates feminist and womanist critiques of King's conception of redemptive suffering, but argues that these critiques obscure a more fundamental agreement: shared conceptions of love as mutual, passionate, and community-creating. Reading

8. For an exception, see Katie G. Cannon, *Black Womanist Ethics* (Atlanta: Scholars, 1988). While acknowledging that King did not "reflect directly on Black women's experience," she nevertheless finds within King's thought resources for a "politics of justice." She names King's understanding of human beings created in the image of God, the relationship between love and justice, and the beloved community as resources that womanists may find helpful. To my knowledge the only other source that reflects on the relationship between King and womanist thought is Noel Leo Erskine, *King Among the Theologians* (Cleveland, OH: Pilgrim, 1994).

King's thought on love alongside that of various feminists and womanists, I uncover a "feminist" trajectory in this distinctly nonfeminist thinker. In so doing, I model a method of engagement with King that simultaneously contributes to his legacy and witness, realist, and feminist projects.

I begin this argument by reading King's thought on love alongside feminist and womanist reflection on love. This reading first reveals that King describes agape primarily as a public form of love. This conception exacerbates an already problematic understanding of agape defined over against philia and eros. Second, I argue that despite inheriting this first understanding of agape from traditional Protestant conceptions, King also espouses an agape that resonates with feminist conceptions. This understanding of agape becomes increasingly prominent as the civil rights movement progresses. This love is a love in action that draws on the self-loving, reciprocal, passionate, and community-creating aspects of philia and eros. Third, I suggest, in relation to womanist thought, that *creativity* rather than strictly love or justice comes to take pride of place in King's theopolitical vision. My reading thus traces a "creative synthesis" in King's thinking between conceptions of agape adopted wholesale from traditional Protestant accounts and a new vision of love that emerges when the traditional conception comes down to earth and hits the ground running.

This reading yields new trajectories for those committed to King's legacy, as well as needed projects within witness and realist stances that would strengthen their own accounts. Witness theologians might find themselves challenged by King to address racism as well as to define the contours of an extra-ecclesial politics consistent with their own approach. Realists, including realist-leaning new Augustinian Eric Gregory, might find themselves challenged to attend to the importance of the church in nurturing loving political actors. And feminists may be challenged to identify in King's theology an unlikely ally for the pursuit of gender justice.

## King and Witness, Realist, and Feminist Traditions

What are witness, realist, and feminist theologians to make of Martin Luther King Jr.'s theological and political legacy? Despite King's synthesis of insights from each of these approaches, he is generally neglected by theologians representing them all. Once again, the debate between witness and realist theologians and the absence of feminist theologies leaves the legacy of King, who incorporates aspects of but does not belong firmly in any of these stances, overlooked.

It is odd that prominent witness theologians neglect King because he is, after all, a paradigmatic Christian witness, firmly grounded in and shaped by the church and its practices, particularly nonviolence. John Howard Yoder gives King sustained attention,[9] but Yoder's celebration of King does not appear among prominent theologians who often claim Yoder's legacy. For example, scholars repeatedly criticize Stanley Hauerwas for failing to engage race-related issues.[10] Although Hauerwas claims that the black church best embodies the ecclesial faithfulness he champions in his work, he elects not to address problems related to race.[11] As noted in chapter 1, he has avoided "us[ing] Martin Luther King Jr. and the church that made him possible, to advance *my* understanding of 'Christian ethics'"

---

9. For two of Yoder's most sustained engagements with King, see "The Power Equation, the Place of Jesus, and the Politics of King," in *For the Nations: Essays Evangelical and Public* (Eugene, OR: Wipf & Stock, 2002), 125–47; and "The American Civil Rights Struggle," in *Nonviolence: A Brief History, The Warsaw Lectures*, ed. Paul Martens, Matthew Porter, and Myles Werntz (Baylor, TX: Baylor University Press, 2010), 27–38.
10. See, for example, James Logan, "Liberalism, Race, and Stanley Hauerwas," *CrossCurrents* 55, no. 4 (Winter 2006), 522–33.
11. Stanley Hauerwas, "Remembering Martin Luther King Jr. Remembering," *Journal of Religious Ethics* 23, no. 1 (Spring 1995): 136.

because "that is not *my* story."[12] While Hauerwas's concern not to appropriate King's thought in ways that disrespect its integrity is laudable, I see no reason why King's witness cannot challenge Hauerwas to address the systemic violence of racism as part of Hauerwas's account of a "peaceable" church. Indeed, given Hauerwas's and King's shared conviction that nonviolence is central to the church's politics, it is strange that Hauerwas does not regard King's story as part of his own.[13] If Hauerwas were alone in neglecting King, one might chalk this up to an unfortunate oversight. But most of the prominent contemporary witness theologians avoid issues related to race.[14]

One might think realists eager to fill this vacuum. Not only does King draw on Niebuhr's analysis of sin and group morality, he also demonstrates Niebuhr's prescience about the success of nonviolent tactics in securing civil rights for African Americans. But Robin W. Lovin is alone among realists in mentioning King. He cites King as an example of both the limits and the possibilities realist analysis identifies at the heart of human ethical action. According to Lovin, King's accomplishments "stand out as rare achievements"; those like him "become heroes precisely because people see in their achievements a possibility that exists in relation to all conflicts, even the perfectly ordinary ones that are settled by prevailing mechanisms of compromise or coercion."[15] But apart from this and a few other small references, King does not feature prominently in realist analysis.

12. Ibid.
13. Logan makes this point in "Liberalism, Race, and Stanley Hauerwas," 527.
14. Some of Hauerwas's students have done so, however. See Jonathan Tran, "Time for Hauerwas's Racism," in *Unsettling Arguments: A Festschrift on the Occasion of Stanley Hauerwas's 70th Birthday*, ed. Charles R. Pinches, Kelly S. Johnson, and Charles M. Collier (Eugene, OR: Cascade, 2010), 246–61.
15. Robin W. Lovin, *Reinhold Niebuhr and Christian Realism*, (Cambridge: Cambridge University Press, 1995), 154–55.

New Augustinian accounts fare better, but they still fail to provide the level of engagement with King one might expect. Although Charles Mathewes does not specifically mention King, he does name the civil rights movement as a powerful demonstration of the kind of hopeful citizenship the church can sustain.[16] Luke Bretherton gives King a cursory nod, mentioning him only as a reference point to argue for the significance not only of "heroic figures such as Martin Luther King" but also the "ordinary political actor."[17] Gregory's account is the exception. Paying particular attention to the role of love in King's political ethic, Gregory illuminates connections between King's discussion of love and those of "care" in feminist political philosophy. In his brief analysis of King as an Augustinian liberal, Gregory highlights a number of significant similarities: a challenge to an exclusive focus on justice as the primary virtue of political life, conceptions of love and care as practices rather than emotions, anthropologies focused on the interrelated nature of human persons and community, and methodologies that draw on personal experience and emphasize the importance of attention to particulars.[18] While illuminating, this discussion does less to acknowledge the elements of King's thought that complicate the comparison. It fails to do justice, for example, to the gender-justice-oriented nature of care theorists' challenge to the liberal divide between public and political life, concealing King's failure to espouse gender justice. It also fails to consider the differences between "love" and "care," overlooking the theological robustness of King's vision.

---

16. Charles Mathewes, *A Theology of Public Life* (Cambridge: Cambridge University Press, 2007), 217.

17. Luke Bretherton, *Christianity and Contemporary Politics: The Conditions and Possibilities of Faithful Witness* (Malden, MA: Wiley-Blackwell, 2010), 213.

18. Eric Gregory, *Politics and the Order of Love: An Augustinian Ethic of Democratic Citizenship* (Chicago: University of Chicago Press, 2008), 188–96.

What about feminists and womanists? What do they make of King's theological and political legacy? On one hand, feminists and womanists can find much to admire in his commitment to justice, his ability to identify connections between various forms of oppression, and his embrace of love as a political practice. On the other, King led one of the most important movements for equal rights in American history yet virtually ignored gender injustice. He spoke often of the "triple evils of poverty, racism, and war" but never identified sexism as an equally pernicious evil.[19] The feminist and womanist literature on King reflects King's ambivalent attitude toward women. Most feminist and womanist responses critique King for connecting agape with redemptive suffering, arguing that views like King's valorize suffering and condone the abuse of women. Feminists Joanne Carlson Brown and Rebecca Parker, for example, criticize King's view of redemptive suffering because it "makes victims the servants of the evildoer's salvation."[20] Reading Jesus' experience on the cross through black women's experiences of surrogacy, womanist Delores Williams argues that, for black women, to glorify the cross is "to render their exploitation sacred."[21] Similarly, Jacquelyn Grant argues that in the context of black women's social, economic, and political disempowerment, the concept of servanthood proves more sinful than salvific. She proposes "discipleship" as an empowering alternative.[22]

Nevertheless, some womanists acknowledge the constructive theological potential of positions like King's. Grant understands King's contention that suffering is redemptive in light of black

19. King, *Strength to Love*, 8.

20. Joanne Carlson Brown and Carole R. Bohn, ed., *Christianity, Patriarchy, and Abuse: A Feminist Critique* (New York: Pilgrim, 1989), 20.

21. Delores S. Williams, *Sisters in the Wilderness: The Challenge of Womanist God-Talk* (Maryknoll, NY: Orbis, 1993), 167.

22. Jacquelyn Grant, "The Sin of Servanthood," in *A Troubling in My Soul: Womanist Perspectives on Evil and Suffering*, ed. Emilie M. Townes (Maryknoll, NY: Orbis, 1993), 216.

women's experiences of God's redemptive love in the midst of oppression.[23] JoAnne Marie Terrell rejects the idea that suffering, sacrifice, and violence are redemptive in and of themselves or that God condones violence. She does, however, propose an account of sacrifice that allows for the possibility of suffering being rendered meaningful if one exercises one's "moral and creative agency" or if others learn from sufferers' experiences. Her account construes those who suffer not as "victims who passively acquiesced to evil" but "empowered, *sacramental*, witnesses."[24] Finally, Karen Baker-Fletcher articulates a broadly held womanist view of the cross as a symbol of the human capacity for evil and the risk involved in pursuing justice rather than as a glorification of sacrifice.[25] She notes that King's concept of agape moves beyond mere sacrifice to express the "victory of God's Agape" in "moments of community across differences."[26] Emphasizing the robust character of King's notion of sacrifice, Baker-Fletcher's analysis clarifies that King does not affirm suffering per se, but voluntary suffering for a just cause.

While some feminists and womanists may understandably remain wary of redemptive suffering as a constructive theological category, it is critical to remember that King's notion of suffering intends not the violation of one's dignity but an affirmation of self and community. Nevertheless, both King's failure to address gender justice and feminist and womanist critiques of redemptive suffering demonstrate the difficulty of appropriating King's thought for a gender-justice-oriented ecclesial politics. Evaluating whether King's thought can sustain such an account requires a close reading of his theological

---

23. Ibid., 213.
24. JoAnne Marie Terrell, *Power in the Blood? The Cross in African American Experience* (Maryknoll, NY: Orbis, 1998), 143, 142.
25. Karen Baker-Fletcher and Garth Kasimu Baker-Fletcher, *My Sister, My Brother: Womanist and Xodus God-Talk* (Maryknoll, NY: Orbis, 1997), 53; and Williams, *Sisters in the Wilderness*, 169.
26. Baker-Fletcher and Baker-Fletcher, *My Sister, My Brother*, 53.

reflection on and practice of love. How does King describe agape, and how is his discussion relevant to feminists and womanists?

## King on Love

King's earliest articulations of agape draw from standard accounts of agape in Protestant social ethics developed by Anders Nygren, Reinhold Niebuhr, Paul Ramsey, and others.[27] These thinkers often contrast agape with the more "worldly" loves of philia and eros, conceptualizing agape through the rubric of divine sacrifice. In these accounts, agape is self-sacrificial, nonreciprocal, disinterested, and spontaneous. It is opposed to self-love, unmotivated by any benefit to the lover, and not prompted by the qualities or merits of the person being loved. It is a pure, otherworldly love, the love of God acting through the vehicle of the human agent.

This understanding laid the foundation for King's own conception of love as a student and continued to inform his understanding of agape throughout his career. In a 1950 Crozer Theological Seminary paper, King cites Nygren's conception of agape. Describing Christ's sacrifice on the cross as an example of agapic love, he argues that "God does not allow his love to be determined or limited by man's worth or worthlessness. . . . It is sacrificial in nature."[28] In January 1952, then pursuing a doctorate at Boston University, King refers again to Nygren. Noting Nygren's contrast between the Greek eros and agape, he describes eros as loving "in proportion to the value of the object," whereas agape is "'spontaneous and uncaused,' . . . 'indifferent to human merit.' . . . It flows down from God into the transient, sinful world."[29]

27. See, for example, the discussion in Kenneth L. Smith and Ira G. Zepp Jr., *Search for the Beloved Community: The Thinking of Martin Luther King, Jr.* (Valley Forge, PA: Judson, 1974).
28. Martin Luther King Jr., "A View of the Cross Possessing Biblical and Spiritual Justification," in *The Papers of Martin Luther King, Jr. Vol. I*, ed. Clayborne Carson, Ralph E. Luker, and Penny A. Russell (Berkeley: University of California Press, 1992), 267.

King often conveys this understanding of agape by appealing to the ancient Greek distinctions between agape, philia, and eros. More problematically, he begins to associate agape with a public form of love, seemingly rendering philia and eros irrelevant to public endeavors. At this point King still refers to love in the Niebuhrian sense of a "regulating ideal," but he also insists on the direct relevance of love in action, connecting agape with public campaigns of nonviolent resistance, such as those of the 1955 Montgomery bus boycott.[30] He frequently notes the public character of agape by describing it as "the type of love that we talk about, and that we are supposed to live about in this method of nonviolent resistance. It is a love that can change individuals. It can change nations. It can change conditions."[31] As late as November 1957, King still refers to the Greek to argue that only agape qualifies as divine love, while philia and eros remain tainted by emotion and reciprocity. In King's words, "Eros is a sort of aesthetic or romantic love. . . . Philia [is] a reciprocal love and the intimate affection and friendship between friends. . . . Agape [is] understanding and creative, redemptive goodwill for all men."[32] But more importantly, King effectively disassociates philia and eros from Jesus' public ministry: "When Jesus bids us to love our enemies, he is speaking neither of eros nor philia; he is speaking of agape."[33] King thus identifies agape as the only kind of love that is relevant beyond friendship and intimate relationships to the political practice

---

29. Martin Luther King Jr., *The Papers of Martin Luther King, Jr., Vol. II*, ed. Clayborne Carson, Ralph E. Luker, Penny A. Russell, and Peter Holloran (Berkeley: University of California Press, 1994), 127.

30. Martin Luther King Jr., "An Experiment in Love," 17. For Niebuhr's view of the relationship between love and justice, see Niebuhr, *The Nature and Destiny of Man: A Christian Interpretation, Vol. II: Human Destiny* (Louisville: Westminster John Knox, 1996), 244–86. See also Martin Luther King Jr., "The Montgomery Story," *The Papers of Martin Luther King, Jr., Vol. III*, ed. Clayborne Carson, Stewart Burns, Susan Carson, Peter Holloran, and Dana L.H. Powell (Berkeley: University of California Press, 1997), 306.

31. King, "Non-Aggression Procedures to Interracial Harmony," in *King Papers, Vol. III*, 327.

32. King, *Strength to Love*, 52.

33. Ibid.

of nonviolence, and to the social, cultural, and political conditions of nations. Agape goes public; philia and eros remain disassociated from public affairs.[34] King certainly revises Niebuhr's conception of the love–justice relationship, affirming the direct relevance of love to the realm of politics. But King makes clear that this love is not the kind one associates with friendship or other intimate relationships. This love is not emotional or sentimental. It is divine, sacrificial, and unearned. King acknowledges the importance of philia and eros, but he baptizes only agape for public, political use.

Unfortunately, because of gendered associations that link men with rationality, spirituality, and public life, and women with emotion, materiality, and private life, this conception of agape carries negative consequences for the role of women in King's theopolitical vision.[35] This plausible connection between King's conception of love and his inability to treat women as equals raises the question of whether feminists and womanists should abandon King as a theopolitical ally. Although King ties his conception of agape to notions of redemptive suffering and continues to hold agape as a public love over against philia and eros, I contend that engaging King's thought remains valuable for feminists and womanists.

In fact, King espouses another strand of thinking that strongly resonates with feminist and womanist insights. If we continue to trace his discussions of love throughout his participation in the civil rights movement, it becomes clear that King draws on the power of philia and eros to inspire participants and appeal to the conscience of the nation. In other words, "The powerful passion that King denies of love in theory is precisely the power that allows him to speak

---

34. As Preston N. Williams notes, "Although he constantly cited the three Greek words for love—eros, philia, and agape—he utilized only the understanding of love as agape in his application of love to society or social change." "An Analysis of the Conception of Love," 23–24.

35. Ibid., 24.

of love as 'a potent force for social change.'"[36] In his appeals to the Greek divisions of love, King clearly seeks to avoid what Niebuhr would characterize as an understanding of love as mere sentiment unrelated to power structures. It is also likely that King employs different understandings of agape at different times for the purpose of justifying or motivating action in particular contexts. King may also have continued to appeal to traditional Protestant conceptions of agape that distinguish agape from eros for an additional purpose: to resist and challenge white stereotypes of African Americans as oversexualized.[37] Whatever reasons King may have had for identifying agape as the only love relevant to the public realm, this conception begins to exist in tension with his reliance in practice on the worldly elements of love typically associated with philia and eros as well as the creative form this love often takes.

King's embrace of love as a political practice constitutes an innovation in the tradition that places him in good stead with feminists who contend that the tradition of twentieth-century Protestant social ethics tends to exile love from the public realm.[38] His political appeal to love draws on the social gospel tradition and marks his departure from Niebuhr's view that love remains relevant to the political realm as an ideal but not as a concrete possibility. Contrary to Niebuhr's dialectic between love and justice, or to those who would position justice as a public norm and love as a private norm, King calls for a "creative synthesis of love and justice" that should endear

---

36. James E. Gilman, *Fidelity of Heart: An Ethic of Christian Virtue* (New York: Oxford University Press, 2001), 186.
37. Thanks to Darryl Trimiew for this insight.
38. This is a common feminist claim about Reinhold Niebuhr's conception of love and justice. See, for example, Barbara Hilkert Andolsen, "Agape in Feminist Ethics," *Journal of Religious Ethics* 9, no. 1 (Spring 1981): 69–83. For an excellent discussion of similar feminist criticisms, see Rebekah L. Miles, *The Bonds of Freedom: Feminist Theology and Christian Realism* (New York: Oxford University Press, 2001).

him to feminists weary of claims about love's irrelevance to public morality.[39]

He also draws heavily on an understanding of divine love that is informed by his own personal experience. In 1950, the same year that King cited Nygren's account of agape, he also described the love of God in familial terms. "It is quite easy for me to think of a God of love," he writes, "mainly because I grew up in a family where love was central. . . . It is quite easy for me to think of the universe as basically friendly mainly because of my uplifting hereditary and environmental circumstances."[40] This account bears remarkable similarities to those of feminist theologians, such as Sallie McFague, who argues for a conception of divine love that draws on one's experience of familial love from a parent (in McFague's account, a mother).[41]

## King and Feminist Conceptions of Agape

The similarities between this strand of King's thinking on love and feminist reconstructions of agape can be categorized according to three broad themes: the importance of self-love, the significance of philia and eros to a proper understanding of agape, and the community-oriented nature of divine love.

### The Importance of Self-Love

An important feminist critique of the tradition's dominant conception of agape rejects the understanding of agape primarily as self-sacrifice. Valerie Saiving Goldstein, Barbara Hilkert Andolsen, and Beverly W. Harrison all issue such critiques.[42] Goldstein, for

---

39. King, *Strength to Love*, 20.
40. King, "An Autobiography of Religious Development," in *King Papers, Vol. I*, 360.
41. Sallie McFague, "God as Mother," in *Weaving the Visions: New Patterns in Feminist Spirituality*, ed. Judith Plaskow and Carol P. Christ (San Francisco: Harper & Row, 1989).

example, argues that agape understood as self-sacrifice reveals a male bias that neglects female experience. She criticizes Nygren and Niebuhr for identifying "sin with self-assertion and love with selflessness," arguing that "specifically feminine forms of sin" tend toward the "underdevelopment or negation of the self."[43] While an understanding of agape as selflessness may speak to men's need to repent of the sin of pride, it only serves to reinforce women's sin of lack of self-assertion. Far from seeing a healthy self-love as detracting from agape, these feminists affirm the importance of self-love. They aim to correct the focus on self-sacrifice by incorporating the loves of philia and eros, which acknowledge the importance of the self in the act of loving. Nearly every feminist reconstruction of agape appeals to friendship, familial relationships, or intimate relationships.[44]

Interestingly, Beverly Harrison cites King as one who understood this power of radical mutual love.[45] While King does not abandon understandings of agape as self-sacrifice, he argues along the same lines as feminists in emphasizing the importance of self-love. During the Montgomery bus boycott, King appealed to the black community to affirm its "somebodyness," to reject the "tragic sense of inferiority resulting from the crippling effects of slavery and segregation," and for each person to recognize their "eternal worth to God."[46] Far from extolling the virtue of selflessness, King recognizes

42. Valerie Saiving Goldstein, "The Human Situation: A Feminine View," *The Journal of Religion* 40, no. 2 (April 1960): 100–112; Andolsen, "Agape in Feminist Ethics," 74; and Beverly W. Harrison, *Making the Connections: Essays in Feminist Social Ethics*, ed. Carol S. Robb (Boston: Beacon, 1985), 28.

43. Goldstein, "The Human Situation: A Feminine View," 100, 108–9.

44. Harrison, McFague, and Linda Woodhead, among others, develop concepts of agape based on mutuality. See Harrison, *Making the Connections*; McFague, "God as Mother"; and Linda Woodhead, "Love and Justice," *Studies in Christian Ethics* 5, no. 1 (April 1992): 44–61.

45. Although an unlikely source for King's "feminist" conception of agape, Daniel Day Williams's *The Spirit and the Forms of Love* also reconstructs agape along lines similar to those of contemporary feminists. As one of Harrison's teachers as Union Theological Seminary, Williams likely influenced Harrison's and other feminists' conceptions of agape. I owe this illuminating suggestion to Glen Stassen.

that most members of the black community need an affirmation of their significance as selves. Indeed, King rejects segregation because it communicates and reinforces a sense of "nobodiness."[47] His appeal to "somebodyness" figures centrally in his 1963 "Letter from Birmingham Jail": "When you are forever fighting a degenerating sense of 'nobodiness,'" King writes, "then you will understand why we find it difficult to wait."[48] These passages reveal that King emphasizes the same kind of redemptive self-love that womanists often champion as a response to "the cultural production[s] of evil"[49] that denigrate black women.

Although King continues to invoke the traditional Protestant conception of agape as a self-sacrificial love, he clearly does not regard self-sacrifice as synonymous with self-abnegation. To the contrary, King's call for the black community to embrace the sacrificial love of agape presumes a self who possesses the power to choose to sacrifice for the sake of others. It also suggests that it is the hope that all persons' "somebodyness" will one day be honored that fuels one's agapic activity. Through voluntary suffering one lays claim to one's dignity as an agent worthy of respect. In this sense, King's account resembles Terrell's in seeing those who risk suffering as "empowered, *sacramental*, witnesses."

## The Role of Philia and Eros in Reconstructing Agape

Feminists also take issue with conceptions of agape that seek to avoid the taint of reciprocity, such as King's description of agape

---

46. On "somebodyness," see Garth Baker-Fletcher, *Somebodyness: Martin Luther King, Jr., and the Theory of Dignity* (Minneapolis: Fortress Press, 1993). Quote from Martin Luther King Jr., *Stride toward Freedom: The Montgomery Story* (New York: Harper & Row, 1958), 190.

47. King, *Strength to Love*, 141.

48. Martin Luther King Jr., "Letter from Birmingham Jail," in *Why We Can't Wait* (New York: Signet, 2000), 70.

49. Emilie M. Townes, *Womanist Ethics and the Cultural Production of Evil* (New York: Palgrave Macmillan, 2006).

as "an overflowing love which seeks nothing in return."[50] Several feminists' constructive turns from agape as self-sacrifice to agape as mutuality reject both the disinterested character of self-sacrifice and the individualist notion of the self that agape as self-sacrifice requires. Claiming that Nygren, Niebuhr, and Gene Outka deprecate mutuality in Protestant Christian ethics, Harrison embraces an embodied, mutual love: "The love we need and want is deeply mutual love, love that has both the quality of a gift received and the quality of a gift given. The rhythm of a real, healing, and empowering love is take and give, give and take, free of the cloying inequality of one partner active and one partner passive."[51] Harrison's embrace of agape as a mutual and interested love echoes King's own "relational ontology" of persons.[52]

In fact, King's references to an "inescapable network of mutuality," a theme that pervades his work, resonate with Harrison's insistence on the "deep, total sociality of all things."[53] King frequently calls attention to the nature of the self as relational and interdependent. His primary battle cry against injustice is that it tears at the fabric of our mutual existence and destiny. The contention that "injustice anywhere is a threat to justice everywhere," that we are "tied in a single garment of destiny,"[54] appears frequently not only in King's writings but in his sermons, where he challenges listeners to see that their own lives and actions are deeply implicated in their neighbors'.[55] Rather than maintaining the fiction of isolated, self-contained selves, King argues along feminist lines for us to recognize our dependence

---

50. King, *King Papers, Vol. III*, 459.
51. Harrison, *Making the Connections*, 17–18.
52. Kathryn Tanner, "The Care That Does Justice: Recent Writings in Feminist Ethics and Theology," *Journal of Religious Ethics* 24, no. 1 (Spring 1996): 179.
53. Harrison, *Making the Connections*, 16.
54. King, *Why We Can't Wait*, 65.
55. See King, "The Man Who Was a Fool," "Transformed Nonconformist," and "On Being a Good Neighbor," in *Strength to Love*.

on others, advocating the mutual love that our reality as interdependent selves requires.

The feminists who challenge understandings of agape as detached and disinterested also draw on eros to reconstruct their concepts of agape.[56] They attribute this privileging of agape over philia and eros to a pernicious dualism in Christian thought that devalues material reality. As Carter Heyward argues, "The traditional Christian understanding of love fails to value adequately the embodied human experience of love among friends and sexual partners because it assumes the negative, dangerous, and nonspiritual character of sensual, erotic, and sexual feelings and expressions."[57] Heyward suggests that experiences of erotic love reveal God's love, that "the erotic is . . . our most fully embodied experience of God as love."[58] Similarly, womanists often use the language of "passion" to express this holistic understanding of love.[59] Rather than defining Christian love apart from our embodied reality, feminists and womanists articulate a concept of Christian love that honors our whole being. In doing so, they not only emphasize the reciprocal nature of love, they also draw on forms of love that are often identified as impure or worldly.

King, too, draws on the language of philia and eros to convey the meaning of God's love. Throughout his career, he invoked the love of family, friends, and lovers to explain the love present in the civil rights movement. King often uses the metaphor of friendship

56. Rita N. Brock, Carter Heyward, and Catherine Keller, among others, reconceptualize agape in terms of eros. See Rita N. Brock, *Journeys By Heart: A Christology of Erotic Power* (New York: Crossroad, 1988); Carter Heyward, *Touching Our Strength: The Erotic as Power and the Love of God* (San Francisco: Harper & Row, 1989); and Catherine Keller, *From a Broken Web: Separation, Sexism, and Self* (Boston: Beacon, 1986).

57. Heyward, *Touching Our Strength*, 98–99.

58. Ibid., 99.

59. See Patricia L. Hunter, "Women's Power—Women's Passion," in *A Troubling in My Soul*, 191–92; and Kelly Brown Douglas, *Sexuality and the Black Church: A Womanist Perspective* (Maryknoll, NY: Orbis, 1999), 119–21.

to describe the movement's goal: the aim is not to "seek to defeat or humiliate the enemy but to win his friendship and understanding."[60] In his 1963 "I Have a Dream" speech, King portrays this goal with an image of the children of former slave owners and the children of former slaves joining hands as sisters and brothers. These familial metaphors appear to be the maturation of ideas already present in King's 1950 essay, "Six Talks Based on *Beliefs that Matter* by William Adams Brown," where he relies on parental metaphors to convey the relationship between God and humanity. "Each Christian should believe that he is a member of a larger family of which God is the Father. . . . We are members of one family, meant to live as brothers and to express our brotherhood in helpfulness."[61] As noted earlier, King also draws on the mutual love of intimate relationships to convey the passion with which civil rights advocates should undertake political action. In 1958, describing the willingness of the practitioner of nonviolent resistance to accept suffering, King wrote, "If going to jail is necessary, he enters it 'as a bridegroom enters the bride's chamber.'"[62] Far from banishing eros from agape, King relies on the experience of eros to enliven our understanding of agape. In this case, it is necessary to accept one's suffering with a passion akin to that of embracing one's lover.

Furthermore, King's friends and colleagues report that the charismatic power of King's presence itself possessed an erotic dimension.[63] Feminists and womanists rightly criticize the abuse of such "sexual power," but these reports nevertheless suggest the integral relationship between the various forms of love. No matter how carefully King tries to differentiate agape from eros, he seems

60. King, *Strength to Love*, 51.
61. King, *King Papers, Vol. I*, 281.
62. King, "An Experiment in Love," 18.
63. Ralph Abernathy, *And the Walls Came Tumbling Down: An Autobiography* (New York: Harper & Row, 1989), 471.

unable in practice to appeal to agape without the explanatory help of eros and philia.

## Agape as Community-Creating

Finally, feminist developments of agape appeal to the centrality of community. Linell E. Cady argues that imagining agape as self-sacrifice not only validates oppression but also obscures the relational character of love. While she acknowledges that friendship comes closer to accurately describing the character of love as relation, friendship is ultimately not expansive enough. Rather, she puts forward "an alternative interpretation of love in which the primary aim is the creation, deepening, and extension of communal life."[64] This account, which imagines love as creating a universal community, mirrors King's own.

The incorporation of mutuality and passion into King's conception of agape leads him, like Cady, to affirm the role of agape in creating community relationships.[65] As he puts it, "*Agape* is love seeking to preserve and create community. . . . *Agape* is a willingness to go to any length to restore community. . . . The cross is the eternal expression of the length to which God will go in order to restore broken community. The resurrection is a symbol of God's triumph over all the forces that seek to block community. The Holy Spirit is the continuing community creating reality that moves through history."[66] This passage indicates that although King continues to describe agape as self-sacrificial, nonreciprocal, and individually oriented, he increasingly relies on a different strand of thinking

64. Linell E. Cady, "Relational Love: A Feminist Christian Vision," in *Embodied Love: Sensuality and Relationship as Feminist Values*, ed. Paula M. Cooey, Sharon A. Farmer, and Mary Ellen Ross (San Francisco: Harper & Row, 1987), 147.

65. The emphasis on community in King's conception of agape also reflects the influence of Paul Ramsey. See *Basic Christian Ethics* (Louisville: Westminster John Knox, 1993), 234–48.

66. King, "An Experiment in Love," 20.

that places him in feminist company. This strand requires an understanding of agape as self-loving, mutual, passionate, and community-creating. Indeed, the notion of agape inherited from the Protestant tradition does not fit well with King's practice of love in the civil rights movement. The love he puts into practice more closely resembles that envisioned by contemporary feminists.

## King and Womanism: Love as a Creative Practice

King's "feminist" conception of agape is not the only new development this comparison of King and feminism uncovers. Comparing King's thought on love with that of womanist theologies also reveals a shared conception of agape that emphasizes its creative capacities. Both construe agape as a love that, when put into action for the sake of justice, draws on the mutual, reciprocal, passionate, and community-creating aspects of philia and eros. Scholars make much of the role of love and its relationship to justice in King's thought, but few attend to King's emphasis on love as a "creative power," and thus the centrality of creativity in King's vision.[67] Although it is now neglected, the theme of creativity became increasingly prominent as King's career progressed. In fact, in the first six volumes of the *King Papers*, separate index references to agape and eros disappear after the third volume and a three-line reference to "creativity/creative will" appears in the sixth under a heading for King's political and social ideas.

Although womanists do not self-consciously name the theme of creativity as a component of their theological approaches, their work often emphasizes the importance of creative power. Much womanist theology and ethics features an emphasis on the dignity of human

---

67. King's understanding of love as a creative power draws not only on Nygren but also on Paul Tillich. See, especially, *Love, Power, and Justice: Ontological Analyses and Ethical Applications* (New York: Oxford University Press, 1972).

beings as creators and a construal of human agency as participation in God's creative activity, an understanding of this activity as involving a critique of the status quo and conformity, and an affirmation that such creative activity is redemptive. These same themes feature prominently in King's thought.

## Human Beings as Creators:
## Agency as Participation in God's Creative Activity

Drawing from a picture of God as Creator, womanist theological anthropologies often affirm the creation of each human being in the image of God and construe human agency as participation in God's creative activity. Expressing this creativity enables one to affirm one's dignity and agency as a human being in situations where others deny that dignity, and to seek wholeness of life. Monica A. Coleman's postmodern womanist account, for example, holds that because of our creation by God, we are cocreators who work with God to carry on God's process of creation. Identifying the womanist concept of "making a way out of no way" with "creative transformation" in process thought, Coleman describes both as articulating an understanding of "how we work with God to implement God's ideals in the world."[68] Similarly, an affirmation of the *imago Dei* undergirds Kelly Brown Douglas's call for the black church to end its silence on important issues related to human sexuality. Douglas argues that "to reflect the image of God is to do nothing less than nurture loving relationships. . . . [Human sexuality] is a central factor in recognizing the human role in God's ongoing creative activity."[69] This same emphasis appears in Baker-Fletcher's work on creation and the environment, where she identifies seven womanist powers,

---

68. Monica A. Coleman, *Making a Way Out of No Way: A Womanist Theology* (Minneapolis: Fortress Press, 2008), 86.
69. Kelly Brown Douglas, *Sexuality and the Black Church*, 115, 121.

each rooted in the *imago Dei*. The powers—"voice, vision, naming, community building, regeneration, rememory, and the interlocking powers of survival, resistance, and liberation"—symbolize "Black women's participation in God's creative activity."[70] In particular, the womanist emphasis on the power of naming harkens back to God's creation of the world through speech, affirming womanists' power to create. Despite their diverse methodologies and topics of concern, all of these womanists root their accounts in an affirmation of the *imago Dei*, where its meaning is expressed as a shared capacity to create.

Reflecting, in part, the influence of Boston Personalism, King's view of God as Creator also leads him to a theological anthropology that highlights human beings' creative capacities. King frequently makes reference to the human task to live creatively and employ our God-given creative powers. In "Creating the Abundant Life," he argues that "life is something that you create. It was always Jesus' conviction that life is worth living and that men through the proper adjustment and attitudes could create a meaningful life. . . . Jesus is saying that part of his mission on earth is to help men create the abundant life."[71] Like the womanists who draw on the *imago Dei* as their source for affirming human beings' creative capacities, King affirms the inherent dignity of human beings as persons who share in God's creative power. "Man," King writes, "that being that God created just a little lower than the angels, is able to think a poem and write it; he's able to think a symphony and compose it. He's able to imagine a great civilization and create it."[72] King declares that God's "creative power is not exhausted by this earthly life," thereby identifying God's creative power as a living force of which human

---

70. Baker-Fletcher and Baker-Fletcher, *My Sister, My Brother*, 149–50.
71. Martin Luther King Jr., *The Papers of Martin Luther King, Jr., Vol. VI*, ed. Clayborne Carson, Susan Carson, Adrienne Clay, Virginia Shadron, and Kieran Taylor (Berkeley: University of California Press, 2000), 188.
72. Ibid., 178.

beings are to partake in struggling against destructive forces in the universe.[73] Just as Coleman, Douglas, and Baker-Fletcher ground their understanding of what it means to participate in God's creative activity in the *imago Dei*, King suggests that doing the will of a loving Creator God requires that humans join God in God's creative activity.

## Participation in God's Creative Activity as a Challenge to Conformity and the Status Quo

The emphasis on human beings' creative capacities also reveals itself in womanist methodologies. For many womanists, participation in God's creative activity means, in Emilie M. Townes's words, "encourag[ing] creativity rather than conformity."[74] Some womanists appeal to the language of revolution to convey how their creative methods break free from oppressive categories and methods of the past to signal new possibilities for the future. Katie G. Cannon describes womanist pedagogy as "challenging conventional and outmoded dominant theological resources" and "creating new modes of inquiry."[75] Stacey M. Floyd-Thomas refers to womanists as "intellectual revolutionaries," who "*created* frames of thinking and ways of being that took Black women being agents of their own destiny as the norm."[76]

In addition to incorporating black women's literature, blues, gospels, and African religious traditions as sources of theoethical reflection, womanists often convey this emphasis by describing their

---

73. King, *Strength to Love*, 95–96.
74. Townes, *Troubling in My Soul*, 9.
75. Katie G. Cannon, *Katie's Canon: Womanism and the Soul of the Black Community* (New York: Continuum, 1995), 137–38.
76. Stacey M. Floyd-Thomas, "Introduction: Writing for Our Lives—Womanism as an Epistemological Revolution," in *Deeper Shades of Purple: Womanism in Religion and Society*, ed. Stacey M. Floyd-Thomas (New York: New York University Press, 2006), 2–3.

methods through the rubric of artistic activities. Williams describes her work with the analogy of creating mosaics;[77] Coleman, with braiding hair;[78] and Cheryl Kirk-Duggan, with quilting.[79] Each activity takes different fragments, scraps, or pieces and brings them together to create something beautiful and whole. The mosaic and quilting metaphors suggest the possibility of doing so with broken or otherwise unusable material. Williams even describes black women's survival strategies as "arts" to emphasize "the high level of skill" required.[80] Memory plays a crucial role in these accounts, indicating that while creativity challenges the status quo, it is not construed as a total break with the past but as a creative retrieval and reappropriation of community traditions, experiences, and wisdom directed toward new, redemptive futures.

This critique of conformity prevalent in the work of both King and a host of womanists is perhaps nowhere so prominent as in their respective critiques of the church. In addition to Douglas's call for black churches to address homophobia, a number of womanists address gender injustice. As noted in chapter 2, Marcia Y. Riggs provides one such example.[81] The womanist critique of the conformity of black churches to sexism is accompanied by calls for churches to be agents of creative action. Grant, for example, connects the agenda of racial, economic, and sexual-gender justice with the vocation of a prophetic church. She argues that "the prophetic church cannot be a part of the status quo" but must "create the new church—an egalitarian church free of racism, sexism, classism, imperialism, a church which is God's Kingdom on Earth."[82] Adding

---

77. Williams, *Sisters in the Wilderness*, 12.
78. Coleman, *Making a Way*, x.
79. Cheryl A. Kirk-Duggan, "Quilting Relations with Creation," in *Deeper Shades of Purple*, 189.
80. Williams, *Sisters in the Wilderness*, 236.
81. Marcia Y. Riggs, *Plenty Good Room: Women Versus Male Power in the Black Church* (Cleveland, OH: Pilgrim, 2003).

environmental justice to the agenda, Baker-Fletcher also advocates creative responses from churches: "If the church is to live into the new creation of a new heaven and a new earth, it must do so by working in harmony with God, Creativity Itself."[83] As these examples indicate, the womanist challenge to traditional methods is of a piece with calls for churches to be voices of creative challenge to the status quo. Both aim to dismantle structures of thought and institutional practices that perpetuate black women's marginalization and detract from the well-being of all people.

Just as these womanists emphasize the importance of creativity as a counter to conformity, King's discussions of nonviolence feature the theme of creativity and its role in attaining the movement's goals. Because scholars usually interpret King's nonviolent practice as the manifestation of how King relates love and justice, few attend to the role of creativity in his methods. King certainly regarded nonviolent direct action as a practical way of putting Jesus' love ethic into action, but here again we should attend to love's creative character. King conceives of nonviolent direct action, first and foremost, as a creative act. The love it relies upon is a "creative force."[84] Acts of civil disobedience are "creative outlet[s]" for discontent.[85] The world is in need of "creative extremists."[86] And, although he does not have gender injustice in mind, King repeatedly critiques churches for their failure to resist the status quo.[87] Each of these descriptions underscores King's familiar contention that nonviolent resistance creates crises that challenge communities to confront their injustices.[88]

---

82. Jacquelyn Grant, "Tasks of a Prophetic Church," in *Theology and the Americas*, ed. Cornel West, Caridad Guidote, and Margaret Coakley (Maryknoll, NY: Orbis, 1982), 137, 141–42.
83. Karen Baker-Fletcher, *Sisters of Dust, Sisters of Spirit: Womanist Wordings on God and Creation* (Minneapolis: Fortress Press, 1998), 57.
84. King, *Strength to Love*, 56.
85. King, *Why We Can't Wait*, 76.
86. Ibid., 77.
87. Ibid., 67.

## The Redemptive Power of Participation in God's Creative Activity

While womanist accounts understand salvation or redemption variously through the rubrics of liberation, survival, and wholeness and quality of life, they often feature a shared conviction that redemption occurs when human beings make creative use of resources God provides. Many describe such activity as the work of the Holy Spirit.[89] This womanist emphasis on "embracing the spirit" and the idea of "making a way out of no way" expresses the ways in which God enables black women to seek "survival, quality of life, and liberating activity" in this life.[90] Coleman's account envisions a central role for creative human agency in attaining salvation. As she puts it, "God offers us the possibilities that introduce newness into the world. . . . Creative transformation is the change that occurs when God's aims toward novelty are accepted and incorporated."[91] Similarly, in her reading of the Hagar story, Williams affirms Hagar's own role in her redemption. Her description of Hagar's relationship with God depicts God as a fellow artist who helps Hagar create her own means of survival. God provides to Hagar "*new vision* to see survival resources where she saw none before," but it is Hagar who must use these resources to craft the means of her survival.[92] Rosetta E. Ross gives the name "womanist work" to such efforts in her studies of black women activists. She notes that these women often understood their work to be dependent upon resources from God, and that womanist theologians view these activists' endeavors as "propelled by belief in the need to radically obey God's direction

---

88. King, *Strength to Love*, 25.
89. See Karen Baker-Fletcher, "More than Suffering: The Healing and Resurrecting Spirit of God," in *Dancing with God: The Trinity from a Womanist Perspective* (St. Louis: Chalice, 2006), 146–69.
90. Emilie M. Townes, ed., *Embracing the Spirit: Womanist Perspectives on Hope, Salvation, and Transformation* (Maryknoll, NY: Orbis, 1997); and Coleman, *Making a Way*, 33.
91. Ibid., 75, 92.
92. Williams, *Sisters in the Wilderness*, 198.

of work and as faith that God makes the work possible."[93] "Making a way out of no way" is thus a joint effort. God initiates the process by providing necessary resources; the women bring it to fruition by using their creative capacities to survive.

Each of these elements is present in King's discussion of the role of creativity in nonviolent protest. King describes nonviolent direct action as creative because it participates in the creating, sustaining, and redeeming capacities of God that seek to lead creation to its proper fulfillment. As cocreators with God, human beings are called to participate in "the creative turmoil of a genuine civilization struggling to be born."[94] Coleman's and Williams's emphasis on the role of God in creating new possibilities echoes King's own discussion of the way in which nonviolent protest allows one to see resources that were not previously available. Speaking of the effect of engaging in such protests, King argues that "the nonviolent approach does something to the hearts and souls of those committed to it. It gives them new self-respect. It calls up resources of strength and courage that they did not know they had."[95] In other words, the nonviolent approach makes a way out of no way. It puts before the person new possibilities, new resources not previously in view. Contending that "human salvation lies in the hands of the creatively maladjusted,"[96] King anticipates the view of these womanists that human participation proves central to God's creative, redemptive activity.

93. Rosetta E. Ross, "Womanist Work and Public Policy: An Exploration of the Meaning of Black Women's Interaction with Political Institutions," in *Embracing the Spirit*, 41; and Ross, *Witnessing and Testifying*, 5–15.
94. King, "Nobel Prize Acceptance Speech," in *Testament of Hope*, 226.
95. King, *Strength to Love*, 151.
96. Ibid., 27.

## Conclusion

But why does any of this matter? Identifying King's "feminist" and "womanist" politics of love reveals a new vision of churches' political roles: churches as communities of creativity. King's definition of agape as "love seeking to preserve and create community" suggests that for King the political need not be limited to nonviolent resistance but may include any "agapic activity" that seeks to create and sustain community. Although King does not explicitly describe churches as such, reading his theopolitical thought alongside feminist and womanist theology enables a vision of just such a political ecclesiology. Indeed, King's critique of the American church suggests that he views churches as potential sites of divine creativity, as creative communities whose calling consists in embodying and ushering in the new creation. While most view King as a prophet of nonviolence whose method puts love into action for the sake of justice, my comparison of King and various feminists and womanists suggests that it is not so much his call for a synthesis between love and justice that is most significant but his call for a "creative" synthesis.

I have traced in King's own thought strands of what can potentially form a creative synthesis between traditional Protestant conceptions of agape and those of contemporary womanist and feminist theologians that emphasize the worldly nature of love as mutual, reciprocal, and community-creating. My comparison of King's account of love with that of various feminists and womanists not only highlights the indispensability of feminist and womanist theologies for illuminating King's theology, it also challenges feminists and womanists to recognize King's theology as a strategic resource despite his personal failure to address the evil of sexism. While feminist critiques of King's conception of redemptive suffering are critical, they also risk concealing the significant overlap that exists between their conceptions of agape.

In this sense, my reading demonstrates a "feminist/womanist" trajectory in King's account of love that may prove useful as a tool of internal critique for feminists and womanists to identify points at which King's theology (and personal behavior) failed to abide by his own best insights. It also enables feminists and womanists to take King's legacy where King himself was not prepared to go: the pursuit of gender justice both inside and outside of the institutional church. Indeed, this reading suggests that a creative synthesis between King's thought and that of a variety of feminists and womanists offers our best resources for future reflection on what might constitute such practices of creativity and how churches might go about their roles as communities of creativity called to give birth to ever-new forms of relationship rooted in love and justice.

My uncovering of this development in King's thought not only benefits feminist and womanists, it also suggests the potential for new lines of inquiry for witness and realist theologians who could contribute more meaningfully to their own internal projects were they to better engage King's thought. Gregory's comparison of King with feminist ethicists of care innovatively highlights affinities between King's thought and feminist political philosophy, but raises the question of King's relationship to feminist and womanist theologies. In its attention to "care," it inadvertently obscures the important connections between King and feminist/womanist theologians on "love" that have been identified here. It is true that King shares with care ethicists the view of justice as an inadequate political norm and affirms the interdependent and dependent nature of human life, as well as the importance of relationships and recognizing people in their full humanness. But King's conception of love carries with it an entire theological framework of meaning. It invokes God's loving creation of the world and human participation in the redemption of the world. Where care theorists speak of sustaining, preserving and repairing the world,[97] King speaks of creating and redeeming it. Where care theorists discuss inclusion and exclusion within the political order,[98] King's discussion of love is on the order of being and nonbeing. And where care theorists embark on political projects as the end of their moral theory, King identifies the political realm as a site of grace that participates in an end that lies beyond history. Although care is similar to love, it falls short of the radical, generative, and transformative capabilities of love. King's discussion of love highlights not only the importance of feminist and womanist theological reconstructions of love to an understanding of King's politics of love, but also the church as an indispensable site for its cultivation.

In fact, attention to the theological robustness of King's thought challenges the tendency of witness and realist theologians to gloss over King. The centrality of the black churches in sustaining the love at the heart of the civil rights movement underscores the need for realists and realist-leaning new Augustinians to heed witness emphasis on the church as a site of moral formation. Moreover, King's example highlights how important it is for witness theologians to acknowledge the realist insight that churches possess indispensable resources for addressing problems in larger political structures, and therefore cannot stop at embodying change within their own ecclesial communities. King's own example and the feminist/womanist trajectory of his thought on love—in spite of his markedly nonfeminist attitudes—provides a powerful reminder to realists of the need to remain hopeful about what can be accomplished this

---

97. See, for example, Joan C. Tronto, *Moral Boundaries: A Political Argument for an Ethic of Care* (New York: Routledge, 1993), 103–4. Tronto excludes "creative activity" from her definition of care.
98. Ibid., 111, 157.

side of history, as well as their responsibility to give voice to those possibilities.

But just as King's thought reveals the importance of the witness emphasis on the church and its practices of moral formation, it also calls prominent witness proposals to account for both their lack of attention to race and their failure to attend as carefully as King's own witness does to the ways embeddedness in the church and its practices often compels a witness that moves beyond the church to engage with larger political structures. It identifies in particular the need for witness theologians to address the racial segregation that still divides the church, particularly in the United States. In its attention to womanist critiques of the sexism of the black church, my reading also challenges Hauerwas's contention that the black church best embodies a faithful witness model. It thereby identifies both race and gender as issues demanding more attention by witness theologians interested in defining the primary identity and mission of the church.

If King's case is any indication, it would also seem that proper formation in the virtue of love necessarily entails political pursuits outside the institutional church, calling attention to the need for witness theologians to think more substantially not only about how to more fully define the first task of the church, but also about the church's subsequent tasks. The development of agape that I trace in this chapter suggests that love, while cultivated in the church, cannot possibility be contained there—that, in the very way God's own creative love spills over into the gratuitous creation of the universe, Christians' own love spills over into extra-ecclesial engagement. In this sense, King perhaps provides a model for witness theologians of how Christians might maintain an authentic witness to Christ while engaging in extra-ecclesial political activity.

Perhaps most importantly, my analysis of King's theology suggests hope for those whose creative maladjustment renders them uneasy in any one stance. In fact, with King it suggests not only that the vitality of work in the field of Christian ethics, but also the possibility of human salvation itself, may lie in the hands of such creatively maladjusted ethicists.

# Conclusion: From the Genuine Community of Argument to the Beloved Community

"The end is reconciliation; the end is redemption; the end is the
creation of the beloved community."
—Martin Luther King Jr.[1]

What would it look like to do Christian ethics as though "the end
is the creation of beloved community?" Does anyone do theology
and ethics with this confidence? Can we even imagine what such
theologies would look like? What difference might it make for our
communities if all of our theologies pursued the beloved community
as their end?

King saw promising signs of unity already present in the church of
his day, despite its discord. Just after criticizing the American church
for its divisive denominationalism in "Paul's Letter to American
Christians," he mentions the increasing interest in ecumenical
concerns, the organization of the National Council of Churches,
and dialogue between Protestants and Catholics as developments that
"will bring all Christians closer and closer together."[2] In light of

1. Martin Luther King Jr., *The Papers of Martin Luther King, Jr., Vol. III: Birth of a New Age, December 1955–December 1956*, ed. Clayborne Carson, Stewart Burns, Susan Carson, Peter Holloran, and Dana L. H. Powell (Berkeley: University of California Press, 1997), 458.
2. Martin Luther King Jr., *Strength to Love* (Philadelphia: Fortress Press, 1981), 140.

my argument in chapter 4, it should come as no surprise that King describes these efforts as "creative." He commends the church for such developments and bids his fellow Christians to "continue to follow this creative path."[3]

I have tried to take King's advice with respect to the "denominations" of academic theology. In addressing the impact of witness-realist polarization and the relative absence of feminist theologies in public theology—particularly in relation to Niebuhr's, Yoder's, and King's thought—I have modeled an approach to Christian ethics in keeping with its end. To put it in both King's and Tanner's respective terms, if the end is "beloved community," then Christian ethicists should engage in a "genuine community of argument." This community honors diversity and approaches difference with an appreciation for "mutual correction and uplift," in the "shared hope of good discipleship, proper faithfulness, and purity of witness." It contends that approaching the academic boundaries that separate "theological ethics" from "social ethics" and "feminist theologies" from "public" and "political" theologies both enables richer assessments of Niebuhr's, Yoder's, and King's contributions to reflection on the relationship between Christianity and public life and enhances the internal agendas of theologians across Christian ethics.

But there is more at stake than the legacies of Niebuhr, Yoder, and King—or even the larger field. How Christian ethicists go about the theological task may determine whether academic theology contributes productively to what Traci C. West has called "our communal moral life." We live, as King did, in a divided world. Economic disparity between rich and poor continues to increase. Environmental devastation wreaks havoc on the hungriest and poorest among us. Wars rage. Sex trafficking flourishes. Racism is alive and well. The supposedly "united" states are split into red and

3. Ibid.

blue, with isolated media outlets preaching to their own ideological choirs. Public and political discussion often champions one of two extremes in response to complex moral issues. Governments shut down for failure to reach political compromise. There is no end to the divisions, enmities, and brokenness we endure each day. In a world of discord, Christian ethicists should model approaches to difference that celebrate them for the resource they are, rather than using them as tools of division.

What, if any, relevance, then, could a "genuine community of argument" have for Christian ethics? What difference might it make for our field, for the academy, for the world? Doing Christian ethics at the boundaries models an approach to difference more in keeping with the beloved community *and* allows more creative, constructive responses to pressing moral problems. When Christian ethicists work at the boundary, new trajectories emerge. Far from compromising existing agendas, such approaches enable theologians to more powerfully embody their own commitments.

My engagement with Niebuhr, for example, identifies ecclesiology as a new agenda for realists. It challenges common witness and feminist assessments of the value of Niebuhr's work, demonstrating how their criticisms might be used to develop his thought in ways that contribute both to realist agendas and their own. In doing so, it identifies a powerful articulation of the church's mission. While witness theologians find fault with Niebuhr's refusal to ground his Christian ethics in ecclesiology, feminists bemoan his underestimation of the moral potential of religious communities. At face value, these criticisms leave Niebuhr in an ecclesiological lurch. But approaching Niebuhr's thought at the boundaries contributes to the development of a Niebuhrian ecclesiology. I argue that realists should be in engaged in ecclesiology, and I show how they can do this without sacrificing the integrity of their own approach.

This Niebuhrian ecclesiology not only enhances realist projects; it also provides a needed corrective to witness and feminist accounts. Dismissing Niebuhr as insufficiently theological and unapologetically uninterested in ecclesiology, as so many witness theologians do, deprives us of the wisdom of Niebuhr's thought for ecclesiological reflection. Although he does not develop a full-blown ecclesiology, his discussions of the church are sorely needed today: Churches are bearers of God's judgment, places where Christians are formed in humility and hope through prayer and other practices of contrition, that train Christians to be keenly aware of the way pride and self-interest mar even the best endeavors, and that remind members that they are called to take creative action in the world in spite of sin. Reading Niebuhr alongside Kathryn Tanner brings into relief prominent themes shared between Niebuhr's discussion of the church and her description of Christianity as productive of self-critical cultures, suggesting the possibility of developing from within Niebuhr's thought a conception of churches as self-critical and creative cultures that witness both to the power of sin and the possibilities of grace. When witness theologians dismiss Niebuhr from the ecclesiological discussion, they neglect these important contributions.

Likewise, feminist interpreters suggest that Niebuhr's emphasis on divine transcendence undercuts innovative social action and neglects the moral potential of religious groups. Although some feminists have appropriated Niebuhr's thought, correcting for this deficiency, neither they nor Tanner develop their insights about the "horizontal transcendence" of religious communities or the self-critical potential of Christian cultures along explicitly ecclesiological lines. The Niebuhrian ecclesiology I have developed here takes Welch's criticisms, Miles's appropriation, and Tanner's reconsideration of one of Niebuhr's early concerns[4] and puts them to work in an ecclesiological framework, emphasizing the church's character as a self-critical culture whose self-critique catalyzes creative moral activity.

If the church embodies a stance of self-criticism and creativity, how might its approach to moral problems differ? To suggest one example, engaging in self-critical and creative action enables the church to demonstrate its solidarity—in the sense of complicity—with the rest of the world in wrongdoing, and to demonstrate its solidarity—in the sense of commitment—to enact creative solutions to seemingly intractable problems. Feminist theologian Margaret Farley has written, for example, of the powerful impact of Pope John Paul II's March 2000 Lenten prayer in Jerusalem, where the pope prayed in the name of the Catholic Church for forgiveness for wrongs against co-believers and those of other traditions:

> This may have been the most important and most effective word spoken in the public forum by a representative of the Roman Catholic Church in a long time. . . . Embodying vulnerability in the expression of truth, never was the church more strong. Acknowledging not only mistakes but real evil, never was the church more prophetic in its commitment to justice . . . whatever word is spoken, whatever action taken, it needs to be formed with this same spirit: of humility, respect, and the deepest compassion.[5]

Farley's discussion of John Paul's prayer provides a vision of the church as a self-critical culture. The power of this moment suggests that the most vital witness often comes from the church's willingness to submit itself to God's judgment, to engage in public self-criticism, to confess its sin, and to ask for the forgiveness that prompts creative

---

4. As noted in chapter 2, Tanner describes her exploration of the possibilities of an internal critique of Christian belief as consonant with interests expressed by Niebuhr in his *Reflections on the End of an Era*. See *The Politics of God: Christian Theologies and Social Justice* (Minneapolis: Fortress Press, 1992), viii.

5. Margaret Farley, "The Church in the Public Forum: Scandal or Prophetic Witness?" *Proceedings of the Catholic Theological Society of America* 55 (2000): 87, 101.

ethical action. Emptying itself of any claim to moral superiority or moral perfection, the church offers a kenotically Christlike witness to the transformative, creative power of contrition, forgiveness, and mercy. Imagine the power of this kind of self-critical and creative action if the church were to confess its sin across its historical and institutional life![6]

My engagement with Yoder identifies feminism as a new agenda for witness theologians. It challenges both realist and feminist assessments of Yoder's work, as well as witness appropriations of it, to demonstrate how these critiques might lead to a Christian pacifism that more readily emphasizes both feminism and extra-ecclesial activity. Neither realists nor feminists think Yoder has anything to offer Christian politics, but doing Christian ethics at the boundary shows that Yoder's account underdevelops—but demands—extra-ecclesial and feminist engagement. Reading Yoder's theology alongside feminist and womanist work reveals that feminists and womanists—particularly in their attention to the internal violence of trauma and the systemic violence of sexism, racism, and classism—are making needed contributions to Yoder's Christian pacifism. My proposal corrects witness theologians' tendency to construe Yoder's theology in more antiliberal and antifeminist directions than Yoder himself did, and it corrects realist tendencies to undervalue the church's role in sustaining extra-ecclesial political activity. All the while, it challenges feminists to recognize the strategic value of Yoder's claims about feminism despite his own profound violation of feminist commitments. Feminists can cite Yoder's identification of feminism as constitutive of Christian identity to invite witness theologians into the feminist fold.

---

6. For a constructive theology that conceives of the church's public mission as "confession of sin unto repentant action," see Jennifer M. McBride, *The Church for the World: A Theology of Public Witness* (New York: Oxford University Press, 2012).

This development of Yoder's thought identifies not only powerful forms of ecclesial engagement in the world, but ways in which the "church" actually becomes itself in the "world." It argues that the church's pacifist politics invites both collaboration with nonchurch partners who engage in what Yoder calls "spin-offs"[7] of ecclesial practices and commitment to resisting systemic forms of violence like sexism and racism. Yoder's discussion of ecclesial practices as "paradigms" and "models" for "secular" practices; his discussion of non-ecclesial practices as "analogical ways" of doing and "non-religious equivalents" of ecclesial practices; and his discussion of "tactical alliances" and the "real common agenda" between Christians and non-Christians, suggests that Christians should collaborate with others whose political practices may not explicitly confess Christ as Lord but nevertheless witness to Christ's lordship. Some have argued that for Yoder the very identity of the church is constituted by encounters with "outsiders."[8] Consequently, "when Christians cease to engage outsiders with receptive generosity, they cease to let the church be the church, they lose sight of Jesus as Lord."[9] That the church's own identity and mission depends on its willingness to engage with those "outside" the tradition—or feminists perceived by witness theologians to be "outside" the tradition—lends a new urgency to their responsibility to pursue Yoder's claim that "Christian identity itself calls for feminist engagement." In detailing analogical

---

7. John Howard Yoder, *Body Politics: Five Practices of the Christian Community Before the Watching World* (Scottdale, PA: Herald, 1992), 58.

8. See Romand Coles, "The Wild Patience of John Howard Yoder: 'Outsiders' and the 'Otherness of the Church'," *Modern Theology* 18, no. 3 (July 2002): 305–31. See also Nathan R. Kerr's account in *Christ, History, and Apocalyptic: The Politics of Christian Mission* (Eugene, OR: Cascade, 2009), which draws on Yoder's theology and "retriev[es] for our time a biblically eschatological, apocalyptic perspective on history" that conceives of ecclesia as a "praxis of missionary encounter with the other by which we are together given over—converted—to the 'more' of Jesus' life, the shape of whose pneumatological excess we cannot possibly control" (11, 178).

9. Coles, "Wild Patience," 307.

practices shared by "church" and "world," Yoder proves himself a truly worldly theologian. He is so concerned with the world's welfare that his theology is free to become itself there. I suspect that, far from taking offense at recent claims of his heterodoxy, Yoder would embrace them as accurate statements of his main theological point: Christ is Lord not only over the church but also over the cosmos.

Yoder's elaboration of the church's "body politics" indicates the kinds of issues on which Christians and non-Christians might partner. His discussion of binding and loosing identifies forgiveness and reconciliation as areas where Christians should work with those outside the church. His discussion of the Eucharist as "a matter of economic ethics"[10] provides clues to identifying non-Christian practices of economic justice that Christians should support. His discussion of the "rule of Paul" suggests that decision-making procedures that prioritize consensus rather than majority rule are consonant with Christian teaching. His description of baptism as a practice that "relativize[s] prior stratifications and classification"[11] suggests that Christians should practice and advocate for egalitarianism. And his reflections on the "fullness of Christ" indicate that Christians should celebrate practices that honor the dignity and gift of each member.

Churches should cultivate the ability to discern a witness to Christ in non-Christian practices not only for the purposes of such collaboration, but also for the benefit of their own integrity of witness. The ability of non-Christians to witness to Christ, to more faithfully enact some of the practices to which the church is called than churches themselves, suggests that churches should regard such occasions as opportunities for recommitment. In his discussion of feminism, for example, Yoder argues that the church abandoned its

10. Ibid., 21.
11. Ibid., 33.

original feminist witness only to be reminded through "the detour of secular post-Christian humanism"[12] of its own belief in the equal dignity of each community member. Churches should thus be prepared to receive as a gift instances when the lordship of Christ is more faithfully witnessed to by those who do not self-consciously confess Christian belief. They should not hesitate to take correction from their non-ecclesial neighbors.

In light of Yoder's own pervasive sexual violence against women, it is imperative to develop what I have called "feminism as Christian politics." Witness theologians cannot do justice to either Yoder's theological vision or their own without incorporating feminist analyses of the expansive forms violence takes. Only then can we think well about ecclesial resources for shaping communities that can prevent sexual violence. In short, incorporating feminist work on sexism, racism, classism and other forms of structural and internal violence would not only strengthen witness theologians' own accounts of the church as pacifist witness, it would better address the problem of sexual violence.

My engagement with King identifies "creative maladjustment" as a productive stance for all Christian ethicists. It also highlights an argument present in my appropriations of Niebuhr's and Yoder's theologies: feminist theologies are indispensable to the creative capacity of Christian ethics. Or to put it in King's terms, feminist theologians have often been the "creative, dedicated minority" that "almost always"[13] makes the tradition better. The chapter on King also highlights another argument that runs throughout the book: one continuing task of feminist theologies is to reconfigure problematic uses of the tradition and direct them to liberating ends. Occasionally, this will challenge feminists themselves to recognize "feminist

12. John Howard Yoder, *The Christian Witness to the State* (Scottdale, PA: Herald, 2003), 18.
13. King, *Strength to Love*, 61.

trajectories" in the theologies of decidedly nonfeminist thinkers, or in the theologies of those like Yoder whose actions violate women's dignity, or in the theologies of those like King who struggled to treat women as equals.

Reading King alongside feminist and womanist theologies highlights provocative similarities in their conceptions of love, demonstrating the power of potential collaboration among ethicists of diverse approaches. While King began his career as a preacher invoking agape in standard ways drawn from the Protestant theology of his seminary studies, the love he talked about and put into practice during the civil rights movement bore increasing similarities to the reconstructions of agape by feminist theologians such as Beverly W. Harrison, Barbara Andolsen, Carter Heyward, and Linell E. Cady. These reconstructions liken agape to the more worldly loves of philia and eros. The "creative" nature of this love as King describes it resonates with an emphasis on the creative power of love in the work of Emilie M. Townes, Monica A. Coleman, Karen Baker-Fletcher, and other womanists. Although feminists and womanists have been critical of King's conception of redemptive suffering, their overlapping thought on love unearths fertile ground for collaboration.

Indeed, identifying these "feminist" and "womanist" elements in the thought of a figure who so clearly neglected gender justice suggests the power of King's thought to challenge witness and realist theologians as well. King's status as the consummate Christian witness bids witness theologians to address racism and the relationship between ecclesial practices and extra-ecclesial politics. The fact that King's very embeddedness in the black church was essential to his success in extra-ecclesial politics also emphasizes the need for realists to attend to how the church's own politics sustains participation in larger political structures. It also reminds them that, on occasion, love is a "possible" possibility. King's failure to address gender injustice renders it all the more important that feminists make strategic use of "feminist" and "womanist" elements within King's thought to address the sexism that still pervades ecclesial and non-ecclesial structures alike.

King's own witness speaks volumes as to how his own creative maladjustment enabled him to lead a movement of diverse persons and constituencies that provided a vision of the beloved community. King frequently spoke about the power of the "creative, dedicated minority"[14] and the need for the church to be such a creative minority. Rather than functioning as an instrument and enforcer of the status quo, King called the church to be "the moral guardian of the community."[15] Rather than operating as a thermometer that measures the current conditions, King thought the church should be a thermostat that determined what the conditions ought to be.[16] But unfortunately, as he recognized,

> Nowhere is the tragic tendency to conform more evident than in the church, an institution which has often served to crystallize, conserve, and even bless the patterns of majority opinion. . . . Called to combat social evils, it has remained silent behind stained-glass windows. Called to lead men on the highway of brotherhood and to summon them to rise above the narrow confines of race and class, it has enunciated and practiced racial exclusiveness.[17]

Nevertheless, King's pursuit of the beloved community serves as a reminder—not only for the church, but also for the academy—that even when internal divisions threaten to detract from the integrity and power of our theologies, there is always new—and distinctively Christian—work to be done at the boundary.

14. Ibid.
15. Ibid., 25.
16. Martin Luther King Jr., *Why We Can't Wait* (New York: Signet, 2000), 80.
17. King, *Strength to Love*, 25.

# Bibliography

Abernathy, Ralph. *And the Walls Came Tumbling Down: An Autobiography.* New York: Harper & Row, 1989.

Albrecht, Gloria. *The Character of our Communities: Toward an Ethic of Liberation for the Church.* Nashville: Abingdon, 1995.

Alexis-Baker, Nekeisha. "Freedom of the Cross: John Howard Yoder and Womanist Theologies in Conversation." In *Power and Practices: Engaging the Work of John Howard Yoder,* edited by Jeremy M. Bergen and Anthony G. Siegrist, 83–97. Scottdale, PA: Herald, 2009.

Andolsen, Barbara Hilkert. "Agape in Feminist Ethics." *Journal of Religious Ethics* 9, no. 1 (Spring 1981): 69–83.

Baker-Fletcher, Garth. *Somebodyness: Martin Luther King, Jr., and the Theory of Dignity.* Minneapolis: Fortress Press, 1993.

Baker-Fletcher, Karen. *Dancing with God: The Trinity from a Womanist Perspective.* St. Louis: Chalice, 2006.

———. *Sisters of Dust, Sisters of Spirit: Womanist Wordings on God and Creation.* Minneapolis: Fortress Press, 1998.

Baker-Fletcher, Karen, and Garth Kasimu Baker-Fletcher. *My Sister, My Brother: Womanist and Xodus God-Talk.* Maryknoll, NY: Orbis, 1997.

Baldwin, Lewis V. *The Voice of Conscience: The Church in the Mind of Martin Luther King, Jr.* Oxford: Oxford University Press, 2010.

Barth, Karl. *Against the Stream: Shorter Post-War Writings, 1946–52.* London: SCM, 1954.

Bretherton, Luke. *Christianity and Contemporary Politics: The Conditions and Possibilities of Faithful Witness.* Malden, MA: Wiley-Blackwell, 2010.

Brock, Rita N. *Journeys By Heart: A Christology of Erotic Power.* New York: Crossroad, 1988.

Brown, Joanne Carlson, and Carole R. Bohn, eds. *Christianity, Patriarchy, and Abuse: A Feminist Critique.* New York: Pilgrim, 1989.

Cady, Linell E. "Relational Love: A Feminist Christian Vision." In *Embodied Love: Sensuality and Relationship as Feminist Values,* edited by Paula M. Cooey, Sharon A. Farmer, and Mary Ellen Ross, 135–49. San Francisco: Harper & Row, 1987.

———. *Religion, Theology, and American Public Life.* New York: State University of New York Press, 1993.

Cahill, Lisa Sowle. *Love Your Enemies: Discipleship, Pacifism, and Just War Theory.* Minneapolis: Fortress Press, 1994.

———. *Theological Bioethics: Participation, Justice, and Change.* Washington, DC: Georgetown University Press, 2005.

Cannon, Katie G. *Black Womanist Ethics.* Atlanta: Scholars Press, 1988.

———. *Katie's Canon: Womanism and the Soul of the Black Community.* New York: Continuum, 1995.

Carbine, Rosemary P. "Ekklesial Work: Toward a Feminist Public Theology." *Harvard Theological Review* 99, no. 4 (2006): 433–55.

Carter, Craig A. *The Politics of the Cross: The Theology and Social Ethics of John Howard Yoder.* Grand Rapids: Brazos, 2001.

Cavanaugh, William T. "Church." In *The Blackwell Companion to Political Theology,* edited by Peter Scott and William T. Cavanaugh, 393–406. Malden, MA: Blackwell, 2004.

———. "A Nation with the Church's Soul: Richard John Neuhaus and Reinhold Niebuhr on Church and Politics." *Political Theology* 14, no. 3 (2013): 386–96.

———. *Torture and Eucharist: Theology, Politics, and the Body of Christ.* Malden, MA: Wiley-Blackwell, 1998.

Chopp, Rebecca S. "Reimagining Public Discourse." In *Black Faith and Public Talk: Critical Essays on James H. Cone's Black Theology and Black Power,* edited by Dwight N. Hopkins, 150–64. Maryknoll, NY: Orbis, 1999.

Coleman, Monica A. *Making a Way Out of No Way: A Womanist Theology.* Minneapolis: Fortress Press, 2008.

Coles, Romand. "The Wild Patience of John Howard Yoder: 'Outsiders' and the 'Otherness of the Church.'" *Modern Theology* 18, no. 3 (July 2002): 305–31.

Collins, Sheila D. *A Different Heaven and Earth.* Valley Forge, PA: Judson, 1974.

Cone, James H. *Martin & Malcolm & America: A Dream or a Nightmare.* Maryknoll, NY: Orbis, 1991.

Conley, Aaron D. "Loosening the Grip of Certainty: A Case-Study Critique of Tertullian, Stanley Hauerwas, and Christian Identity." *Journal of the Society of Christian Ethics* 33, no. 1 (Spring/Summer 2013): 21–44.

Cramer, David, Jenny Howell, Paul Martens, and Jonathan Tran. "Scandalizing John Howard Yoder," *The Other Journal,* July 7, 2014, http://theotherjournal.com/2014/07/07/scandalizing-john-howard-yoder/.

———. "Theology and Misconduct: The Case of John Howard Yoder." *Christian Century* 131, no. 17 (August 20, 2014): 20–23.

Crouter, Richard. *Reinhold Niebuhr on Politics, Religion, and Christian Faith.* New York: Oxford University Press, 2010.

Dackson, Wendy. "Reinhold Niebuhr's Outsider Ecclesiology." In *Reinhold Niebuhr and Contemporary Politics: God and Power,* edited by Richard

Harries and Stephen Platten, 87–101. Oxford: Oxford University Press, 2010.

Daggers, Jenny. "The Prodigal Daughter: Orthodoxy Revisited." *Feminist Theology* 15, no. 2 (2007): 186–201.

———, ed. *Gendering Christian Ethics*. Newcastle: Cambridge Scholars, 2012.

Daly, Lois K., ed. *Feminist Theological Ethics: A Reader*. Louisville: Westminster John Knox, 1994.

Daly, Mary. *Beyond God the Father: Toward a Philosophy of Women's Liberation*. Boston: Beacon, 1973.

Dean, William, Mark A. Noll, Mary Farrell Bednarowski, and J. Bryan Hehir. "Forum: Public Theology in Contemporary America." *Religion and American Culture* 10, no. 1 (Winter 2000): 21–27.

DeHart, Paul J. *The Trial of the Witnesses: The Rise and Decline of Postliberal Theology*. Malden, MA: Wiley-Blackwell, 2006.

Doak, Mary. *Reclaiming Narrative for Public Theology*. New York: State University of New York Press, 2004.

Dorrien, Gary. *Social Ethics in the Making: Interpreting an American Tradition*. Malden, MA: Wiley-Blackwell, 2009.

Douglas, Kelly Brown. *Sexuality and the Black Church: A Womanist Perspective*. Maryknoll, NY: Orbis, 1999.

Elie, Paul. "A Man for All Reasons." *The Atlantic Monthly* 300, no. 4 (November 1, 2007): 82–96.

Elshtain, Jean Bethke. *Women and War*. Chicago: University of Chicago Press, 1987.

Elshtain, Jean Bethke, and Sheila Tobias, eds. *Women, Militarism, and War: Essays in History, Politics, and Social Theory*. Savage, MD: Rowman & Littlefield, 1990.

Erskine, Noel Leo. *King Among the Theologians*. Cleveland, OH: Pilgrim, 1994.

Erwin, Scott R. *The Theological Vision of Reinhold Niebuhr's The Irony of American History: "In the Battle and Above It."* Oxford: Oxford University Press, 2013.

Farley, Margaret. "The Church in the Public Forum: Scandal or Prophetic Witness?" *Proceedings of the Catholic Theological Society of America* 55 (2000): 87–101.

Floyd-Thomas, Stacey M. "Introduction: Writing for Our Lives—Womanism as an Epistemological Revolution." In *Deeper Shades of Purple: Womanism in Religion and Society*, edited by Stacey M. Floyd-Thomas, 1–14. New York: New York University Press, 2006.

Fulkerson, Mary McClintock. "Feminist Theology." In *The Cambridge Companion to Postmodern Theology*, edited by Kevin J. Vanhoozer, 109–25. Cambridge: Cambridge University Press, 2003.

———. *Places of Redemption: Theology for a Worldly Church*. Oxford: Oxford University Press, 2007.

Fulkerson, Mary McClintock, and Sheila Briggs, eds. *The Oxford Handbook of Feminist Theology*. Oxford: Oxford University Press, 2012.

Garrow, David J. *Bearing the Cross: Martin Luther King, Jr., and the Southern Christian Leadership Conference*. New York: Vintage, 1988.

Gilkey, Langdon. *On Niebuhr: A Theological Study*. Chicago: University of Chicago Press, 2001.

Gilman, James E. *Fidelity of Heart: An Ethic of Christian Virtue*. New York: Oxford University Press, 2001.

Goldstein, Valerie Saiving. "The Human Situation: A Feminine View." *The Journal of Religion* 40, no. 2 (April 1960): 100–112.

Goossen, Rachel Waltner. "'Defanging the Beast': Mennonite Responses to John Howard Yoder's Sexual Abuse." *Mennonite Quarterly Review* 89, no. 1 (January 2015): 7–80.

Graham, Elaine. *Between a Rock and a Hard Place: Public Theology in a Secular Age*. London: SCM, 2013.

Grant, Jacquelyn. "The Sin of Servanthood." In *A Troubling in My Soul: Womanist Perspectives on Evil and Suffering*, edited by Emilie M. Townes, 199–218. Maryknoll, NY: Orbis, 1993.

———. "Tasks of a Prophetic Church." In *Theology and the Americas*, edited by Cornel West, Caridad Guidote, and Margaret Coakley. 136–42. Maryknoll, NY: Orbis, 1982.

Gregory, Eric. *Politics and Order of Love: An Augustinian Ethic of Democratic Citizenship*. Chicago: University of Chicago Press, 2008.

Guth, Karen V. "Churches as 'Self-Critical Cultures': Reinhold Niebuhr, Kathryn Tanner, and the Church's Politics." In *Gendering Christian Ethics*, edited by Jenny Daggers, 23–50. Newcastle: Cambridge Scholars, 2012.

———. "Doing Justice to the Complex Legacy of John Howard Yoder: Restorative Justice Resources in Witness and Feminist Ethics." *Journal of the Society of Christian Ethics* 35, no. 2 (Fall/Winter 2015). Forthcoming.

———. "The Feminist-Christian Schism Revisited." *The Journal of Scriptural Reasoning* 13, no. 2 (November 2014). http://jsr.shanti.virginia.edu/volume-13-number-2-november-2014-navigating-john-howard-yoders-the-jewish-christian-schism-revisited/the-feminist-christian-schism-revisited/.

———. "Reconstructing Nonviolence: The Political Theology of Martin Luther King Jr. after Feminism and Womanism." *Journal of the Society of Christian Ethics* 32, no. 1 (Spring–Summer 2012): 75–92.

Hampson, Daphne. "Reinhold Niebuhr on Sin: A Critique." In *Reinhold Niebuhr and the Issues of Our Time*, edited by Richard Harries, 46–60. Grand Rapids: Eerdmans, 1986.

———. *Theology and Feminism*. Oxford: Basil Blackwell, 1990.

Harrison, Beverly Wildung. *Justice in the Making: Feminist Social Ethics*. Edited by Elizabeth M. Bounds, Pamela K. Brubaker, Jane E. Hicks, Marilyn J. Legge, Rebecca Todd Peters, and Traci C. West. Louisville: Westminster John Knox, 2004.

———. *Making the Connections: Essays in Feminist Social Ethics.* Edited by Carol S. Robb. Boston: Beacon, 1985.

Hauerwas, Stanley. *A Community of Character: Toward a Constructive Christian Social Ethic.* Notre Dame, IN: University of Notre Dame Press, 1981.

———. "Failure of Communication *or* A Case of Uncomprehending Feminism." *Scottish Journal of Theology* 50, no. 2 (1997): 228–39.

———. *The Hauerwas Reader.* Edited by John Berkman and Michael Cartwright. Durham, NC: Duke University Press, 2001.

———. *The Peaceable Kingdom: A Primer in Christian Ethics.* Notre Dame, IN: University of Notre Dame Press, 1983.

———. "Remembering How and What I Think: A Response to the *JRE* Articles on Hauerwas." *Journal of Religious Ethics* 40, no. 2 (2012): 296–306.

———. "Remembering Martin Luther King Jr. Remembering: A Response to Christopher Beem." *Journal of Religious Ethics* 23, no. 1 (Spring 1995): 135–48.

———. *Vision and Virtue: Essays in Christian Ethical Reflection.* Notre Dame, IN: Fides, 1974.

———. *With the Grain of the Universe: The Church's Witness and Natural Theology.* 2001. Reprint, Grand Rapids: Baker Academic, 2013.

Hess, Cynthia. *Sites of Violence, Sites of Grace: Christian Nonviolence and the Traumatized Self.* Lanham, MD: Lexington, 2009.

Heyer, Kristin E. "How Does Theology Go Public? Rethinking the Debate between David Tracy and George Lindbeck." *Political Theology* 5, no. 3 (2004): 307–27.

Heyward, Carter. *Touching Our Strength: The Erotic as Power and the Love of God.* San Francisco: Harper & Row, 1989.

Hines, Mary E. "Ecclesiology for a Public Church." *Proceedings of the Catholic Theological Society of America* 55 (2000): 23–46.

Hollenbach, David. *The Global Face of Public Faith: Politics, Human Rights, and Christian Ethics*. Washington, DC: Georgetown University Press, 2003.

Holmes, Arthur F., ed. *War and Christian Ethics: Classic and Contemporary Readings on the Morality of War*. Grand Rapids: Baker Academic, 2005.

Huebner, Chris K. *A Precarious Peace: Yoderian Explorations on Theology, Knowledge, and Identity*. Scottdale, PA: Herald, 2006.

Hunter, Patricia L. "Women's Power—Women's Passion." In *A Troubling in My Soul: Womanist Perspectives on Evil and Suffering*, edited by Emilie M. Townes, 189–98. Maryknoll, NY: Orbis, 1993.

Hyman, Gavin. "Postmodern Theology and Modern Liberalism: Reconsidering the Relationship." *Modern Theology* 65 (2009): 462–74.

Isasi-Díaz, Ada María. *En La Lucha: Elaborating a Mujerista Theology*. Minneapolis: Fortress Press, 2004.

Jenson, Robert W. "The Hauerwas Project." *Modern Theology* 8, no. 3 (July 1992): 285–95.

Johnson, Elizabeth A. *She Who Is: The Mystery of God in Feminist Theological Discourse*. New York: Crossroad, 1992.

Jones, Serene. *Feminist Theory and Christian Theology: Cartographies of Grace*. Minneapolis: Fortress Press, 2000.

———. *Trauma and Grace: Theology in a Ruptured World*. Louisville: Westminster John Knox, 2009.

Kegley, Charles W., and Robert W. Bretall, eds. *Reinhold Niebuhr: His Religious, Social, and Political Thought*. New York: Macmillan, 1956.

Keller, Catherine. *From a Broken Web: Separation, Sexism, and Self*. Boston: Beacon, 1986.

———. *God and Power: Counter-Apocalyptic Journeys*. Minneapolis: Fortress Press, 2005.

Kerr, Nathan R. *Christ, History and Apocalyptic: The Politics of Christian Mission*. Eugene, OR: Cascade, 2009.

King, Martin Luther, Jr. *The Papers of Martin Luther King, Jr., Vol. I: Called to Serve, January 1929–June 1951.* Edited by Clayborne Carson, Ralph E. Luker, and Penny A. Russell. Berkeley: University of California Press, 1992.

———. *The Papers of Martin Luther King, Jr., Vol. II: Rediscovering Precious Values, July 1951–November 1955.* Edited by Clayborne Carson, Ralph E. Luker, Penny A. Russell, and Peter Holloran. Berkeley: University of California Press, 1994.

———. *The Papers of Martin Luther King, Jr., Vol. III: Birth of a New Age, December 1955–December 1956.* Edited by Clayborne Carson, Stewart Burns, Susan Carson, Peter Holloran, and Dana L. H. Powell. Berkeley: University of California Press, 1997.

———. *The Papers of Martin Luther King, Jr., Vol. IV: Symbol of the Movement, January 1957–December 1959.* Edited by Clayborne Carson, Susan Carson, Adrienne Clay, Virginia Shadron, and Kieran Taylor. Berkeley: University of California Press, 2000.

———. *The Papers of Martin Luther King, Jr., Vol. V: Threshold of a New Decade, January 1959–December 1960.* Edited by Clayborne Carson, Tenisha Hart Armstrong, Susan Carson, Adrienne Clay, and Kieran Taylor. Berkeley: University of California Press, 2005.

———. *The Papers of Martin Luther King, Jr., Vol. VI: Advocate of the Social Gospel, September 1948–March 1963.* Edited by Clayborne Carson, Susan Carson, Susan Englander, Troy Jackson, and Gerald L. Smith. Berkeley: University of California Press, 2007.

———. *The Papers of Martin Luther King, Jr., Volume VII: To Save the Soul of America, January 1961–August 1962.* Edited by Clayborne Carson and Tenisha Hart Armstrong. Berkeley: University of California Press, 2014.

———. *Strength to Love.* 1963. Reprint, Philadelphia: Fortress Press, 1981.

———. *Stride Toward Freedom: The Montgomery Story.* New York: Harper, 1958.

————. *A Testament of Hope: The Essential Writings and Speeches of Martin Luther King, Jr.* Edited by James M. Washington. New York: HarperCollins, 1986.

————. *Why We Can't Wait.* 1963. Reprint, New York: Signet Classic, 2000.

Kirk-Duggan, Cheryl A. "Quilting Relations with Creation." In *Deeper Shades of Purple: Womanism in Religion and* Society, edited by Stacey M. Floyd-Thomas, 176–90. New York: New York University Press, 2006.

Krall, Ruth Elizabeth. *The Elephants in God's Living Room, Volume Three: The Mennonite Church and John Howard Yoder, Collected Essays.* http://ruthkrall.com/downloadable-books/volume-three-the-mennonite-church-and-john-howard-yoder-collected-essays/.

Lasch, Christopher. *The True and Only Heaven: Progress and its Critics.* New York: W. W. Norton & Company, 1991.

Lee, Hak Joon. *The Great World House: Martin Luther King, Jr. and Global Ethics.* Cleveland, OH: Pilgrim, 2011.

Lindbeck, George A. *The Nature of Doctrine: Religion and Theology in a Postliberal Age.* Philadelphia: Westminster, 1984.

Lischer, Richard. *The Preacher King: Martin Luther King, Jr. and the Word that Moved America.* New York: Oxford University Press, 1995.

Logan, James. "Liberalism, Race, and Stanley Hauerwas." *CrossCurrents* 55, no. 4 (Winter 2006): 522–33.

Lovin, Robin W. *Christian Faith and Public Choices: The Social Ethics of Barth, Brunner, and Bonhoeffer.* Philadelphia: Fortress Press, 1984.

————. *Christian Realism and the New Realities.* Cambridge: Cambridge University Press, 2007.

————. *An Introduction to Christian Ethics: Goals, Duties, and Virtues.* Nashville: Abingdon, 2011.

————. *Reinhold Niebuhr and Christian Realism.* Cambridge: Cambridge University Press, 1995.

——, ed. *Religion and American Public Life: Interpretations and Explorations.* New York: Paulist Press, 1986.

Martens, Paul. *The Heterodox Yoder.* Eugene, OR: Cascade, 2012.

Marty, Martin E. *The Public Church: Mainline–Evangelical–Catholic.* New York: Crossroad, 1981.

Mathewes, Charles. *The Republic of Grace: Augustinian Thoughts for Dark Times.* Grand Rapids: Eerdmans, 2010.

——. *A Theology of Public Life.* Cambridge: Cambridge University Press, 2007.

McBride, Jennifer M. *The Church for the World: A Theology of Public Witness.* New York: Oxford University Press, 2012.

McDougall, Joy Ann. "Keeping Feminist Faith with Christian Traditions: A Look at Christian Feminist Theology Today." *Modern Theology* 24, no. 1 (January 2008): 103–24.

McFague, Sallie. "God as Mother." In *Weaving the Visions: New Patterns in Feminist Spirituality,* edited by Judith Plaskow and Carol P. Christ, 139–50. San Francisco: Harper & Row, 1989.

Milbank, John. *The Word Made Strange: Theology, Language, Culture.* Oxford: Blackwell, 1997.

Miles, Rebekah L. *The Bonds of Freedom: Feminist Theology and Christian Realism.* Oxford: Oxford University Press, 2001.

——. "Uncredited: Was Ursula Niebuhr Reinhold's Coauthor?" *Christian Century* 129, no. 2 (January 25, 2012): 30–33.

Miller, Richard B., ed. *War in the Twentieth Century: Sources in Theological Ethics.* Louisville: Westminster John Knox, 1992.

Monro, Anita, and Stephen Burns, eds. *Public Theology and the Challenge of Feminism.* London: Routledge, 2015.

Muers, Rachel. "Bonhoeffer, King, and Feminism: Problems and Possibilities." In *Bonhoeffer and King: Their Legacies and Import for Christian*

*Social Thought*, edited by Willis Jenkins and Jennifer M. McBride, 33–42. Minneapolis: Fortress Press, 2010.

———. "Doing Traditions Justice." In *Gendering Christian Ethics*, edited by Jenny Daggers, 7–22. Newcastle: Cambridge Scholars, 2012.

Murphy, Debra Dean. "Community, Character, and Gender: Women and the Work of Stanley Hauerwas." *Scottish Journal of Theology* 55, no. 3 (2002): 338–55.

Nation, Mark Thiessen. *A Comprehensive Bibliography of the Writings of John Howard Yoder*. Goshen, IN: Mennonite Historical Society, 1997.

———. "Feminism, Political Philosophy, and the Narrative Ethics of Jean Bethke Elshtain." In *Virtues and Practices in the Christian Tradition: Christian Ethics After MacIntyre,* edited by Nancey Murphy, Brad J. Kallenberg, and Mark Thiessen Nation, 289–305. Harrisburg, PA: Trinity Press International, 1997.

———, with Marva Dawn. "On Contextualizing Two Failures of John Howard Yoder," September 23, 2013, Anabaptist Nation Blog, http://emu.edu/now/anabaptist-nation/2013/09/23/on-contextualizing-two-failures-of-john-howard-yoder/.

Niebuhr, H. Richard. *The Social Sources of Denominationalism.* 1929. Reprint, New York: Meridian, 1957.

Niebuhr, Reinhold. *Beyond Tragedy: Essays on the Christian Interpretation of History*. New York: Charles Scribner's Sons, 1937.

———. *Discerning the Signs of the Times: Sermons for Today and Tomorrow.* New York: Charles Scribner's Sons, 1946.

———. *Essays in Applied Christianity: The Church and the New World.* Edited by D. B. Robertson. New York: Meridian, 1959.

———. *Faith and History: A Comparison of Christian and Modern Views of History*. New York: Charles Scribner's Sons, 1949.

———. *Justice and Mercy.* Edited by Ursula M. Niebuhr. New York: Harper & Row, 1974.

———. *Leaves from the Notebook of a Tamed Cynic*. New York: Willett, Clark & Colby, 1929.

———. *The Nature and Destiny of Man: A Christian Interpretation, Vol. I: Human Nature*. 1941. Reprint, Louisville, KY: Westminster John Knox, 1996.

———. *The Nature and Destiny of Man: A Christian Interpretation, Vol. II: Human Destiny*. 1943. Reprint, Louisville, KY: Westminster John Knox, 1996.

———. *Reflections on the End of an Era*. New York: Charles Scribner's Sons, 1934.

———. "Reply to Interpretation and Criticism." In *Reinhold Niebuhr: His Religious, Social, and Political Thought*, edited by Charles W. Kegley and Robert W. Bretall, 429–51. New York: Macmillan, 1956.

———. "Why the Christian Church is Not Pacifist." In *War in the Twentieth Century: Sources in Theological Ethics*, edited by Richard B. Miller, 28–46. Louisville: Westminster John Knox, 1992.

Nugent, John C. *The Politics of Yahweh: John Howard Yoder, the Old Testament, and the People of God*. Eugene, OR: Wipf & Stock, 2011.

Oppenheimer, Mark. "A Theologian's Influence, and Stained Past, Live On." *New York Times*, October 11, 2013, A14.

Ottati, Douglas F. *Hopeful Realism: Recovering the Poetry of Theology*. Eugene, OR: Wipf & Stock, 2009.

Parsons, Susan Frank, ed. *The Cambridge Companion to Feminist Theology*. Cambridge: Cambridge University Press, 2002.

Placher, William C. "Revisionist and Postliberal Theologies and the Public Character of Theology." *Thomist* 49 (1985): 392–416.

———. *Unapologetic Theology: A Christian Voice in a Pluralistic Conversation*. Louisville: Westminster John Knox, 1989.

Plantinga Pauw, Amy. "The Word is Near You: A Feminist Conversation with Lindbeck." *Theology Today* 50, no. 1 (April 1993): 45–55.

Plaskow, Judith. "Feminist Anti-Judaism and the Christian God." *Journal of Feminist Studies in Religion* 7 (Fall 1991): 99–108.

———. *Sex, Sin, and Grace: Women's Experience and the Theologies of Reinhold Niebuhr and Paul Tillich.* Washington, DC: University Press of America, 1980.

Price, Tom. "A Known Secret: Church Slow to Explore Rumors Against a Leader." *The Elkhart Truth,* July 14, 1992, B1.

———. "Teachings Tested: Forgiveness, Reconciliation in Discipline." *The Elkhart Truth,* July 16, 1992, B1.

———. "Theologian Accused: Women Report Instances of Inappropriate Conduct." *The Elkhart Truth,* July 13, 1992, B1.

———. "Theologian Cited in Sex Inquiry." *The Elkhart Truth,* July 29, 1992, B1.

———. "Theologian's Future Faces a 'Litmus Test': Yoder's Response to Allegations Could Determine Standing in the Field." *The Elkhart Truth,* July 12, 1992, B1.

Pui-lan, Kwok. "Feminist Theology, Southern." In *The Blackwell Companion to Political Theology,* edited by Peter Scott and William T. Cavanaugh, 194–209. Malden, MA: Blackwell, 2004.

Ramsey, Paul. *Basic Christian Ethics.* Louisville: Westminster John Knox, 1993.

Rasmussen, Larry, ed. *Reinhold Niebuhr: Theologian of Public Life.* San Francisco: Harper & Row, 1989.

Reno, R. R. "Feminist Theology as Modern Project." *Pro Ecclesia* 5, no. 4 (Fall 1996): 405–26.

Riggs, Marcia Y. *Plenty Good Room: Women Versus Male Power in the Black Church.* Cleveland: Pilgrim, 2003.

Ross, Rosetta E. "John Howard Yoder on Pacifism." In *Beyond the Pale: Reading Ethics from the Margins,* edited by Stacey M. Floyd-Thomas and

Miguel A. De La Torre, 199–207. Louisville: Westminster John Knox, 2011.

———. *Witnessing and Testifying: Black Women, Religion, and Civil Rights.* Minneapolis: Fortress Press, 2003.

———. "Womanist Work and Public Policy: An Exploration of the Meaning of Black Women's Interaction with Political Institutions." In *Embracing the Spirit: Womanist Perspectives on Hope, Salvation, and Transformation,* edited by Emilie M. Townes, 41–53. Maryknoll, NY: Orbis, 1997.

Ruether, Rosemary Radford. "The Emergence of Christian Feminist Theology." In *The Cambridge Companion to Feminist Theology,* edited by Susan Frank Parsons, 3–22. Cambridge: Cambridge University Press, 2002.

———. "Feminist Theology: Where Is It Going?" *International Journal of Public Theology* 4 (2010): 5–20.

———. *New Woman, New Earth: Sexist Ideologies and Human Liberation.* New York: Seabury, 1975.

———. *Sexism and God-Talk: Toward a Feminist Theology.* Boston: Beacon, 1983.

———. *Women-Church: Theology and Practice of Feminist Liturgical Communities.* San Francisco: Harper & Row, 1985.

Russell, Letty M. *Church in the Round: Feminist Interpretation of the Church.* Louisville: Westminster John Knox, 1993.

Schlabach, Gerald W. "The Christian Witness in the Earthly City: John H. Yoder as Augustinian Interlocutor." In *A Mind Patient and Untamed: Assessing John Howard Yoder's Contributions to Theology, Ethics, and Peacemaking,* edited by Ben C. Ollenburger and Gayle Gerber Koontz, 221–44. Telford, PA: Cascadia, 2004.

———. "Only Those We Need Can Betray Us: My Relationship with John Howard Yoder and His Legacy." GeraldSchlabach.net, July 14, 2014.

http://www.geraldschlabach.net/2014/07/10/only-those-we-need-can-betray-us-my-relationship-with-john-howard-yoder-and-his-legacy/.

Schüssler Fiorenza, Elisabeth. *Bread Not Stone: The Challenge of Feminist Biblical Interpretation.* Boston: Beacon, 1984.

————. *Discipleship of Equals: A Critical Ekklēsia-logy of Liberation.* New York: Crossroad, 1993.

————. *In Memory of Her: A Feminist Theological Reconstruction of Christian Origins.* 10th anniversary edition. New York: Crossroad, 1994.

————, ed. *The Power of Naming: A Concilium Reader in Feminist Liberation Theology.* Maryknoll, NY: Orbis, 1996.

Schweiker, William. *Theological Ethics and Global Dynamics: In the Time of Many Worlds.* Malden, MA: Wiley-Blackwell, 2004.

Smith, Kenneth L., and Ira G. Zepp Jr. *Search for the Beloved Community: The Thinking of Martin Luther King, Jr.* Valley Forge, PA: Judson, 1974.

Soskice, Janet Martin, and Diana Lipton, eds. *Feminism and Theology.* Oxford: Oxford University Press, 2003.

Stackhouse, Max L. "Civil Religion, Political Theology and Public Theology: What's the Difference?" *Political Theology* 5, no. 3 (2004): 275–93.

————. *Public Theology and Political Economy: Christian Stewardship in Modern Society.* Grand Rapids: Eerdmans, 1987.

Stout, Jeffrey. *Democracy and Tradition.* Princeton, NJ: Princeton University Press, 2004.

Tanner, Kathryn. "The Care That Does Justice: Recent Writings in Feminist Ethics and Theology." *Journal of Religious Ethics* 24, no. 1 (Spring 1996): 171–91.

————. *The Politics of God: Christian Theologies and Social Justice.* Minneapolis: Fortress Press, 1992.

————. "Public Theology and the Character of Public Debate." *The Annual of the Society of Christian Ethics* (1996): 79–101.

———. "Social Theory Concerning the 'New Social Movements' and the Practice of Feminist Theology." In *Horizons in Feminist Theology: Identity, Tradition, and Norms*, edited by Rebecca S. Chopp and Sheila Greeve Davaney, 179–97. Minneapolis: Fortress Press, 1997.

———. *Theories of Culture: A New Agenda for Theology*. Minneapolis: Fortress Press, 1997.

Terrell, JoAnne Marie. *Power in the Blood? The Cross in African American Experience*. Maryknoll, NY: Orbis, 1998.

Thiemann, Ronald F. *Constructing a Public Theology: The Church in a Pluralistic Culture*. Louisville: Westminster John Knox, 1991.

———. *Religion in Public Life: A Dilemma for Democracy*. Washington, DC: Georgetown University Press, 1996.

Tillich, Paul. *Love, Power, and Justice: Ontological Analyses and Ethical Applications*. 1954. Reprint, New York: Oxford University Press, 1972.

Townes, Emilie M., ed. *Embracing the Spirit: Womanist Perspectives on Hope, Salvation, and Transformation*. Maryknoll, NY: Orbis, 1997.

———, ed. *A Troubling in My Soul: Womanist Perspectives on Evil and Suffering*. Maryknoll, NY: Orbis, 1993.

———. *Womanist Ethics and the Cultural Production of Evil*. New York: Palgrave Macmillan, 2006.

Tracy, David. *The Analogical Imagination: Christian Theology and the Culture of Pluralism*. New York: Crossroad, 1981.

Tracy, Kate. "Christian Publisher: All of Top Theologian's Books Will Now Have Abuse Disclaimer." *Christianity Today*, December 18, 2013. http://www.christianitytoday.com/gleanings/2013/december/publisher-john-howard-yoder-books-abuse-women-mennonite.html?paging=off.

Tran, Jonathan. "Time for Hauerwas's Racism." In *Unsettling Arguments: A Festschrift on the Occasion of Stanley Hauerwas's 70th Birthday*, edited by Charles R. Pinches, Kelly S. Johnson, and Charles M. Collier, 246–61. Eugene, OR: Cascade, 2010.

Tronto, Joan C. *Moral Boundaries: A Political Argument for an Ethic of Care*. New York: Routledge, 1993.

Walton, Heather. "You Have to Say You Cannot Speak: Feminist Reflections Upon Public Theology." *International Journal of Public Theology* 4 (2010): 21–36.

Weaver, J. Denny, ed. *John Howard Yoder: Radical Theologian*. Eugene, OR: Cascade, 2014.

———. *The Nonviolent Atonement*. Grand Rapids: Eerdmans, 2011.

Webster, John. "Theology after Liberalism?" In *Theology After Liberalism: A Reader*, edited by John Webster and George P. Schner, 52–61. Oxford: Blackwell, 2000.

Welch, Sharon D. *A Feminist Ethic of Risk*. Revised edition. Minneapolis: Fortress Press, 2000.

Wells, Samuel. "The Nature and Destiny of Serious Theology." In *Reinhold Niebuhr and Contemporary Politics: God and Power*, edited by Richard Harries and Stephen Platten, 71–86. Oxford: Oxford University Press, 2010.

West, Cornel. *The Cornel West Reader*. New York: Basic Books, 1999.

West, Traci C. "Constructing Ethics: Reinhold Niebuhr and Harlem Women Activists." *Journal of the Society of Christian Ethics* 24, no. 1 (2004): 29–49.

———. "Gendered Legacies of Martin Luther King Jr.'s Leadership." *Theology Today* 65 (2008): 41–56.

Williams, Daniel Day. *The Spirit and the Forms of Love*. Lanham, MD: University Press of America, 1981.

Williams, Delores S. *Sisters in the Wilderness: The Challenge of Womanist God-Talk*. Maryknoll, NY: Orbis, 1993.

Williams, Preston N. "An Analysis of the Conception of Love and Its Influence on Justice in the Thought of Martin Luther King, Jr." *Journal of Religious Ethics* 18, no. 2 (Fall 1990): 15–31.

Wills, Richard Wayne Sr. *Martin Luther King, Jr. and the Image of God.* Oxford: Oxford University Press, 2009.

Woodhead, Linda. "Can Women Love Stanley Hauerwas? Pursuing an Embodied Theology." In *Faithfulness and Fortitude: In Conversation with the Theological Ethics of Stanley Hauerwas,* edited by Mark Thiessen Nation and Samuel Wells, 161–88. Edinburgh: T&T Clark, 2000.

———. "Love and Justice." *Studies in Christian Ethics* 5, no. 1 (April 1992): 44–61.

———. "Spiritualising the Sacred: A Critique of Feminist Theology." *Modern Theology* 13, no. 2 (April 1997): 191–212.

Yoder, John Howard. *Body Politics: Five Practices of the Christian Community Before the Watching World.* Scottdale, PA: Herald, 1992.

———. *The Christian Witness to the State.* Scottdale, PA: Herald, 1964.

———. *Discipleship as Political Responsibility.* 1964. Reprint, Scottdale, PA: Herald, 2003.

———. "Feminist Theology Miscellany #1: Salvation Through Mothering?" (October 1990): 1–7.

———. "Feminist Theology Miscellany #2: What Kind of Feminist Was Jesus?" (October 1990): 1–4.

———. *For the Nations: Essays Evangelical and Public.* 1997. Reprint, Eugene, OR: Wipf & Stock, 2002.

———. *The Fullness of Christ: Paul's Vision of Universal Ministry.* Elgin, IL: Brethren, 1987.

———. "How H. Richard Niebuhr Reasoned: A Critique of *Christ and Culture.*" In *Authentic Transformation: A New Vision of Christ and Culture,* edited by Glen H. Stassen, D. M. Yeager, and John Howard Yoder, 31–89. Nashville: Abingdon, 1996.

———. *The Jewish-Christian Schism Revisited.* Edited by Michael G. Cartwright and Peter Ochs. Scottdale, PA: Herald, 2008.

———. *Nonviolence—A Brief History: The Warsaw Lectures.* Edited by Paul Martens, Matthew Porter, and Myles Werntz. Waco, TX: Baylor University Press, 2010.

———. *The Original Revolution: Essays on Christian Pacifism.* 1971. Reprint, Scottdale, PA: Herald, 2003.

———. *The Politics of Jesus: Behold the Man! Our Victorious Lamb.* Grand Rapids: Eerdmans, 1972.

———. *The Priestly Kingdom: Social Ethics as Gospel.* Notre Dame, IN: University of Notre Dame Press, 1984.

———. "Reinhold Niebuhr and Christian Pacifism." *Mennonite Quarterly Review* 29 (April 1955): 101–17.

———. *The Royal Priesthood: Essays Ecclesiological and Ecumenical.* Edited by Michael G. Cartwright. Scottdale, PA: Herald, 1994.

———. *The War of the Lamb: The Ethics of Nonviolence and Peacemaking.* Edited by Glen Stassen, Mark Thiessen Nation, and Matt Hamsher. Grand Rapids: Brazos, 2009.

———. "Yoder Suspended." *Christian Century* 109, no. 24 (August 12, 1992): 737–38.

# Index